BOB MARLEY AND THE WAILERS

THE ULTIMATE ILLUSTRATED HISTORY

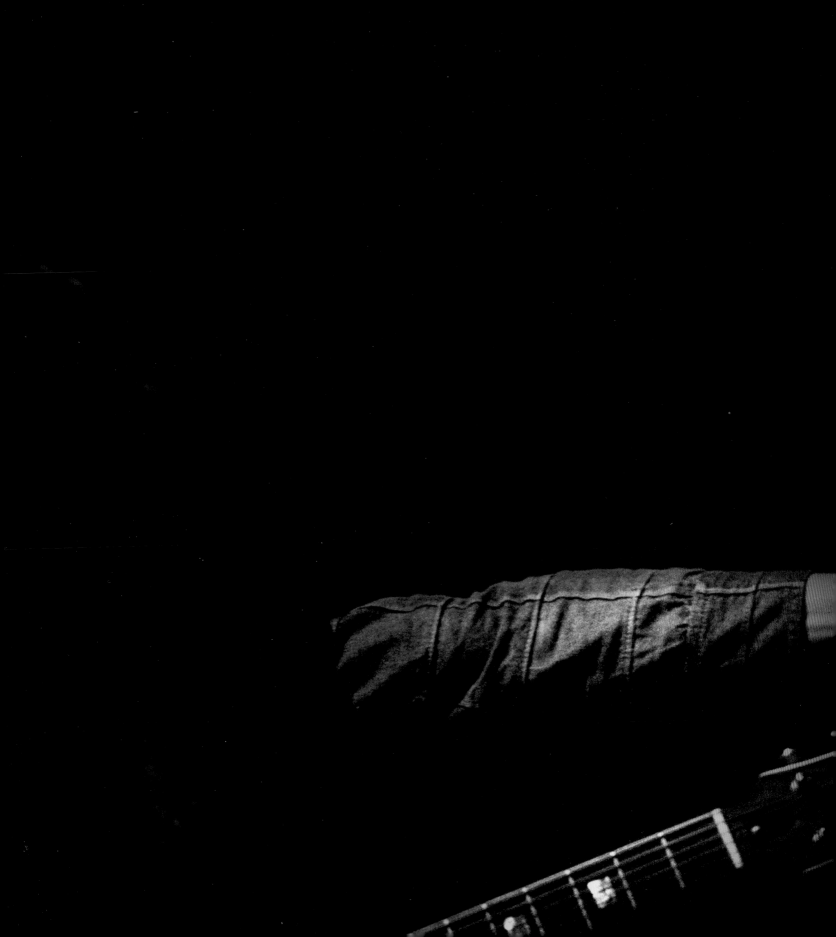

BOB MARLEY AND THE WAILERS

THE ULTIMATE ILLUSTRATED HISTORY

RICHIE UNTERBERGER

with

GARTH CARTWRIGHT
PAT GILBERT
GILLIAN G. GAAR
DAVE HUNTER
HARVEY KUBERNIK
and
CHRIS SALEWICZ

VOYAGEUR
PRESS

First published in 2017 by Voyageur Press, an imprint of The Quarto Group,
401 Second Avenue North, Suite 310, Minneapolis, MN 55401 USA.
Telephone: (612) 344-8100 Fax: (612) 344-8692

QuartoKnows.com

Voyageur Press titles are also available at discounts in bulk quantity for industrial or sales-promotional use. For details contact the Special Sales Manager by email at specialsales@quarto.com or by mail at The Quarto Group, 401 Second Avenue North, Suite 310, Minneapolis, MN 55401 USA.

10 9 8 7 6 5 4 3 2 1

ISBN: 978-0-7603-5241-0

Library of Congress Cataloging-in-Publication Data

Names: Unterberger, Richie, 1962- author. | Cartwright, Garth. | Gilbert, Pat. | Gaar, Gillian G.,
    1959- | Hunter, Dave, 1962- | Kubernik, Harvey, 1951- | Salewicz, Chris.
Title: Bob Marley and the Wailers : the ultimate illustrated history / Richie Unterberger, with Garth
    Cartwright, Pat Gilbert, Gillian G. Gaar, Dave Hunter, Harvey Kubernik, and Chris Salewicz.
Description: Minneapolis, MN : Voyageur Press, 2017. | Includes bibliographical references and index.
Identifiers: LCCN 2017004255 | ISBN 9780760352410 (paper over board)
Subjects: LCSH: Marley, Bob. | Wailers (Reggae group) | Reggae musicians--Jamaica--Biography. |
    Marley, Bob--Portraits. | Wailers (Reggae group)--Pictorial works
Classification: LCC ML420.M3313 U57 2017 | DDC 782.421646092 [B] --dc23
LC record available at https://lccn.loc.gov/2017004255

ACQUIRING EDITOR: Dennis Pernu
PROJECT MANAGERS: Madeleine Vasaly and Alyssa Bluhm
ART DIRECTOR: Cindy Samargia Laun
COVER AND PAGE DESIGN: Beth Middleworth
LAYOUT: Kim Winscher

FRONT COVER: *Mike Prior/Redferns/Getty Images*
BACK COVER: *Michael Ochs Archives/Getty Images*
TITLE PAGES: New York, New York, May 1, 1976. *Richard E. Aaron/Redferns/Getty Images*
COPYRIGHT PAGES: Chicago, Illinois, May 27, 1978. *Paul Natkin/Getty Images*
TABLE OF CONTENTS: Birmingham, England, July 19, 1975. *Ian Dickson/Redferns/Getty Images*

Printed in China

Contents

Introduction

Pop music stars usually fade from public consciousness when two generations have passed since the end of their careers. Yet thirty-five years after Bob Marley's death, the reggae pioneer is bigger than ever.

His music is widely played all over the world—not just in the North American and European nations responsible for the bulk of sales by English-speaking performers, but in every continent. His songs are performed by artists of all age groups and dozens of nationalities and ethnicities. His record sales—impressive, but not among the top echelon of superstars during his lifetime—now number in the hundreds of millions, even without counting the many pirated cassettes and CDs of his work that have circulated for decades, especially in Third-World countries. His best-selling disc, *Legend: The Best of Bob Marley and the Wailers*, has sold about twenty-five million copies, and as of this writing has spent more than four hundred consecutive weeks on the *Billboard* album chart.

Marley is everywhere, especially if you take into account the massive numbers of T-shirts, handbags, and other paraphernalia bearing his image. His most important legacy, however, is not in the massive merchandise he generates, but in his status as a symbol of empowerment for the underprivileged. Especially in Africa, he's revered as a spokesperson for the rights of the oppressed. He gained this position not only through the messages of his many songs, but also through the courageous stances he often took in his public life.

Even without these considerations, Marley's purely musical accomplishments were remarkable. With the Wailers—especially Peter Tosh and Bunny Wailer, who were nearly as important to the group as Marley in the band's first decade—he was crucial to developing and popularizing reggae, the music that remains Jamaica's most renowned export. He and the Wailers were the first reggae act to make albums as unified statements rather than more or less random collections of tracks. Those albums, in turn, were among the first reggae records to gain a wide listenership among rock fans outside of Jamaica, with reggae going on to influence countless musicians, rock and otherwise.

Marley has often been deified as a saint or even a Christ-like figure. But while his achievements were in some respects miraculous, he was, like any idolized artist, a very human and flawed figure. He was not an ideal husband or father, and did not always practice the peace and love extolled in many of his songs.

And despite his enormous fame and legacy, many of the details of his life remain surprisingly mysterious, especially for the years before his rise to international fame in the mid-1970s. Even some of the most prominent Marley biographies report events in different sequences, or give different months or even years for the same pivotal moment. One source, for instance, will report a Wailers single becoming a hit in Jamaica half a year before the month in which another source states it was recorded in the studio. Different close associates of Marley will have substantially different memories of what happened when or where, or why it happened.

It's virtually certain, however, that Marley was born on February 6, 1945, in the village of Nine Mile, Jamaica. It's even more certain that before leaving his teens, he helped spearhead a musical revolution that still echoes around the globe.

Staffordshire, England, June 22, 1978. TRINITY MIRROR/MIRRORPIX/ALAMY STOCK PHOTOS

BEGINNINGS 1945–1962

1

When Bob Marley was born, no one would have predicted that a boy of his background could become a musical revolutionary. His race, nationality, and modest family assets all seemed to work against the likelihood of his even rising out of poverty. Yet those same factors may well have fueled his burning desire to better not just himself, but the lot of millions of others with similar disadvantages.

One of those disadvantages was his color. Economic and political power in Jamaica was almost exclusively concentrated in a small white minority, often descendants of the British, who were still running Jamaica as a colony in which the gap between the ruling elite and a large black underclass was huge. Although his father was white, Marley was considered part of that underclass. It had been part of Jamaican life since slaves were forced to move to the country from their African homes starting in the early sixteenth century, though Jamaica finally abolished slavery in 1838.

Marley's mother, Cedella Malcolm, was reasonably well off by the standards of rural black Jamaicans. In the village of Nine Mile in the parish of Saint Ann, her father ran small businesses and owned

A group of Jamaican musicians plays a small local dance in 1946, the year after Marley's birth. MICHAEL OCHS ARCHIVES/GETTY IMAGES

INSET: "Judge Not" was credited to Marley when it was issued as his debut single. He was just sixteen.

some property. Her family became known to Norval Marley, a Jamaican of British descent who was, by most accounts, an overseer of land administered by the government in the area, though it's been suggested that his position was more modest than that.

Indeed, considerable mystery surrounds Norval's origins. He was known as Captain Marley, but doesn't seem to have attained that rank in his travels and various occupations in Jamaica, Britain, and Nigeria. When he first crossed paths with Cedella, he was aged anywhere from his late forties to his early sixties, depending

Marley's mother, Cedella Malcolm, was from the village of Nine Mile, where her father ran small businesses and owned some property. Marley's boyhood home there is now a museum. A MEDIA PRESS/ALAMY STOCK PHOTO

on the account. Certainly the middle-aged man was quite a bit older than the teenaged girl, who was seventeen when she became pregnant by him. Conferring legitimacy on the child they were expecting, Captain Marley married Cedella in June 1944.

Although Norval moved to Kingston shortly afterward, he did name the son that Cedella gave birth to on February 6, 1945, Nesta Robert Marley. For much of his early youth, the future Bob Marley would be known as Nesta. He seldom saw his father, and when the youngster was sent to live with Norval at around the age of five, Captain Marley ended up arranging for his boy to live with a woman not even related to his parents. Cedella Marley ended up taking her son back to Nine Mile about a year later. He'd see little of his father before Norval Marley died in the mid-1950s.

Marley's father Norval was a white Jamaican of British descent and, by most accounts, a government land administrator.

"Captain did not prove himself a good father," Cedella understated in her book, *Bob Marley, My Son* (written with Anthony C. Winkler). "Mostly, he stayed away from his son, writing the occasional letter but visiting only rarely. He seemed to take little or no interest in Nesta's upbringing."

If his mixed racial background was an embarrassment to his father's family, and the possible source of some teasing from his peers as he grew up in black Jamaican society, Marley never let it hold him back. "My father's white, my mother's black," he acknowledged in *Melody Maker* in 1975. "You know what them call me, half caste or wh'ever. Well, me don't dip on nobody's side, me don't dip on the black man's side nor the white man's side, me dip on God's side, the man who create me, who cause me to come from black and white, who give me this talent."

FORMING THE WAILERS

As a single mother in a small town, Cedella found it hard to support herself and her son, taking domestic work in Kingston and leaving Bob in the care of relatives in Nine Mile for spells. Shortly before Bob's teens, the two moved to Kingston, by far the largest city in Jamaica. There she took up with Toddy Livingston, who ran a bar and often visited her and Bob in Trench Town, a large ghetto even more impoverished than its counterparts in the United States.

Here Bob became reacquainted with Livingston's slightly younger son, Neville, known as Bunny since his birth on April 10, 1947. The pair had first become friends when Bunny and his father lived in Nine Mile several

Marley's former home on First Street in Trench Town as seen in 2000. COLLIN REID/AP PHOTO

years earlier. Their friendship grew as they discovered a mutual interest in music and as their parents' affair intensified, resulting in a daughter, Pearl, born in 1962. With a half-sister in common, Bob and Bunny were not just friends; they were family, cementing a bond that would help in the formation of their own singing group.

Even for bright boys like Bob—a name, rather confusingly, that he was increasingly being called, along with Robert, Robbie, and Nesta—educational opportunities for the overwhelmingly black and poor population of Trench Town were limited. Around the age of fifteen, he left school with no qualifications and, apparently, little to expect in terms of economic advancement. He at least had plenty of time to sing and play rudimentary guitar with Bunny.

Their chief inspirations were not the calypso music popular in Jamaica and throughout much of the Caribbean, nor mento, its somewhat similar Jamaican variation. Their real passion was for American rock 'n' roll and rhythm and blues, which made their way into the poorest neighborhoods of Jamaica via radio and records. As Bob confirmed in interview footage used in *Rebel Music: The Bob Marley Story*, "We couldn't afford to buy records, so we listened to the radio."

In particular, they were inspired by the young, black American harmonizing vocal groups—sometimes called doo-wop acts, in honor of the frequent nonsense syllables they employed—that were merging pop and R & B into a style that would lay a foundation for 1960s soul music. Frankie Lymon and the Teenagers had been one of the first such groups to score a big rock 'n' roll hit in the mid-1950s with "Why Do Fools Fall in Love." The more polished Platters updated the kind of smooth arrangements used by pre-rock acts like the Ink Spots. And the Drifters, with ever-shifting members, added more elaborate, sometimes orchestrated production as the 1950s turned into the 1960s. All were cited by Bunny Livingston (in the *Marley* documentary) as key early influences on the group that, with the addition of a third member, evolved into the Wailers.

The third teenager was Peter Tosh, born Winston Hubert McIntosh on October 19, 1944. Peter spent his early years in the coastal town of Savanna-la-Mar before moving at a young age to Kingston, living with an uncle in Trench Town when he entered his teens. A more accomplished instrumentalist, Tosh ran into the pair while playing and singing in Trench Town. By the early 1960s, they formed a trio, naming themselves the Teenagers, in honor of Frankie Lymon's group. After briefly working as a welder, Bob's resolve to make music his living was stiffened when a piece of metal flew into his eye at work. Although the debris was removed without complications, Marley quit welding to focus on music. The accident gave Tosh an excuse to give up his welding job as well.

Giving up a trade to sing, in a town with high unemployment among black youth, must have seemed foolhardy to much of their family and friends, especially considering there wasn't

As teens in Trench Town, Marley and Bunny Livingston were inspired not by the local calypso music, but by black American vocal groups like (from top) Frankie Lymon and the Teenagers, the Platters, and the Drifters.

THE DRIFTERS

yet much of a Jamaican music industry. Yet at precisely this time, opportunities to make a living at music—and even to make records—were opening up for young Jamaicans.

Even back in the 1950s, the zeal for American rock and R & B was such that some Jamaicans began bringing back large quantities of 78s and 45s to play in their homeland. Perhaps the fervor was greased by the lack of a language barrier, Kingston being the largest English-speaking city south of the United States in the Western Hemisphere. The new sounds could also be heard, if erratically and with static, on US radio stations, if conditions permitted the reception of signals from cities such as Miami and New Orleans. For the most part, this music was not available on behind-the-times Jamaican radio; some poor households couldn't even afford a radio set.

With Jamaican radio behind the times, entrepreneurs found ways to bring the hottest sounds to the masses, giving rise to Jamaica's competitive sound system and DJ culture.

To meet the demand, some entrepreneurs started playing their precious American discs on the loudest sound equipment available at the time, presenting public events at which revelers could pay a small admission to dance to the records. Often staged in outdoor settings, the apparatus the organizers traveled with became known as sound systems, sidestepping the usual channels to bring the music to the people. Such was the cutthroat competition between sound systems that DJs often scratched out the labels on records so the performers and songs couldn't be identified, giving them "exclusives" of a sort.

The hunger for "exclusives" among DJs and audiences grew so intense that it became difficult for the supply to keep up with the demand. Some sound system operators realized that one way to keep one jump ahead was to make their own records with Jamaican artists. The sound-system-guys-turned-record-producers were quick to realize that the discs could be played at dances *and* on the radio, and sold to stores and jukeboxes, opening a much more lucrative stream of revenue.

The artists, however, couldn't quite replicate the American R & B they craved. Instead, what came out was something of a hybrid of American rock/R & B and indigenous Jamaican sounds. The rhythm accentuated insistent, jerking offbeats; the brass and guitar, often played by musicians older than the singers, betrayed their backgrounds in jazzier pre-rock; and the vocals, though approximating the feel of American soul singers, couldn't help but be infused with Jamaican dialect.

On top of everything was the fervor of a post–World War II generation boasting a new pride and self-determination after Jamaica declared independence from the United Kingdom on August 6, 1962. The result was ska, the direct predecessor of the reggae with which Bob Marley and his group would become so strongly associated. After changing their name first to the Wailing Rudeboys and then to the Wailing Wailers, they settled on the Wailers (though perhaps unbeknownst to them, a Tacoma, Washington, rock band with the same name had already scored an American instrumental hit with "Tall Cool One" in 1959).

Marley, Livingston, and Tosh were not among the very first wave of ska artists to make records, however. They were still in their midteens and in need of some refinement and experience, even as they were already beginning to toy with writing their own material. Before they changed their name to the Wailers, they began rehearsing under the tutelage of Joe Higgs. Already a national star in the pre-reggae style, Higgs had been recording since the late 1950s and would, for a brief time, sing with the Wailers onstage more than a decade later, when they were on the cusp of international stardom.

The Wailers, Higgs told Roger Steffens in *Option* magazine in 1986, "weren't even conscious of sound when I started to deal with them. To hear that 'Joe assisted with the Wailers'—this is foolishness. The Wailers weren't singers until I taught them. . . . It took me years to teach the Wailers." Additionally, Higgs asserted, "They would be going to make a record and I would go with them and there is somebody making constant mistakes. I would just have to take his part in order to get the record finished in time." Marley, noted Higgs in Stephen Davis's *Bob Marley*, "was the leader of the group, but the lead *singer* of the group in those days was Junior Braithwaite," who joined the Wailers before they made their first record. "But person to person, they were each capable of leading at any given time because I wanted each person to be a leader in his own right, able to lead anyone, or to be able to wail."

The young Wailers fell under the tutelage of Joe Higgs, often called the "Father of Reggae," who had begun recording in the 1950s. Seen here circa 1980, he would join the Wailers for a time in the 1970s.
LEE JAFFE/GETTY IMAGES

However large Higgs's role in shaping their harmonies, the Wailers were, with his help, hitting on a distinctive and effective blend. Tosh, who at six foot five towered over the others, had the grittiest and deepest voice; Livingston had the sweetest and highest. Marley combined qualities of both, as if he were the earthy mix of Tosh's toughness and Livingston's airiness. Many feel their vocal differences reflected differences in their personalities and, a few years down the line, their songwriting, Peter affecting the most militant tone, Bunny the most spiritual, and Marley something of a more commercial midpoint.

There were exceptions to these categorizations, of course, but even at this early stage, it was clear that they had more of an impact together than as soloists. "Me and Bunny together had a kind of voice that could decorate Bob's music and make it beautiful," declared Tosh in the documentary *Rebel Music*. "So we just did that wholeheartedly."

RECORDING DEBUT

It was as a soloist, however, that Marley would make his recording debut. Around early 1962, he was recommended to budding producer Leslie Kong, who'd started his Beverley's label as an outgrowth of his combination restaurant/ice cream parlor—itself an indication of how primitive the Jamaican music business was at ska's inception. Two early ska stars, Desmond Dekker (who'd have one of the first big international reggae hits in the late 1960s with "The Israelites") and Derrick Morgan (who was also a talent scout for Kong), have been credited with making Marley aware of an opportunity to cut a single with Kong.

Also on the scene was a teenage Jimmy Cliff, later to become one of reggae's most popular singers. As Cliff later remarked to the Experience Music Project, "Desmond Dekker went back to Bob and said, 'I've found this guy, Jimmy Cliff, and I got my songs passed, and I'm going to record, so you should go and see him.'" When Marley met Cliff, Cliff added, Marley "sang some of his songs, and among the songs that he sang, three of them I chose, and then when Derrick [Morgan] come, he liked those as well, which was 'One Cup of Coffee,' 'Judge Not,' and 'Terror.' And at Leslie Kong's next session, he recorded those three songs. And that was the start of Bob Marley."

Released when Bob was just sixteen, "Judge Not" was credited to Robert Marley when it was issued as his debut single. A quite respectably infectious and catchy slice of early-1960s ska, with a wheezing flute, it also bore a trace of the moral compass that would feature in many of his later compositions, urging others not to judge him before they judged themselves. As Cliff observed in the documentary *Marley* (2012), "Judge Not" was "[an] evolutionary song defending his rights as an individual. It occurred to me, well, this guy's really a good poet."

It sold little at the time, however, and nor did its follow-up, "One Cup of Coffee" (on which Bob was billed as "Bobby Martell"), based on a recent American country hit by Claude Gray.

Marley was likely more comfortable as part of the Wailers and also likely realized that his prospects were greater as part of a group with two talented friends. Not long after his pair of singles with Kong, however, came a turn of events that could have short-circuited the band's career almost as soon as it had started. Her relationship with Toddy Livingston (who'd been married to another woman during their affair) having soured, Bob's mother, Cedella, went to stay with relatives in Delaware. Intending to move to the US permanently if she could, she likely would have wanted her son to come with her. But Bob remained behind in Jamaica, determined to make it with the group even though he lacked a permanent residence and slept for a while on a kitchen table in a friend's place.

Bob would eventually join his mother in Delaware. In the three years or so before that extended visit, however, the Wailers—sometimes embellished by one, two, or even three other members—became one of the biggest acts in Jamaica.

LEFT: Ska star Desmond Dekker, sporting classic rude boy garb on this sleeve of his late-1960s hit, "The Israelites," is credited with steering the young Marley to producer Leslie Kong.

BELOW: Marley's debut single, "Judge Not" (see page 10) fared poorly at the time, as did its follow-up, "One Cup of Coffee," based on a recent American country hit.

Famous promotional photo of the Wailing Wailers depicts, from left, Livingston, Marley, and Tosh.

THE STUDIO ONE SKA YEARS 1963–1966

2

When Cedella Marley married an American man, Edward Booker, in October 1963, she became a permanent legal resident of the United States. That would have made it easier for Bob to also emigrate, which could well have spelled the end of the Wailers. Yet he continued to rehearse with the group's growing lineup, without a record deal and at a time when Jamaican labels were rapidly expanding their output as ska boomed.

While the date (like so much early Marley chronology) is indefinite, at some point in the early 1960s, a fourth singer, Junior Braithwaite, started to sing with Marley, Livingston, and Tosh. Younger than the other three, Braithwaite already knew Joe Higgs, as Braithwaite's grandmother had raised Higgs's duet partner, Roy Wilson, and Higgs and Wilson rehearsed in his yard. At some point, the budding Wailers were also joined by a young woman, Cherry Green (real name Ermine Ortense Bramwell) and a teenage girl, Beverley Kelso, who wasn't much older than Braithwaite.

Perhaps the Wailers were influenced by favorite American doo-wop groups such as the Platters in incorporating both male and female singers into the act. Although the Platters' lead singer was Tony Williams and their personnel largely male, Zola Taylor added a woman's voice to the mix, as did some other US vocal groups such as the Miracles, who in their early years included leader Smokey Robinson's wife, Claudette.

It could also be that the Wailers simply hadn't settled upon a lineup, or even an approach. The four- to six-person lineup remained rather fluid in the year or two they sang together, probably starting around 1963. They didn't use the same personnel for all of their performances or even on their records, though it was a while before they managed to cut any. Labels might have been reluctant because the ska scene was oriented toward solo singers and duos rather than groups.

Complicating matters for Marley, in May 1963, Cheryl Murray gave birth to his daughter, Imani Carole, though little is known of either mother or child. Imani Carole would be the first of many children Bob fathered, although exactly how many were born to how many mothers varies according to the source. Most accounts place the number at about a dozen offspring, birthed by almost as many women.

CONTRACT WITH COXSONE DODD

Their constant practicing, whether with Joe Higgs or on their own, meant the Wailers had undergone quite a bit of preparation before the opportunity to record finally arrived. Egged on by Higgs, percussionist Seeco Patterson took them to audition at a new Kingston facility, Studio One. The studio was run by Clement "Coxsone" Dodd, a sound system operator who'd started his own label, also called Studio One.

He didn't get excited, however, until they launched into "Simmer Down," with some reluctance from Marley, who didn't think much of the tune. The audition could have been held anytime between late 1963 and mid-1964; even the most widely distributed accounts of Marley's history are not in agreement.

Whenever the audition took place, it's pretty certain that Dodd quickly offered the Wailers a deal: twenty pounds for every track of theirs he released. It wasn't a very good deal for the group—should the discs sell well, as many of them did, they wouldn't see many or any royalties. It was, however, a more or less standard deal for Jamaican artists of the time, in a young record business that routinely exploited its young performers. It was also more money than they would see *without* a deal, especially as Bunny and Bob didn't have much cash coming in, though Tosh had a job at a dry cleaner.

There was also a definite advantage to recording with Dodd, however. He often employed some of Jamaica's best musicians, including several players who were crucial to supplying the supple drive behind many of the best early ska records. From their first Studio One sessions, the Wailers were backed by top instrumentalists such as trombonist Don Drummond, tenor saxophonists Tommy McCook and Roland Alphonso, trumpeter

Johnny Moore, drummer Lloyd Knibbs, guitarist Ernest Ranglin, and keyboardist Jackie Mittoo. Most of these artists also released records under their own names, sometimes collecting substantial sales. All of them save Ranglin were also founding members of the Skatalites, Jamaica's top instrumental ska group.

Dodd himself, as Livingston emphasized in the *Marley* documentary, "might not be an instrument player, he might not even know if a guitar is [in] tune. But he knows when the sound is *right*!"

It was also spontaneous. "We would try to get two takes. One that is the right one, and then one for luck," Bunny said in an interview included in the same film's DVD edition. As Marley wittily put it in *Rolling Stone*, "Jamaicans go slow, everything is 'soon come,' but if there's one thing Jamaicans rush about, it's making a recordin'!"

Reports vary as to whether "Simmer Down" was recorded at their first session (which seems probable), or even whether it was the first Wailers single Dodd released. It *can* be confidently stated, however, that in the last half of 1964, "Simmer Down" became the Wailers' first Jamaican hit. Kicked off by blaring brass reminiscent of themes for western movies featuring galloping horses, "Simmer Down" had an irresistible propulsive energy, Marley's vocals backed by raw yet exuberant harmonies from his fellow Wailers—or most of his fellow Wailers, at any rate. Cherry Green, already in her early twenties, had to miss the session due to work and would sing on just a handful of their releases (and perform onstage with them just once).

Even at this early juncture, Marley's writing was infused with social commentary, if relatively mild in comparison to his famous 1970s anthems. By the mid-1960s, a youth cult of "rude boys" had emerged in Kingston. Like the Mods emerging at the same time in England, they had their own codes of hipster dress and slang, and espoused a rebellious attitude toward authority. More than the Mods, they were often deemed troublemakers, both by authorities and many Jamaicans, for engaging in gangster-type behavior. Those activities had a direct impact on the ska scene, with the rude boys sometimes disrupting sound system dances with violent fights.

"Simmer Down," the first side the Wailing Wailers cut with Clement "Coxsone" Dodd at Studio One.

"Simmer Down" was a plea, if a subtle one, to rude boys to control themselves—though, ironically, the song was likely a favorite among rude boys as well as everyday young Jamaicans, such was its infectious danceability. "I knew from the minute I heard 'Simmer Down' at their audition that the Wailers had that *intelligent* teenage sound that was needed in Jamaica," Coxsone Dodd claimed in an interview with Timothy White for *The Beat*. "Telling the youth, 'Don't slip up or else.'"

Sales reports and even chart positions (such as charts were in Jamaica at the time) need to be taken with a grain of salt, given how unreliable such figures were in the country's market, but "Simmer Down" is usually reported to have made #1 and sold seventy thousand to eighty thousand copies. On an island with a population of a little less than two million, it was the equivalent of selling roughly five million copies in the United States.

The Wailers didn't see much money from the sales, of course, but Coxsone Dodd probably did. Which meant that the Wailers were soon back in the studio churning out more sides for the producer and would cut plenty more for Studio One over the next couple years or so. Indeed, they worked at a furious rate, resulting in about three dozen 45s through the end of 1966. No comparable American or British group was releasing singles at such a rapid-fire pace. But the crush of product was as much a reflection of the Wild West nature of the Jamaican record industry as the Wailers' prolific generation of fresh material. Several Jamaican labels were saturating the small national market with vinyl as fast as they could press it, in part to continue to satisfy the demand of the sound systems, which were still integral to getting the music out to the public.

THE STUDIO ONE SIDES

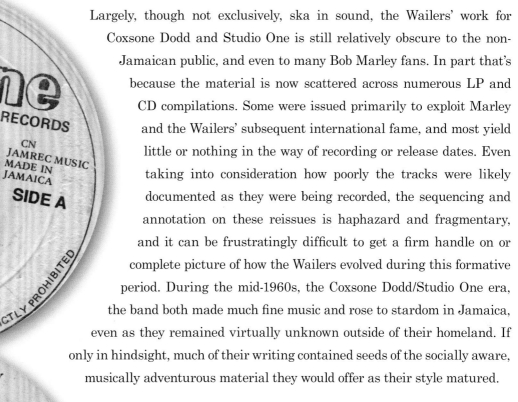

Largely, though not exclusively, ska in sound, the Wailers' work for Coxsone Dodd and Studio One is still relatively obscure to the non-Jamaican public, and even to many Bob Marley fans. In part that's because the material is now scattered across numerous LP and CD compilations. Some were issued primarily to exploit Marley and the Wailers' subsequent international fame, and most yield little or nothing in the way of recording or release dates. Even taking into consideration how poorly the tracks were likely documented as they were being recorded, the sequencing and annotation on these reissues is haphazard and fragmentary, and it can be frustratingly difficult to get a firm handle on or complete picture of how the Wailers evolved during this formative period. During the mid-1960s, the Coxsone Dodd/Studio One era, the band both made much fine music and rose to stardom in Jamaica, even as they remained virtually unknown outside of their homeland. If only in hindsight, much of their writing contained seeds of the socially aware, musically adventurous material they would offer as their style matured.

While admirably eclectic, the Studio One sides were also at times wildly uneven, partly because their personnel was in flux almost from the era's start. Not long after "Simmer Down" made the Wailers one of the hottest acts in ska, Junior Braithwaite left the group. Far from being a peripheral member, Braithwaite had taken some lead vocals on some of their earliest tracks, most notably another 1964 hit, "It Hurts to Be Alone." The standout among Braithwaite's slim body of Wailers leads, this gripping soul ballad featured piercingly pleading singing from Junior, the fifteen-year-old's tenor still so high that some listeners could mistake it for a woman's voice.

The Wailers recorded several records for Coxsone Dodd. The Wailers' "It Hurts to Be Alone" was a gripping soul ballad featuring fifteen-year-old Junior Braithwaite on lead vocal. "Dancing Shoes," meanwhile, featured a deft lead vocal by Bunny Livingston.

From doo-wop to Dylan, the Wailers made stabs at several styles while recording for Dodd. Their take on the Impressions' "I Made a Mistake" was more effective than most. The Impressions and their leader, Curtis Mayfield (right), would remain the Wailers' biggest influence. AFRO AMERICAN NEWSPAPERS/GADO/GETTY IMAGES

Shortly after it was recorded, Braithwaite immigrated to Chicago with his family. Had he stayed, he quite possibly could have taken a stronger role with the Wailers, at least in their early work. Cherry Green told one of Marley's biographers, Chris Salewicz, that she thought Braithwaite had the finest voice in the group. With his departure, yet more of the focus fell on the founding trio of Marley, Tosh, and Livingston.

"With the Wailers, it was Junior Braithwaite at that time who had the voice and the drive," opined Coxsone Dodd in Roger Steffens's liner notes to the *Climb the Ladder* compilation. "I loved how he delivered 'Don't Ever Leave Me' and 'It Hurts to Be Alone.' If he hadn't left for Chicago to join his parents, maybe he would still have been the lead singer of the Wailers. I appointed Bob as leader when he left."

With and without Braithwaite, the Wailers' Studio One recordings encompassed almost ridiculously wide-ranging stabs at several styles. Some of this could be attributed to the sheer volume of tracks they were laying down (some not even issued at the time), as if Coxsone Dodd was throwing as much as he could at the wall to see what would stick. The early Wailers can sound yet more exotic—at least to non-Jamaican ears—owing to the relatively primitive state of Jamaican recording, which lent the tracks an oft-murky, slightly lo-fi sound that could seem several years behind what was being taped at studios in the United States and United Kingdom. Studio One was just a one-track studio when the Wailers first set foot there, and, though Dodd (along with the rest of the Jamaican recording industry) would soon update his technology, the country's facilities lagged behind those in North America and Europe for quite some time.

At Studio One, they covered an improbable gamut of hits ranging from Harvey and the Moonglows' 1950s doo-wop classic "Ten Commandments of Love" to Dion and the Belmonts' "Teenager in Love" and "Lemon Tree," the folk tune that had been an early-1960s hit for Peter, Paul, and Mary. Some of the covers were quite good, given the surprising sources: their mutation of the Beatles' "And I Love Her" into a mournful ska ballad was extremely enjoyable, and their more expected choice of the Impressions' "I Made a Mistake" (written by that group's leader-singer-songwriter, Curtis Mayfield) was effective and haunting. Others were more dubious, such as their version of Tom Jones's campy "What's New Pussycat," which was neither as weird nor as interesting as one might guess. Sometimes they took great liberties with the lyrics of the classics they interpreted, such as "White Christmas," Bob Dylan's "Like a Rolling Stone," and "And I Love Her," in which they wail "'cause I love her, oh yes siree!" at the end of the verses.

There were some cool moments in their covers, but the Wailers' ultimate strength lay in their originals, at this point mostly composed and sung by Marley. Yet as strong as the first of those to catch on ("Simmer Down") had been, a good number of the others were on the callow and derivative side. Some of the songs remained quite indebted to slow, dreamy, mid-1950s doo-wop, a style that by 1965 was dated to the point of being passé. Sometimes they even used melodies and lyrics from big American hits, "Dance with Me" appropriating bits of the Drifters' "On Broadway" and "Ska Jerk" taking a lot from Junior Walker's "Shotgun."

A natty young Bob.

The Wailers were at their best not as balladeers or faux American soulsters, but as forceful skasters. From their very first sessions, "I Don't Need Your Love" and "I Am Going Home" have a frenetic, joyful energy that almost slides the discs off the turntable, stopping just shy of careening out of control. Peter Tosh proves himself capable of helming a similar stomper on "Maga Dog," the first recording on which he takes lead vocals. With some other hits (though none as big as "Simmer Down") in the Wailers' clutch of early singles, Dodd became somewhat more generous with his new stars, putting them on a weekly salary of three pounds each. He also let Marley sleep in the audition/rehearsal room of Studio One, partly in appreciation for his extra work in helping to rehearse other artists recording there.

In their lyrics and appearance, the Wailers were still fairly conventional. The words they sang largely stuck—as most American soul acts of the time did—to declarations of love and celebrations of partying. They wore the same kind of conservative suits and ties (and, when Kelso and Green were still aboard, dresses) as most US soul artists did, even if they couldn't afford anything close to the fancy wardrobes of the Supremes or the Temptations. Marley, Tosh, and Livingston sported short, natural haircuts that wouldn't have been out of place in any visiting soul ensemble, though Tosh's extreme height, compared to his relatively diminutive bandmates, did something to make them stand out from the crowd.

Yet as they gained more writing and recording experience, their songs started to reflect more of the Trench Town culture in which they were immersed. It was a lifestyle, and area of

Kingston, of which very few tourists of Jamaica's famous resorts were even aware. Even in their good-time party songs and fashionable outfits, they gave voice to the rude boy culture of which they were a part, if only as entertainers and observers.

"Simmer Down" had been a message of sorts to rude boys, and in 1965, some of the Wailers' songs were more explicitly inspired by that part of their constituency. After a power outage at their Christmas 1964 concert at Kingston's Palace Theatre ignited a mini-riot, they sang about the event, if a bit obliquely, in "Hooligans," a kinetic stomper complete with dramatic opening brass fanfare and drum bashes. Hooligans and the Palace melee were also referenced in "Jumbie Jamboree," another of the first Wailers tracks to prominently feature Tosh on vocals.

This was but a warmup for their hit "Rude Boy," largely sung in unison more as a hypnotic ska-rhythm chant than a conventional tune. Significantly, it also in parts used the Jamaican patois—sometimes using "me" in place of the more standard "I"—that would have made it impenetrable to American listeners had it been played in the States at the time. By using local slang and manners of speech, the Wailers were becoming spokespersons of sorts for younger Jamaicans who had little voice in the media. After the group became internationally famous, their (in particular Marley's) use of patois in interviews, however, would often make their spoken statements difficult to understand for many non-Jamaicans.

In *Bob Marley: The Untold Story*, Skatalites trumpeter Johnny Moore, speaking of the Wailers' early work, remarked, "The uniqueness of the sound they projected was specifically local and really good. The subject matter was clean, and the lyrics were really educative. The statements might be a bit serious, but the way they projected it you could absorb what they were saying. There were some good lessons, we had to admit that."

Not all of the Wailers' first socially conscious songs were about rude boys and riots. "One Love," the earliest of their songs that would find a much wider audience when it was re-recorded in the 1970s, gave thanks to a deity and urged love among a community rather than love between a boy and a girl. With "One Love," the Wailers were likely influenced by Curtis Mayfield, several of whose songs for the Impressions were starting to carry a message of black pride and optimistic exhortations for justice, often with gospel overtones. Marley would combine "One Love" with Mayfield's "People Get Ready" when he recorded it more than a decade later for the *Exodus* album, and the Wailers covered Mayfield's "I Made a Mistake" not long after they committed "One Love" to tape. The Impressions, Bob's soon-to-be wife, Rita, goes as far as saying in *Rebel Music*, were "all they listened to most of the time."

"One Love" was the earliest of several Wailers songs that would find a much wider audience when re-recorded in the 1970s. Here it was the B-side of "Donna" by the Blues Busters.

THE WAILING WAILERS

Review by Richie Unterberger

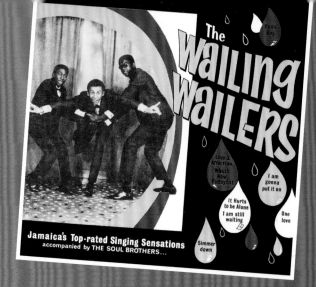

As the only LP issued by the group in the 1960s, some listeners might expect *The Wailing Wailers* to be the cream of their early work. While it contains generally fine music, it isn't the strongest representation of their ska-era tracks that could have been assembled, though it does have some of their greatest early efforts. Instead, it's an uneven and rather arbitrary selection of a dozen songs cut at Studio One, covering the group's roughly first year and a half as a recording act. The Wailers' lineup isn't the same across all twelve cuts, either, adding to its slight stylistic inconsistency.

If these were the only sides the Wailers ever recorded, the disc would still be strong enough to ensure their standing as one of the best and most important ska acts ever. "Simmer Down," "Lonesome Feeling," and "Love and Affection" are the early Wailers at their simplest and most joyful, their effervescent harmonies backed by an irresistibly danceable ska beat. "Put It On" and "Rude Boy" have similar musical strengths, adding to the mix strong hints of their soon-to-blossom spiritually and socially conscious lyrics.

In a slower, more romantic mode, "I'm Still Waiting" might be explicitly derivative of Chicago soul greats Curtis Mayfield and the Impressions, but it's one of the best Impressions knockoffs ever cut anywhere. "It Hurts to Be Alone," with Wailer-for-just-a-while Junior Braithwaite on lead vocals, also testifies to their way with a tear-jerking soul ballad. The original version of "One Love," here done to a ska rhythm slightly less frenetic than their most exuberant party tunes, is by far the most famous song on the album. And even if it would change a great deal by the time it was featured on Bob Marley's 1977 album, *Exodus*, this version is no less worthy (and far more danceable).

Other tracks on *The Wailing Wailers* seem tacked on to fill out the LP. The ghostly cover of Harvey and the Moonglows' classic 1958 doo-wop hit "Ten Commandments of Love," though sung well by Marley, was by the mid-1960s so stylistically dated as to sound ancient. "I Need You" is an average soul slowie, and the cover of Tom Jones's "What's

New Pussycat" an awkward misstep, especially considering how many superior tracks from the same period were available for inclusion.

"When the Well Runs Dry," which has some similarities to William Bell's early-1960s soul classic "You Don't Miss Your Water," is a solid soul lament, but (like some of their other Studio One sides) is marred by a muddy sound, even by early Jamaican ska standards. According to Roger Steffens and Leroy Jodie Pierson, writing in *Bob Marley and the Wailers: The Definitive Discography*, this track was recorded around mid-1966, featuring Peter Tosh on lead vocal and Bunny Livingston, Vision Walker, and Rita Marley on backup vocals in Bob Marley's absence. If this indeed was the personnel, the LP likely couldn't have come out earlier than spring 1966, shortly after Marley left for an extended trip to the United States.

As some compensation for the numerous mid-1960s goodies missing from *The Wailing Wailers*, the album boasted fun if rudimentary cover art featuring the song titles enclosed in teardrops. It also featured a picture of Marley, Tosh, and Livingston—the trio composing the Wailers by the end of 1965, although Beverley Kelso and Cherry Green can be clearly heard on some of the tracks' background vocals (and, as mentioned, Junior Braithwaite on lead for "It Hurts to Be Alone"). In keeping with the generally haphazard modus operandi of the early Jamaican record business, two different sleeves with similar designs were issued, one with a photo of the Wailers crouching and smiling, the other picturing them somberly standing.

For all its assets, *The Wailing Wailers* lacks some of the group's best early cuts, from "Hooligans," "I Am Going Home," "Maga Dog," "I Made a Mistake," and "I Don't Need Your Love" to their goofily endearing cover of the Beatles' "And I Love Her." These and many other Studio One tracks have since been compiled on several reissues (see Discography), but have sometimes been subjected to overdubs—some as late as the 1990s, according to Steffens and Pierson—that diminish their integrity. Such is the importance and quality of the Wailers' Studio One tracks that they really deserve a comprehensive box set that puts them in chronological sequence with thorough annotation, warts and all—without the overdubs.

While the Wailers were heavily Impressions-influenced at their inception, as Johnny Moore is quoted as remarking in *Bob Marley: The Untold Story*, "they were dissuaded from going along that line, and influenced to go inside themselves, however silly or simple they feared what they found there might sound like. They were simply urged to try and cultivate their own thing. And it worked. Even at that age they knew what they wanted. From the time that they realized that trying to be the Impressions was not what they should be doing, they really checked themselves and got into it."

"One Love" was also featured on the Wailers' first LP, *The Wailing Wailers*, probably issued around the end of 1965 or beginning of 1966. Like so many rock and soul full-lengths from all over the world before the Beatles, Bob Dylan, and others started to transform the rock album into an art form, the LP was something of a grab bag of previously released singles and tracks that had yet to be issued as 45s. While it had big hits such as "Simmer Down" and "Rude Boy," it featured neither all of the very best nor all of the most popular of their pre-1966 recordings. It was nonetheless an honor for a group to even release an LP, as the Jamaican scene was so singles oriented, with many Jamaicans unable or unwilling to buy albums.

The cover photos of *The Wailing Wailers* made it clear the group had undergone some serious changes since they cut their first discs. No matter which of the two different sleeves you picked up, only Marley, Tosh, and Livingston were pictured—Beverley Kelso and Cherry Green had drifted out of the group, probably sometime in 1965.

Kelso left, in part, because Marley could be such a tough taskmaster at rehearsals. "Things were getting strictly professional," commented Livingston to *The Beat* many years later, "an' Beverley an' Cherry couldn't cope." Green, as noted, sang on hardly any Wailers sessions, but Kelso sang quite audible harmonies on a couple dozen or so tracks, her high if somewhat shrill vocals adding to the group's overall sense of joie de vivre. Still, cutting back to a trio not only put the emphasis back on the original members, but also allowed them to more closely emulate the all-male Chicago soul stars who were their biggest influence, the Impressions.

MARLEY MARRIES AND LEAVES FOR DELAWARE

In early 1966, one of the more recent recordings on *The Wailing Wailers*, "I'm Gonna Put It On," continued the group's series of sizable Jamaican hits. With its gripping ascending-descending riff, gossamer harmonies, and almost giddily religious sense

ABOVE: Accounts of jobs Marley held in Delaware vary but must certainly included stints as waiter, dishwasher, parking lot attendant, lab assistant at DuPont chemical company, forklift operator at a Chrysler plant, and janitor here, at the Hotel du Pont.

RIGHT: With Marley in Delaware with his mother, the Wailers make a strong showing in the May 23, 1966, Jamaican charts. ROGER STEFFENS' REGGAE ARCHIVE

UK/JAMAICAN TOP TWENTY Week Ending May 23rd.

TOP TWENTY

1. DANCING SHOES (R. 116)	The Wailers
2. DO THE TEASY (WIP 6010)	Joyce Bond
3. 007 – SHANTY TOWN (PYR 6004)	Desmond Dekker
4. MUSICAL TRAIN (R. 115)	The Clarendonians
5. I AM THE TOUGHEST (WI 3042)	Peter Touch
6. SAD MOVIES (DB 1057)	Gloria Crawford
7. YOU CAN'T BE HAPPY (WI 3041)	The Clarendonians
8. DON'T BE A RUDE BOY (R. 105)	The Wailers
9. DANCING MOOD (WI 3013)	Delroy Wilson
10. DON'T STAY AWAY (DB 1061)	Phillis Dillon
11. KEEP THE PRESSURE ON (PYR 6002)	Winston & George
12. GUNS OF NAVARONE (WI 168)	Skatalites
13. COME BACK GIRL (WIP 6009)	Jackie Edwards
14. BEND DOWN LOW (WI 3043)	The Wailers
15. COPASETIC (R. 107)	The Rulers
16. PHOENIX CITY (DB 1020)	Rolando Al & The Soul Bros
17. CLUB SKA '67 (LP 948)	Various Artists
18. SAD WORLD (DB 1051)	Lloyd Williams
19. I'M GONNA TAKE OVER NOW (R. 114)	The Ethioplans
20. WISE MAN (PYR 6003)	Desmond Dekker & The Aces

of joy, it continued a winning streak. But the original Wailers would go on hiatus just as it rose into the Jamaican Top 5 in February. The same month, Bob Marley decided to join his mother in Delaware after all. It must have been frustrating for the Wailers to see such limited financial return for their burgeoning catalog. Despite hits and concerts, their material circumstances weren't all that much different than those of their fans, rude boys and otherwise. Tied to a contract with Coxsone Dodd and no longer as easily assuaged by wages and other perks, it might have seemed to them as though they were hitting a brick wall in terms of career advancement. The Jamaican scene, for all its vibrancy, was a small one. There was little hope of more listeners, or greater riches, unless they somehow found a way to make their music heard beyond their native island.

Several factors likely influenced Marley's decision to join his mother. By working abroad, he might be able to raise enough money to launch the Wailers' own record label back in Jamaica. It was a sky-high ambition, but one that might be necessary if they were to break free of their dependence upon the meager rewards doled out by producers like Dodd. It's even possible that Marley wanted to get a sense of whether the Wailers might be able to perform in or release records in the States, though ska was virtually unknown there. After settling in Delaware, he wrote Livingston asking him and Tosh to come to the US to resume the Wailers' career there.

On February 10, 1966, before leaving for Delaware, Bob married Rita Anderson (seen here later, in the 1970s). The marriage came as a surprise even to some of his closest friends. Rita was a member of the Soulettes, who took their cues from early American soul groups. MICHAEL OCHS ARCHIVES/GETTY IMAGES

Uninterested in relocating, Livingston didn't reply. (One source dates this as occurring later in the 1960s on a subsequent visit by Bob to the United States.)

Or, career prospects aside, Marley might simply have wanted to appease his mother by reuniting with her. Cedella Booker, as she was now known, had gone to Jamaica to help him get a passport, on which a bureaucrat listed his first name as Robert. From that point onward, Marley would seldom be called Nesta by anyone but his family. To everyone else—and eventually many millions throughout the world—he would be known simply as Bob Marley.

There was one order of business Bob made sure to take care of before leaving Jamaica. On February 10, 1966, he married Rita Anderson, a nineteen-year-old singer with whom he had recently gotten involved. Although their relationship had grown increasingly serious over the past few months, the marriage came as a surprise even to some of his closest friends, such as Tosh and Livingston, who weren't even invited to the ceremony. A couple days later, he was in Wilmington, not to return to Jamaica for another eight months or so.

One of the most important figures in Bob's life and music, Rita Anderson was born on July 25, 1946, in Cuba, and moved to Kingston at a young age with her Jamaican father and Cuban mother. Also a singer, Rita was part of the Soulettes, who as their name signified, took their cues from early American soul groups. Through Bob and Peter, the Soulettes began recording at Studio One, both as backing singers and as a group releasing discs under their name. Bob got to know Rita through his Studio One work rehearsing other acts on the label, though it still came as a surprise to her when Bunny told Rita that Bob was in love with her. She was interested in Peter too, and vice versa. But it was Bob with whom she became serious, the pair starting to live together at her aunt's house, along with Rita's infant daughter Sharon from a previous relationship.

It's been speculated that Bob married Rita to make sure she'd be waiting for him when he returned from the States. It's known that Coxsone Dodd encouraged him to tie the knot, maybe so that it would be easier to bring Rita over if he moved there for good. Whatever the rationale, the union seems to have been hastily arranged. There

wasn't time for a honeymoon; the very evening of the wedding, the Wailers played their biggest concert to date at the National Stadium at Kingston. The marriage also came as a surprise to Bob's mother, who only found out on the drive with Bob from the Philadelphia airport to Wilmington, Delaware.

Bob's sojourn in Delaware probably didn't work out as anyone had hoped. It says much about the state and size of the Jamaican economy that he could make more money finding menial work abroad than he could at home as one of ska's hottest stars. It would have been inconceivable, for instance, to find Curtis Mayfield quitting the Impressions to work in an auto plant out of economic necessity just as they were tasting the heights of success. Yet work in an auto plant Marley did, among other things.

Peter Tosh's "Rasta Shook Them Up" (2016 reissue seen above) was inspired by the Ethiopian Emperor Haile Selassie's visit to Jamaica on April 21, 1966. Here, Selassie (second from left) greets a delegation of Rastafarian leaders in Kingston. MICHAEL OCHS ARCHIVES/GETTY IMAGES

Lists of the various occupations he held in Delaware vary according to the source (and are perhaps conflated with temporary work he might have taken on subsequent shorter visits), but include stints as a janitor at the Hotel du Pont, a waiter, a dishwasher, a parking lot attendant, a lab assistant at DuPont chemical company, and a forklift operator at a Chrysler assembly line.

Bob didn't like the weather, either, which for at least the first part of his visit was far colder than anything he'd experienced in Jamaica. His displeasure was alleviated when Rita joined him in August, but as she wrote in her memoir, the explosion of a vacuum cleaner at one of his jobs, like the welding accident a few years earlier, was the last straw, heightening his resolve to make music his livelihood. Although Bob wasn't a US citizen, as a long-term resident he risked becoming eligible for American military service. Some reports suggest the arrival of a letter from the selective service, either instructing him to register for the draft or actually drafting him—at a time when call-ups for service in the Vietnam War were rapidly increasing—made up his mind to return home. (Some reports date this event to the late 1960s or early 1970s rather than 1966.)

RETURN TO KINGSTON

By late 1966, the Marleys were back in Kingston. Bob had saved just seven hundred dollars from his various American jobs, and though that went pretty far in Jamaica back then, it would by no means be easy to launch a label on those funds alone. Having done little that was music-related in Delaware besides playing guitar and writing songs at his mother's home, Bob was also eager to reunite with the Wailers.

As Bob had written and sung lead on most of the Wailers' material, it might have been assumed the group would disband, wait around for his return, or sputter badly had they tried to continue without him. Yet far from remaining inactive, Bunny and Peter had kept on recording and performing, and also kept on making strong singles, some of which were quite popular. In addition, those 45s gave Tosh and Livingston the chance to shine in a fashion that might not have been possible had Marley remained in Kingston, proving there was more to the Wailers than Bob and whoever else was in the band.

With Rita's fourteen-year-old cousin Constantine Walker (sometimes nicknamed "Dream" or "Vision") often singing in Bob's place, and Rita herself occasionally contributing backup vocals, some of the singles the Wailers cut without Bob in 1966 were among their strongest early work. "Sinner Man" was an exceptionally brooding interpretation of an oft-covered spiritual, with haunting unison lead vocals by Bunny and Peter. Tosh took the lead on a fine cover of the Temptations' "Don't Look Back," a song that would become one of his most famous recordings when he rerecorded it as a duet with Mick Jagger in the late 1970s. Peter was also to the fore on "Can't You See," a surprisingly effective fusion of uptempo Motown soul and the kind of raw British rock being played by the Rolling Stones, although neither Tosh nor the Wailers would follow up on that promising direction.

For his part, Bunny took a deft lead vocal on the terrific ebullient party number "Dancing Shoes." A Jamaican hit as fine as anything the Wailers did at Studio One, it also demonstrated that for all their increasingly wide lyrical focus, the group could always turn on the charm and make music suitable for lovemaking or dancing. For those who wanted something more serious, there was "The Toughest," a solo single credited to "Peter Touch" that marked the first blossoming of Tosh's rough 'n' tumble public image.

More serious than this burst of braggadocio was Peter's "Rasta Shook Them Up," inspired by the Ethiopian Emperor Haile Selassie's visit to Jamaica on April 21, 1966. For the first time, a Wailers disc was informed by their growing interest in Rastafarian religion. Its teachings would have a huge and permanent influence on their music and lifestyle, even after Marley, Tosh, and Livingston had gone their separate musical ways. Just how deeply they'd immerse themselves in Rastafari teachings, however, wouldn't become evident until after Bob had rejoined his musical brothers.

"During that period when Bob was absent from the group, the members who stood their ground proved that we were the Wailers with or without Bob," Livingston declared in John Masouri's *Steppin' Razor: The Life of Peter Tosh*. "Those recordings are there to show that no member of the Wailers was indispensable. Every one of us was fully clad, and ready and able to deliver themselves so that the group became the Wailers, no matter what. Looking back, it's good to know that we'd grown into each other in such a way so that if one member's missing, you don't even feel it."

There's little indication that Bob was jealous of the Wailers' success in his absence, or annoyed that they'd carried on without him. Similarly, there's little indication the Wailers were tempted to keep on going without him after he came back to Kingston. Soon the trio were again recording and performing as the Wailers. Although it would take another half-dozen years before they'd make an impact outside Jamaica, those years would see some of their finest work—and help ska evolve into the style famed as reggae.

FROM ROCK STEADY TO REGGAE 1967–1971

3

Bob Marley's life in the five years following his return to Jamaica from Delaware is nearly as hazily documented as his pre-1967 career. The most thorough sources sometimes disagree on what happened when and in what order. His recorded output during that time was, if anything, more haphazard than the Wailers' mid-1960s sides, involving numerous labels and producers. Like the Wailers' mid-1960s work, it's not nearly as well-known as his mid- to late-1970s albums, and unknown even to many Marley fans.

Yet these years were vital to Bob's artistic and commercial progress. During this period, the Wailers made the transition from ska to rock steady music and then to reggae, a style they were vital in shaping. They also made some key connections that would enable their music to be heard outside of Jamaica, even if they wouldn't truly hit pay dirt until 1972 and 1973. They also recorded the original versions of numerous famous songs they'd recut in more widely heard renditions on their 1970s albums, some Marley devotees finding the originals as good or better than the more famous remakes.

A young Marley in Jamaica.
PHOTO 12/ALAMY STOCK PHOTO

ROCK STEADY AND RASTAFARI

When Marley resumed working with the Wailers in late 1966, there were two immediate changes to the group's direction. The first was purely musical. Even in Bob's relatively short absence, the Jamaican music scene as a whole had changed. Ska, with its frantic beats, playful lyrics, and almost jazzy brass, was mutating into the slower, more languid form that would become known as rock steady. Some historians have speculated that the beat slowed down when an unusually hot 1966 Jamaican summer made dancers and musicians want to pace themselves. But it seems more likely that the musical evolution was a natural reflection of the artists growing older, more reflective, and influenced as always by similar changes in American and British soul and rock as those styles matured in the late 1960s.

The second change was more subtle and spiritual, and more difficult for outsiders (and even many Jamaicans) to grasp. The Wailers, and Rita Marley, were becoming followers of Rastafari, a religion rapidly growing in popularity among black Jamaicans. The precise date at which they became interested in the practice is hard to pin down, though they almost certainly would have at least been aware of it since the early 1960s. However, the event that intensified their fervor, as it did for many Jamaicans, was Ethiopian Emperor Haile Selassie's visit to Kingston on April 21, 1966, though Bob was in Delaware at the time.

Since Selassie became emperor in the early 1930s, the Rastafari movement had grown from a small cult in Jamaica to a faith that in some ways was regarded as both a political and cultural threat to the status quo. Rastafari took the position that blacks of African ancestry—and, by extension, many Jamaicans—were in exile from their African ancestry and would one day return to their rightful African homeland. A powerful figure in a continent and world dominated by white imperialists, Selassie was regarded as the holy manifestation of a higher power on earth—Jah, as it's often called in Jamaica. Rastafari had, and still has, great appeal among a Jamaican black population descended from African slaves whose identity and self-empowerment had been eradicated by centuries of white rule.

More controversially, many Rastafari (also called Rastas or Rastafarians) used cannabis as a religious sacrament, often with a zeal that could seem hedonistic. Many Rastas also grew their hair, as the Wailers did, into dreadlocks. Now that dreadlocks are sported by youngsters of several races on several continents, it can be difficult to imagine a time when the establishment considered them not only unusual, but degenerate. Yet such was the situation when the Wailers and many Jamaicans, including many reggae musicians,

By 1966, the Wailers and Rita Marley were becoming followers of Rastafari, a religion rapidly growing in popularity among black Jamaicans. Here, crowds of Rastafarians await the arrival of Ethiopian Emperor Haile Selassie I at Kingston's Palisadoes Airport on April 21, 1966. MICHAEL OCHS ARCHIVES/GETTY IMAGES

adopted dreadlocks and openly advocated Rastafari beliefs, including prodigious consumption of ganja.

"In Jamaica, Rasta was the *last* thing you wanted your children to be involved with," Rita Marley wrote in *No Woman No Cry: My Life with Bob Marley* (coauthored with Hettie Jones). "People said it turned its followers worthless, that besides smoking ganja Rastas didn't eat properly, wash their hair, or brush their teeth. Only the worst things were said about them—no one mentioned the Rasta message of peace and love and understanding and justice, its refusal of pain and abuse, although they silently agreed with its message of black pride."

THE WAIL'N SOUL'M LABEL

It would take a while for the Wailers' Rastafari sentiments to become evident, and sometimes blatant, in their music. When he returned to Kingston in late 1966, Bob's first priority was to set up his own label, Wail'N Soul'M. As another declaration of independence, the Wailers cut their ties to Coxsone Dodd, finally fed up with their low financial return for their long run of popular discs with Studio One. They did cut their first Wail'N Soul'M single, "Bend Down Low," at Studio One, but used different facilities for subsequent discs.

"Coxsone wasn't the kind of person at the time to argue money unless you were ready to go to war," explained Bunny Livingston in the *Marley* documentary. In *Rebel Music: The Bob Marley Story*, Bunny added, "The producers weren't paying the artists the justice that was due them, and a lot of people couldn't take that. They got frustrated and backed out of it. A lot of them. The Wailers didn't. The Wailers decided that no frustration ain't gonna stop the Wailers. So we took frustration as an inspiration to write songs to get us out of the frustrations."

Although Wail'N Soul'M increased the Wailers' autonomy, like any artist-run operation, it also involved added responsibilities. They not only had to press their own records, but distribute them to stores, disc jockeys, and sound system operators, as well as collect money in a business not known for paying promptly in full. Lacking capital, the Wailers and Rita even took their singles around Kingston by bicycle, balancing boxes of 45s on the handlebars and having at least a few accidents in the process.

As an adjunct to the label, the Marleys also ran a Wail'N Soul'M record store, though in reality this was more a part of Bob and Rita's home, and geared toward selling Wail'N Soul'M discs directly to the public to sidestep the usual distribution hassles. "Some days we'd sell three, some days six, sometimes as many as twenty-five, out of a cashier's booth, a little cage we'd constructed," wrote Rita Marley in her memoir. "I never imagined that cage as part of history, but there are two replicas of it now, one at the Bob Marley Museum in Kingston and the other at Universal Studios in Orlando, Florida."

It wasn't easy to compete with the bigger Jamaican labels, and Wail'N Soul'M petered out around the end of the 1960s. "We were too young for producing," reflected Tosh in Steven Davis's Marley biography. "We never understood certain important things, like how to get on the radio or sell our records. We only knew how to make them. And the other producers were holding us down as little producers, as usually big guy control small guy."

The dozen or so singles the Wailers issued on the imprint, however, were generally impressive and showed significant musical progress. Besides slowing the tempo into a dreamier rhythm (or "riddim," as it's often called in reggae), the arrangements sanded off the rougher edges of the ska with smoother musical and instrumental execution. These tracks are among the most overlooked in the Wailers' canon, but contain a good number of highlights, as well as the original versions of a couple of their signature songs. Often splattered in an unfortunately fragmentary manner over many reissue compilations, most of them were, fortunately, gathered on the 2005 anthology *Wail'N Soul'M Singles Selecta*.

The most celebrated of these was "Stir It Up," an unabashedly sensual ode to romantic pleasure (even if the 1967 single wasn't nearly as polished as the re-recording featured on their 1973 breakthrough album, *Catch a Fire*). Another gem was the Peter Tosh–sung "Steppin' Razor," whose ominous snake-charming melody and "don't mess with me" lyrics would gain a second life when Peter featured it on one of his early solo albums almost a decade later. So synonymous did it seem with Tosh's personality that many naturally assumed he was the song's author, though it was actually composed by the band's early mentor, Joe Higgs.

Other fine late-1960s Wail'N Soul'M singles included the supremely sad lament "I'm Hurting Inside"; the suggestive "Bend Down Low," which bore the strongest links to their ska days; and "Don't You Rock My Boat," with its ethereal vocal harmonies and bouncy organ. These all stuck to romantic topics, but other tracks on the 45s reflected a growing musical and lyrical scope. "Freedom Time" urged listeners to prepare for oncoming liberation. "Hypocrites," "Bus Dem Shut," and "Them Have Fi Get a Beatin'" used the kind of patois heard in Trench Town, mixing in messages, if general ones, about oppression, Jah, and ghetto life. Their update of the traditional spiritual "This Train" was almost more folk than rock steady, while "Lyrical Satirical" seemed influenced by the nyabinghi-styled acoustic percussive music made at Rasta rituals. With its reference to Babylon—the name given by Rastafari to the side of the world ruled by the wicked—the burning "Fire Fire" also gave voice to new attitudes.

The bonds among the Wailers were forged yet deeper by the June 1967 birth of a son to Peter and Bunny's younger sister, Shirley. Bunny was not present on quite a few Wail'N Soul'M releases. The following month, he was busted for marijuana possession. Unsuccessfully pleading innocence, he served more than a year in prison. Rita Marley sang on studio sessions in his absence, in essence replacing Bunny until his release from prison in September 1968. She also sang lead, and quite well, on the delightfully slinky Wail'N Soul'M 45 "Play Play Play," credited to the Soulettes, though Bob and Peter sang harmony vocals on the track.

While Livingston was incarcerated, the Wailers' circumstances underwent some other unexpected changes. The Marleys had a daughter, Cedella, in August 1967. As in so many things Marley, the chronology is indefinite, but not long before this, they and the other Wailers had moved from Kingston back to Bob's hometown, Nine Mile. In part this was to farm some land Bob's mother had inherited; in part it was to escape the stressful Trench Town environment. Livingston's prison sentence and the more urban-minded Tosh's quick return to Kingston seemed to threaten the Wailers' very existence, though it wasn't long before Bob and Rita moved back to the city too. It was probably shortly after their return that they made an unexpected connection to the American record business. It would be the first major step in exposing their music outside of Jamaica.

JOHNNY NASH AND DANNY SIMS

Since the late 1950s, Texan Johnny Nash had been a journeyman singer with only mild American chart success, often recording in a style reminiscent of adult pop superstar Johnny Mathis. By the late 1960s, he and his manager, Danny Sims, were spending more time in Jamaica. Sims later claimed he relocated to escape getting killed by the CIA and FBI after using the phrase "burn, baby, burn" in a commercial for Nash's Top 5 R & B hit

American singer Johnny Nash met Bob in Kingston in 1968 and quickly recommended Marley to his manager Danny Sims, who signed Bob, Peter, and Rita to a songwriting/publishing deal. Nash had enjoyed a Top 5 R & B hit "Let's Move and Groove Together" (English pressing seen here).
REDFERNS/GETTY IMAGES

The Wailers certainly had plenty of material to offer Sims's and Nash's JAD company, and some recordings employed celebrated session musicians, as well as star South African jazz trumpeter Hugh Masekela. MICHAEL OCHS ARCHIVES/GETTY IMAGES

"Let's Move and Groove Together." Less fancifully, it's also been suggested he wanted to record in Kingston as it was far cheaper than using American studios.

Whatever their motivation, Nash's enthusiasm for early Jamaican reggae was genuine and began influencing his own recordings. On January 7, 1968, he met Bob Marley at a Rastafari ceremony for Ethiopian Christmas Day and was deeply impressed by Bob's songs. (Some sources cite this meeting as having taken place a year earlier, though the later date seems more likely.) Nash quickly recommended Marley to Sims, who signed Bob, Peter, and Rita to a songwriting/publishing deal. Each would receive one hundred dollars a week—a lifeline at a time when they were struggling merely to survive, let alone keep cutting tracks and running a record label. Still in prison, Bunny was not part of the contract.

It's not entirely clear what Sims and Nash hoped, or at least hoped most, to gain by the association. Probably they wanted to place some of their songs—especially Marley's—with American artists, as the publishing royalties for US hits could mean a big payoff. They were also probably considering some of the material for Nash (who would indeed make one of Marley's songs a big hit, though not for nearly five more years). As a longer shot, there was the possibility of getting hits in North America and Europe for records performed by Marley and/or the Wailers themselves, though they were unknown in those territories, and reggae itself was barely known anywhere outside of Jamaica.

Probably starting around early 1968, Bob, Peter, and Rita began cutting demos for Sims and Nash's JAD company. It's unclear whether these were intended to be shopped to other artists, to be considered for interpretation on Nash's own releases, to secure a deal for the Wailers and/or Marley, or, if the demos were good enough, to gain overseas release. It was probably some combination of all of these alternatives.

The Wailers certainly had plenty of material to offer for consideration. Many tracks were cut for JAD-211, according to a 2004 Universal Music press release announcing a licensing deal between the two companies. Some used instrumentation by celebrated American soul and jazz session musicians such as guitarist Eric Gale (who'd contributed to Van Morrison's earliest solo recordings) and drummer Bernard Purdie, as well as South African star jazz trumpeter Hugh Masekela. By using American musicians, perhaps Sims and Nash were trying to Americanize the Wailers a bit to make them more commercial in the United States.

They might have had similar thoughts when having them cut some material by American songwriters, including Jimmy Norman, whose most famous credit was supplying lyrics for the soul tune "Time Is on My Side," covered by the Rolling Stones for their first stateside Top 10 hit. Accounts differ as to whether the contributions by non-Wailers were recorded in New York or Jamaica, but according to some sources, Sims flew the Wailers to New York at some point in 1968, maybe trying to give them an introductory taste of the United States should they eventually break into the American market. This would have been Peter Tosh's first visit to the States.

Though remakes of "Bend Down Low" and "Mellow Mood" were released on a Canadian single, Sims encountered little interest in issuing Wailers music in the United States. The Jamaican dialect and diction of the Wailers' vocals might have had something to do with it. Sims told *MOJO* that when he brought a Wailers record to New York DJs, "They said, 'Danny, you bring your gun, your dope, your money, but with this material here, you gotta bring a translator! It'll never be played on R & B stations!' That broke my heart." The rejection wasn't totally defensible on those grounds, as then and later, the group usually sang in a manner reasonably understandable to English speakers of any nationality (and certainly more understandable than the patois in which they often spoke).

It's also curious that Nash did not record any of Marley's songs in the late 1960s. Nash made #5 in both the US and UK with a breakthrough hit, "Hold Me Tight," that drew heavily (and quite skillfully) upon Jamaican rock steady music. Bob's material would have fit in well with his new direction. Nash *did* cover a Peter Tosh song, "Love," on his *Hold Me Tight* album, marking the first high-profile cover of a Wailers song abroad.

Largely unreleased at the time, many of the JAD tracks have since come out on archival releases, with documentation so fragmentary it's sometimes difficult to confirm whether they're even JAD demos, let alone ascertain where and when they were done. Featuring some remakes of songs issued on Wail'N Soul'M and Studio One (going all the way back to "It Hurts to Be Alone" in one instance), these include the anthemic "Soul Rebel" (later revived as the title track to an early-1970s Wailers album) and the lilting "Rocking Steady," two of the best tracks that have been dated as 1968 outtakes. Both sound like they might have been recorded without any non-Jamaican musicians.

There's nonetheless the sense that the Wailers might have been holding back some of their best songs and not recording material in as uncompromisingly personal a style as they were on their Jamaican releases. And some of the compositions supplied to them by American writers hardly seem indicative of their true feelings, musical or otherwise. It's hard to imagine Marley or any of the Wailers, for instance, writing a song about "Milk Shake and Potato Chips," to name one number penned by Jimmy Norman.

BUNNY LIVINGSTON REJOINS

Bunny Livingston got out of jail in time to sing on at least a few of the JAD demos, probably from around late 1968 (taking the lead on one of the better Norman compositions, "Treat You Right"). Having now put out good records during prolonged absences by both Bob and Bunny, the Wailers looked set to see out the 1960s on full batteries. Instead, they floundered. They recorded little in 1969, even as rock steady completed its transition to reggae in Jamaica with the heightened use of more jagged, irregular beats and increasingly serious, sophisticated lyrics. Their friends Desmond Dekker and Jimmy Cliff had their first big international hits around this time as well, but it wasn't certain the Wailers would even be around to capitalize on reggae's budding worldwide visibility.

Dates given in different books (sometimes by actual participants in the Wailers saga) are frustratingly variable, but it seems that Bob went to live with his mother in Delaware for at least a few brief stretches in the late 1960s and early 1970s, even taking on some of the same kinds of menial work he'd labored at during his 1966 visit. When in Jamaica, he was spending some time in Nine Mile, away from Kingston and the other Wailers.

Why he needed to work in the United States if he and Rita were still getting one hundred dollars a week from Sims, or even whether they were still drawing a salary, isn't clear. He might have been feeling pressure to support his growing family, which now included a new son, David (subsequently known to everyone as "Ziggy"), born October 17, 1968. With the Sims/Nash/JAD deal having yielded little in the way of released material, he might have been considering US citizenship for himself and his family, which he probably could have secured, with his mother now a permanent resident.

As always, music won out, and as the 1960s turned into the 1970s, Marley was again recording with Tosh and Livingston in Kingston. On sporadic recordings from around this time, however, they seemed to be at a loss for direction. They cut covers of the Box Tops' hit "The Letter" (retitled "Give Me a Ticket") and, even more strangely, the Archies' bubblegum smash "Sugar Sugar" (American soul giant Wilson Pickett had a small hit with a funkified version of the tune around the same time). They did another version of "This Train"; reactivated the Wail'N Soul'M label for the obscure, bittersweet "Trouble on the Road Again"; and, most bizarrely, cut "Black Progress," a semi-rapped funk-meets-reggae hybrid that quotes from James Brown's "Say It Loud (I'm Black and I'm Proud)" at its finish. Without Bob, Bunny and Peter cut "Tread-O," with its ghostly Tosh organ and the weird lyric "you're like a stick of macaroni in bed."

As the Wailers' deal with JAD gave them the freedom to record and release product with whomever they wished in Jamaica, they placed these recordings with various labels, even issuing "Give Me a Ticket" under the pseudonym of the Mad Dogs.

LESLIE KONG AND *THE BEST OF THE WAILERS*

For all the recording the Wailers had done in the last half of the 1960s, no album of their material had been issued since Studio One's half-baked *The Wailing Wailers* LP. Getting something of a proper album together—in a world where albums were taking over from singles as the prime medium of expression in popular music—might have been on the Wailers' mind when they decided to work with Leslie Kong in spring 1970.

Way back in 1962, Kong had recorded Marley's first single. Since then, he'd found success with several reggae giants, including Toots and the Maytals and Desmond Dekker, whose "Israelites" had recently been a #1 UK hit (and hit the US Top 10). The tracks the Wailers did with Kong in May would not be parceled out on a bunch of 45s, but mostly used for a full-length album that would not, like *The Wailing Wailers*, simply be a fairly arbitrary selection of tracks cut over the span of a year and a half or so.

Recorded with Kong's talented in-house band, the Beverley's All-Stars (named after his Beverley's label), the sessions had a generally more consistent, clearer sound than the sides the Wailers had done for Wail'N Soul'M and other labels in the late 1960s. On much of the material, there was a brighter, bouncier feel than the group had previously managed. Upbeat tracks included "Soul Shakedown Party," "Cheer Up," and Tosh's "Stop the Train" (later remade as "Stop That Train," a standout on 1973's *Catch a Fire*). Organ (by Winston Wright) was employed more than it had been on the Wailers' 1960s records, and the trio's harmonies were tighter and lighter than ever on numbers such as "Soul Captives."

Some of the group's graver concerns, however, were addressed in "Caution," with marvelous jittery guitar and harmonies. There was also time for sex ("Do It Twice"), spirituality ("Go Tell It on the Mountain"), and quality Tosh-helmed tracks to vary the pace ("Soon Come"). Tosh also redid one of the standout Studio One sides he'd sung a few years ago, "Can't You See," with a slower, more reggae-fied approach. Throughout the rest of their career, the Wailers (and Tosh and Livingston as solo artists) would often re-record previously issued songs with substantially different arrangements, a much more common practice in reggae than rock.

Recorded with Leslie Kong's talented in-house band, the Beverley's All-Stars, the Beverley's sessions had a generally more consistent sound than the sides the Wailers had done for Wail'N Soul'M and Coxsone.

After the cream of the sessions was assembled into a ten-track LP, however, the Wailers weren't happy with how it was packaged. Although all of the material was previously unreleased, Leslie Kong misleadingly titled it *The Best of the Wailers*, probably hoping to deceive at least a few buyers into thinking they were getting a greatest hits collection. Bunny Livingston was particularly angry, feeling that such a title should be used only at the end of an act's life. As several Wailers biographers have related, Bunny told Kong that as he, Bob, and Peter were in good health, the decision to use such a title must mean that the producer's life would soon end. Kong shrugged off the pronouncement as mumbo-jumbo—and died of a heart attack in August 1971, just thirty-eight years of age.

THE LEE PERRY SESSIONS

Not long after recording *The Best of the Wailers*, the band began working with another top Jamaican producer, Lee "Scratch" Perry. One of the most eccentric figures in reggae, if not all of twentieth-century popular music, Perry entered the music business as an assistant to Coxsone Dodd before establishing himself as a producer and recording artist. The tracks the Wailers cut with Perry would usually come out on the producer's own label, Upsetter. The rhythm section on many of these recordings, bassist Aston "Family Man" Barrett (who'd helped connect Marley with Perry) and his brother Carlton "Carly" Barrett on drums, would eventually become full-time Wailers, though not for several years.

After *The Best of the Wailers*, the band began working with another top Jamaican producer, Lee "Scratch" Perry, one of the most eccentric figures in all of twentieth-century popular music.
MICHAEL OCHS ARCHIVES/GETTY IMAGES

Perry later took some credit for keeping the Wailers intact at this precarious stage. "Bob didn't want to go back with the Bunny and Peter thing," he told Bruno Blum in a 1997 interview quoted in David Katz's Lee Perry biography, *People Funny Boy*. "I say, 'Well, I think you should do it with this soul revolution for special reason, because the three of your voice blend very good like an angel, to manifest your work on this soul revolution.' That was a revolution—a spiritual revolution, fighting against government pressure and things like that, so he say, 'I'll take your advice and call 'em back.' . . . Bob wanted to sing with me alone without them, but I said, 'No, you need them for special work like "Sun Is Shining," you need the harmony.'"

Added Perry in Christopher John Farley's *Before the Legend: The Rise of Bob Marley*, "We take it to a spiritual level. Because him did not have any songs that could hit international or any songs of spiritual size. So me take him into a zone and start to create those vibration for him, and that what the people them want to hear."

Exact dates are not available, but as far as can be surmised, the Wailers worked with Perry for about half a year, or a bit more, in the last few months of 1970 and the first few months of 1971. They were quite prolific in this period, laying down enough sides to fill a couple albums and several singles. It's fuzzy whether those LPs were intended as fully developed standalone statements or simply vehicles for tracks recorded in the same period of time.

But while their records continued to emerge in a rather piecemeal, disorganized fashion, the quality of the music was impressive. Sparer and starker than their outings for Wail'N Soul'M and Leslie Kong, they were also more identifiably reggae in their gently ebbing rhythms, some echo (and, on the single "Mr. Brown," horror-movie organ) adding a slightly otherworldly aura. It's been suggested by some critics that this is the point where their vocal harmonies finally escaped the doo-wop and soul influences that had shaped them, though they'd been moving away from these and toward more distinctively idiosyncratic wails and phrasing for two or three years. Some more purist-minded reggae aficionados consider these the best Wailers recordings, though they weren't as accessible as the internationally distributed tracks the band would do after hooking up with Island Records.

Some of the most significant recordings from the Perry sessions would emerge not on LPs, but as singles. "Small Axe" (which would be re-recorded for the 1973 album *Burnin'*) was an only slightly veiled attack against powerful Jamaican reggae producers Coxsone Dodd, Duke Reid, and Prince Buster. The big three—or "big tree" in the song—had a heavy-handed influence on the country's music industry, the Wailers and Perry thus representing the "small axe" cutting down the tree.

ABOVE: Scratch Perry–produced "Small Axe" (later re-recorded for the 1973 album *Burnin'*) was a veiled attack against Jamaican reggae producers Coxsone Dodd, Duke Reid, and Prince Buster (seen here)—the big three, or "big tree." Here it's backed with "Down the Road" by Perry's Upsetters.
LARRY ELLIS/*DAILY EXPRESS*/HULTON ARCHIVE/GETTY IMAGES

RIGHT: Another Upsetter single, "Duppy Conqueror" (also later redone for *Burnin'*) gave the Wailers a big Jamaican hit.

That may be true, but as Marley explained to Carl Gayle in *Let It Rock*, the song had a more universal meaning. "'Small Axe' was about righteousness against sin," he elaborated. "It says 'Why boasteth thyself oh evil men/Playing smart and not being clever.' It didn't encourage violence, it didn't mean you should go out and cut a man down, it was a power, a world power. It's a victory, it's a small axe." It was also a manifesto of sorts for the kind of nonviolent struggle for justice Bob would often advocate in his lyrics over the next decade.

Another Upsetter single, "Duppy Conqueror," also to be redone for *Burnin'*, gave the Wailers a big Jamaican hit with a much different lyrical slant on justice. Boasting that bars could not contain them, the song alluded to the increasing harassment (and sometimes spells in jail) the Wailers and Rastafari in general suffered, owing to their unconventional appearance and ganja use. As Marley confirmed in *Let It Rock*, "It was really for every prisoner who came out at that time, because it was so good just to be back on the street again." Adding another level of intrigue, in Jamaica a "duppy" is an evil ghost or spirit, "Duppy Conqueror" ascribing supernatural powers to the Wailers by association.

Soul Rebels, the first of the two LPs to emerge from the Upsetter/Perry era, included some songs that would find a wider audience via subsequent remakes. "It's Alright" was later reworked as "Night Shift" on 1976's *Rastaman Vibration* and might have been inspired by Marley's autoworker job in Delaware. "Soul Rebel," first recorded (but not released) by the group in the late 1960s, played up their image—grounded in plenty of reality—as antiestablishment types.

Peter Tosh might not have been as prolific a songwriter as Bob Marley, but his two contributions were of an equally high standard. His "400 Years" urged liberation centuries after black Africans had been sold into slavery, and was re-recorded for *Catch a Fire*. "No Sympathy," with its slicing rhythms and eerie backup harmonies, would find a bigger audience after its remake for Tosh's 1976 solo debut. Another excellent Tosh track, "Downpresser," updated the moody spiritual "Sinner Man" (which the Marley-less Wailers had done previously at Studio One) with new lyrics. Only appearing on 45 at the time, it too would be remade on an early Tosh solo album, retitled "Downpressor Man" on 1977's *Equal Rights*.

"Peter is another good writer," Perry emphasized in a 1975 issue of *Black Music*. "He writes how he feels. Any time Peter writes a tune he writes it for a reason. He doesn't do it just because he wants to sing a song, he does it because it means something to him, because you done something to him or he's saying something about somebody or something. He doesn't do things for a quick price. He does it because he wants to send a message."

THE BEST OF THE WAILERS

Review by Richie Unterberger

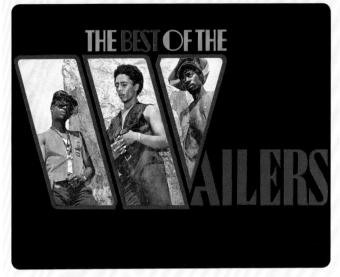

SOUL SHAKE DOWN PARTY • SOUL CAPTIVES • CAUTION
GO TELL IT ON THE MOUNTAIN • CHEER UP • CAN'T YOU SEE
STOP THAT TRAIN • BACK OUT • DO IT TWICE • SOON COME

beverley's

The misleadingly titled album *The Best of the Wailers* has caused endless confusion among fans. This was not a greatest-hits compilation, instead comprising recordings made in spring 1970 for an LP that was issued shortly afterward.

In fact, *The Best of the Wailers* was only the second full-length disc by the Wailers, and the first for which the tracks were cut with the intention of getting placed on the same album. However, the title that producer Leslie Kong bestowed upon it gave the false impression it was a compilation of the most popular material they'd cut in their first half dozen or so years. After the Wailers' rise to international fame, countless listeners were no doubt puzzled by its failure to include standards like "I Shot the Sheriff" and "No Woman, No Cry."

Unfortunately, its disingenuous title has obscured the record's considerable significance as the Wailers' first standalone album, and one that did much to reinvigorate their career. After a series of generally stellar late-'60s singles on their own Wail'N Soul'M label, the group was floundering—cutting subpar, rather directionless 45s and uncertain they'd even stay together. For all the quality of many of their '60s singles, much of the material had muffled fidelity well below the standards of typical US and UK recordings.

With the help of Kong and the Beverley's All-Stars, *The Best of the Wailers* immediately closed that gap. The clean sonics also boasted admirable balance between the instruments as well as between the lead and backup vocals. The harmonies especially benefited from the increased clarity, vocals gliding and blending in unison on tracks like "Soul Captives" or wah-wahing with a haunting idiosyncrasy on "Caution."

While much of their approach remained grounded in rock-steady beats and American soul, the Wailers were developing melodic hooks with a wider international appeal. Several of the songs on this album would no doubt count among the Wailers' more popular tunes had they appeared on a higher-profile LP, especially the sunnier ones like "Soul Captives" and "Soul Shakedown Party." Indeed "Stop the Train" (redone a few years later as "Stop That Train" on *Catch a Fire*) and Peter Tosh's "Soon Come" (reprised for his 1978 album *Bush Doctor*) would find much wider audiences after the Wailers became internationally famous.

Most critics view the Wailers' subsequent early-'70s LPs with producer Lee Perry as their best pre–*Catch a Fire* albums. Yet even if it's a somewhat transitional record, *The Best of the Wailers* has a lot going for it. Airily soulful yet distinctively Jamaican in its rhythms and harmonies, and featuring consistently strong songs, it set the Wailers on the track as album-oriented artists whose messages were ready to be appreciated by a worldwide audience.

The title of the second Perry-produced album, *Soul Revolution*, might have led listeners to expect a more political, militant record. While some of the songs broadly fell into that category, it was actually another mix of political and personal, romantic and Rasta. The Wailers paid tribute to perhaps their heaviest early influence by covering Curtis Mayfield's "Keep on Moving." There were a couple hymns in praise of pot, "Kaya" (later remade as the title track of a late-1970s Marley album) and "African Herbsman," actually a cover of American folk-rocker Richie Havens. "Don't Rock My Boat," a remake of a late-1960s single, would later show up as "Satisfy My Soul" on the *Kaya* album, which also included a remake of another *Soul Revolution* track, "Sun Is Shining."

Tosh had a disappointingly low profile as a songwriter and lead singer on *Soul Revolution*, but a couple tracks gave Livingston a chance to shine in those roles. Their Studio One favorite, "Put It On," made another showing in a slower reggae arrangement. (The Wailers were not done with the tune, redoing it for 1973's *Burnin'*.) The melodica-driven instrumental "Memphis" and a quirky, less vocal-oriented mix of "Duppy Conqueror" gave the impression that the disc was fleshed out with filler to create a full LP. Separate instrumental "versions," as they were dubbed, of vocal tracks were becoming a trend in reggae—Perry even issued an album of *Soul Revolution*'s backing tracks sans vocals.

The Wailers-Perry combination seemed a good one. Perry was certainly a champion of their main figure's talents, telling *Black Music*, "Every song that Bob Marley sing is good. That is the only artist in Jamaica that I really admire and nothing Bob can do can be wrong as far as I'm concerned." But their collaboration ended in 1971, mostly for nonmusical reasons. The band again had cause to be unhappy with a producer's packaging of their LP, Perry putting a rather exploitative picture of an open-shirted, gun-toting female revolutionary on the cover of *Soul Rebels*. Of greater concern to the group, Perry wasn't sticking to an unwritten agreement to split profits evenly with the band, instead offering (according to Livingston) only a 10 percent royalty. Frustration over yet another dispute with the record industry might have played a part in Marley leaving Jamaica altogether to pursue another opportunity.

A selection of Peter Tosh singles from 1971—some released under the alias "Peter Touch." "Downpresser" (see Upsetter label) would be remade as "Downpressor Man" on Tosh's 1977 solo album, *Equal Rights*.

MARLEY IN SWEDEN

The Wailers' deal with Danny Sims and Johnny Nash had yielded little in the way of overseas covers or record releases, and, by the early 1970s, they seemed to have almost disappeared from the picture. In early 1971, however, they offered Marley the chance to write material for the soundtrack of a Swedish movie in which Nash was starring. Around springtime, he went to Stockholm to work on material, sharing a home with Sims, Nash, and a white Texan keyboard player, Rabbit Bundrick. As only Marley was flown over, it seems Sims and Nash might have viewed him as the primary and possibly only asset in their deal with the Wailers. Never even mentioning Peter and Bunny to Bundrick in his two months or so in Sweden, it's possible Bob was thinking of becoming a solo act.

The peculiar Swedish jaunt was disappointingly unproductive. Not finding the country's climate or cuisine to his liking, Marley spent much of the time in his room with his guitar writing songs—probably not all of which he intended to propose for the movie. "It was like a songwriting factory," remembered Bundrick in the liner notes to the 1992 Marley box set *Songs of Freedom*. "As you walked through the house you would hear a conglomeration of different types of music all fighting for the same ear space. . . . Although Bob was such a tremendous songwriter, singer, performer, and artist, I did occasionally wonder if he was ever going to tune his guitar, or just leave it like it was, because with all the harmonics flying around the house, maybe he thought I was out of tune, or Johnny."

None of Bob's material was used in the film, *Vill så gärna tro* (known as *Love Is Not a Game* or *Want So Much to Believe* in English), which played for just a week in Sweden (though Marley did appear in a party scene as an extra). When the wages ran out and (according to Bundrick) Sims failed to win them back in a poker game, Marley went back to Jamaica. In lieu of the money he was owed, as some accounts have it, he took Johnny Nash's rented guitar and tape recorder. The only music issued from his Swedish trip (on *Songs of Freedom*) is an informal tape of Bob on acoustic guitar, singing a medley of sorts that included some of the Wailers' better tunes, such as "Stir It Up" and "I'm Hurting Inside."

SOUL REBELS

Review by Chris Salewicz

Soul Rebels and *Soul Revolution*, the recordings made by the Wailers with Lee "Scratch" Perry in 1970, resulted in the finest work done by both parties, at any stage of their careers. "Though it may never be known who influenced whom," wrote author and reggae expert Steve Barrow, "the recordings they made together constitute a significant turning point for the participants and for Jamaican music."

In September 1969, Bob Marley returned to Kingston from his mother's home in the United States, where Bob had absorbed the mood of black militancy and written similarly political material. He would break away, he decided, from Bunny Livingston and Peter Tosh.

Bob asked the eccentric Lee "Scratch" Perry to produce his new music. Perry and Bob worked on the material that Bob had written. Scratch had a powerful, affecting voice, redolent with the timbre of the roots

and earth of Jamaica. As he worked with Perry, Bob's own voice mutated, taking on a distinctly similar tone.

Despite the new songs' form, the pair did not consider them reggae music, but "revolutionary soul." When the first album emerged from the ensuing recording sessions, it was titled *Soul Rebels*, the first Bob Marley record envisaged in its entirety as a long-player. And it was credited to the Wailers, Scratch having persuaded Marley that he should bring the other Wailers in on the project. "You need the harmony," he told him.

Perry worked with the Wailers, rehearsing them, reconstructing them. He persuaded them to drop their doo-wop harmonizing and follow the feel of the sound in their own heads, literally to find their own voices.

With the Barrett brothers, part of Scratch Perry's house band, providing the rhythm section, the songs were recorded at Randy's, the four-track studio above the prestigious record store of the same name.

The entire *Soul Rebels* album was "voiced" in one day; eight of the instrumental tracks had been recorded twenty-four hours previously: "Rebel's Hop," "Corner Stone," "400 Years," "No Water," "Reaction," "No Sympathy," "Soul Almighty," and "Soul Rebel." The vocals for "My Cup" and "Try Me" had been recorded at a previous session. There were three microphones, one for each of the Wailers, who were experimenting freely with their singing, lifting parts from Temptations and James Brown vocals, dropping in bird sounds or anything that seemed appropriate to give the music an extra notch of appeal. At the end of the day's session, everyone involved felt thrilled at what they had achieved—they believed something magical had taken place.

The songs were put on the *Soul Rebels* LP in the order they were recorded.

Like Marley's previous trips to Delaware, and Livingston's previous stint in prison, the Swedish interlude could easily have spelled the end of the Wailers. Tosh recorded some solo singles in Bob's absence, sometimes credited to "Peter Touch" or "Peter Toush." But as with those previous interruptions, upon Bob's return, the Wailers resumed without much of a hitch.

EARLY TUFF GONG RELEASES

On their own Tuff Gong label, formed in 1970, the Wailers put out a few singles featuring some of their strongest material yet. Foremost among these was the original version of "Trench Town Rock" (revived a few years later for Marley's *Live!* album), which, far from being a gritty list of ghetto realities, was a tense celebration of the music heard in the Kingston slum. The choppy, circular two-stroke rhythm that Marley plays on guitar on this track has been credited for originating a style that would become prevalent throughout reggae in the 1970s. In *Let It Rock*, Marley later claimed the song "was a message to the police, we told them not to come and cold [us] up, don't brutalize us. Because in JA [Jamaica], when the police see guys like us on the street they come over and start stumbling all over you."

Tuff Gong became one of the most important recording studios in Jamaica. In January 2017 the label announced it would resume pressing vinyl records to meet current demand.

BELOW: "Nice Time" b/w "Hypocrites" was a Tuff Gong reissue of a 1967 Wail'N Soul'M release. PHIL CLARKE HILL/IN PICTURES VIA GETTY IMAGES

The grimmer side of the Trench Town experience was depicted in "Concrete Jungle," with more ghostly production than the famous remake that kicks off *Catch a Fire*. "Lively Up Yourself," on the other hand, celebrated pure joy, though the arrangement was a bit hollow compared to the subsequent version on Marley's 1974 album *Natty Dread*. "Man to Man" was yet another tune that found a new life down the line, getting reworked as "Who the Cap Fit" for the 1976 *Rastaman Vibration* LP.

This series of Tuff Gong singles wasn't solely notable as source points for songs that would find a home on more widely heard LPs. "Guava Jelly" was one of the Wailers' most delicate romantic tunes, and one of its most explicit, with sexual allusions so juicy it's hard to imagine it getting much commercial airplay abroad. Combined with the likes of "Concrete Jungle," "Lively Up Yourself," and "Trench Town Rock," it could have helped form the core of an album stronger than any of the Wailers' previous full-lengths.

Forming Tuff Gong, Marley asserted in *Let It Rock*, "was the greatest thing we ever did. The first label [Wail'N Soul'M] went down but we had some big hits on Tuff Gong. The big boys didn't like it, but it meant we didn't have to go to a guy knowing he was gonna rob us. And win or lose we just dug having our own business, we didn't have to go and hustle a guy for our money." Other branches of Tuff Gong reached into other parts of the music business, including a small record store and, eventually, a studio.

But as 1971 ended, the Wailers were in much the same position as they'd been since the mid-1960s. Stars in their homeland, they were virtually unknown elsewhere. Even though some of their records sold well in Jamaica, they were far from rich and constantly battling some combination of producers, labels, and distributors for a fairer piece of the pie. Although the international rock (and, starting in the early 1970s, soul) market had shifted from singles to albums, they hadn't yet managed a powerful, unified LP-length disc that fully lived up to their potential. Reggae itself, some sporadic hits aside, was still rarely played in the United States. Although it had a thriving niche market in the United Kingdom's large Jamaican community, it had made only slightly greater incursions into the British pop mainstream.

All of this might have tempted the Wailers to give up, especially when Marley was called away for yet another overseas task at the beginning of 1972. Yet that trip would, at long last, make the connection that would make the Wailers international stars.

SOUL REVOLUTION

Review by Garth Cartwright

BOB MARLEY and the WA

For certain Bob Marley fans, *Soul Revolution* stands as the best album he ever made. Paradoxically, it's also his most obscure. As the second album the Wailers recorded with Lee "Scratch" Perry, *Soul Revolution* was released in Jamaica in 1971 on Perry's Maroon record label. It attracted little attention there and almost no international sales. Trojan Records, the UK label that licensed and distributed the vast majority of reggae in Europe, refused to release it (Trojan boss Lee Gopthal famously told Perry, "Forget these guys. They'll never make it"). The lack of revenue generated led to a split between the Wailers and Perry. Marley, who had seen Scratch as a father figure and let the producer shape his singing and direct his songwriting, remained on friendly terms, but Peter Tosh and Bunny Wailer both loathed the man (partly, one imagines, because he pushed Bob out front).

Beyond the bad blood that resulted from the poor sales and overdue royalties, *Soul Revolution* remains masterful, a template for things to come.

Following 1970's *Soul Rebels* LP (the first with Perry producing), *Soul Revolution* should have won the trio greater acclaim. The twelve songs included are strong, the trio's voices—both out front and in harmony—have a greater intensity than ever before, while the Upsetters (as Perry had named his studio band: Aston and Carlton Barrett on bass and drums, respectively; guitarist Alva "Reggie" Lewis; and keyboardist Glen Adams) are remarkable in their precision and power. The sound is sparse and intense, drums and bass underpinning everything, with Marley testifying strongly ("Sun Is Shining," now one of his most loved songs, debuts here). Bunny Wailer takes lead vocal on "Riding High" and "Brain Washing," while Peter Tosh is a background presence. This is roots reggae that still looks to America—Curtis Mayfield, Richie Havens, and Cole Porter songs get "adapted" here—while emphasizing Rastafari beliefs and the jerky rhythms unique to Jamaica.

Soul Revolution's commercial failure pushed the trio to reach out to Chris Blackwell of Island Records—he, at least, was impressed by the LP—and steal the Barrett brothers from Perry. Marley would later re-record three songs from *Soul Revolution* for *Kaya* (1978), hinting at the value he placed on these sessions.

Soul Revolution is confusing in the sense that the original LP covers came stamped *Soul Revolution Part II*—in a very Jamaican tradition, Scratch was preparing a dub mix of the LP, and covers for this project came to house the original LP. Today both the vocal and dub mixes tend to be packaged together—appropriately, as *Soul Revolution* is the most intense roots reggae album Bob Marley ever made.

THE INTERNATIONAL BREAKTHROUGH 1972–1974

4

As 1972 dawned, Bob Marley and the Wailers were in some ways at the peak of their productivity. They were continuing to write and record some of the tracks that were most crucial to establishing reggae as *the* major form of Jamaican music. Yet in some ways, they were as close to breaking up as ever.

After nearly a decade of recordings, they had yet to attract any significant notice outside of their native Jamaica. They had yet to perform in North America or the United Kingdom, and their few, scattered releases in those regions had attracted scant attention. They'd fallen out with three of the leading producers in Jamaica, and there was increased pressure on Marley to support his growing family.

The prospect of bringing his family to join his mother in Delaware—where better-paying, if menial, work might be available—might well have crossed his mind, even if he'd vowed to make music his life on more than one occasion after mishaps on his industrial jobs. Instead, 1972 would be the year in which the Wailers finally got the big break that put Marley on the road to international superstardom. Ironically, complications from the first fruits of that record deal would seal the split of the original Wailers, with Bob Marley, Bunny Livingston, and Peter Tosh going their separate ways within a couple years.

Marley and the Wailers pose for a promotional photo. From left: Bunny Livingston, Bob Marley, Carly Barrett, Peter Tosh, and Family Man Barrett.
CHARLIE GILLETT/REDFERNS/GETTY IMAGES

FIRST US AND UK TOURS

The first hours of the new year, in fact, marked their first concert on American soil, even if they had no record sales or airplay to speak of in the United States. The details behind the Wailers' first, brief US "tour" remain sketchy, and its purpose indefinite. At least a couple of the gigs were promoted by Tony Spaulding, a powerful figure in Jamaica's People's National Party (PNP). The Wailers had recently done a few shows in support of the leftist party, and Spaulding might have been trying to repay the favor by giving them some US exposure.

Regardless of why it was arranged, it's known that their first American show (with support by the Debonaires) took place on New Year's Eve of 1971 at the Concourse Plaza Hotel in the Bronx before an audience of three thousand. Also on the bill was a more popular Jamaican reggae artist, John Holt, and the event seems to have been targeted toward New York's sizable Jamaican community. This may have also been true of concerts a week later in Brooklyn and the Manhattan Center, with yet more ill-documented shows following in Pennsylvania and Delaware.

If the idea behind this junket was to somehow "break" them in the United States, it didn't break much ground. Soon the Wailers were back in Jamaica, continuing to play PNP Bandwagon shows, sort of a touring revue. Their determination to remain a unit seemed to solidify with a decision to make multi-instrumentalist Aston "Family Man" Barrett and

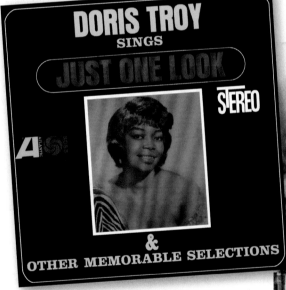

Produced by Johnny Nash, the half-dozen cuts Bob recorded in London in spring 1972 featured Ghanaian percussionist Rebop Kwaku Baah (seen here playing with Traffic in 1973) and American soul singer Doris Troy (above), best known for her 1963 hit, "Just One Look."
BRIAN COOKE/REDFERNS/GETTY IMAGES

his younger brother drummer, Carly, semiofficial Wailers onstage and in the studio. Almost right after that, however, Marley was on his way to London, out of the country for the third time in less than a year. His wife, Rita, and their children would not accompany him; they lived in Delaware for the time being with his mother, while Rita found work as a nurse's aide.

Now coming up on its fifth year, Bob's association with manager-of-sorts Danny Sims and his fellow client Johnny Nash hadn't yielded much in the way of tangible results. Yet for all his problems with them, they remained his only lifeline to the international music business. Now there was a chance Bob could sign with CBS Records' Epic subsidiary, for whom Nash was now recording. In mid-February, Marley flew to London, not only to play on the album Nash was recording there, but also to do some tracks for CBS under his own name.

Produced by Nash, the half-dozen cuts Bob laid down around early spring 1972 seem like attempts to somehow make reggae palatable for the pop audience. Joining were keyboardist Rabbit Bundrick, familiar to both Marley and Nash from work on the ill-fated Swedish film soundtrack; Ghanaian percussionist Rebop Kwaku Baah, known for playing with top British rock group Traffic; and, on harmony vocals, Nash and American soul singer Doris Troy, who'd had a big 1963 US hit with "Just One Look" and recorded a solo LP for Apple (and would soon sing on Pink Floyd's *Dark Side of the Moon*). Some fuzzy, distorted guitar features on the reasonably catchy, if lyrically slight, soul-rock concoction "Reggae on Broadway," which was issued as a flop British single in May.

About half an album's worth was recorded, all but two of the tracks remaining unissued until just after Marley's death in 1981. While they have their moments, they seem indecisive, as if the producers couldn't figure out whether to aim them at the soul, pop, or rock audience. In the process, the reggae at the core of Bob's sound was diluted. Not all of the results were inconsequential; the gently seductive "Stay with Me,"

Though Marley's instrumental and vocal contributions went uncredited on Johnny Nash's *I Can See Clearly Now*, the LP included three Marley compositions and one Johnny and Bob wrote together. "Stir It Up" became a big hit for Nash, reaching the Top 15 in both the US and UK.

which would have made a better choice for a single, had genuine hit-worthy hooks, as well as a loping reggae beat and soulful female backup vocals (though some sources intimate this could have been recorded earlier than 1972 for JAD). But for the most part, Marley seemed adrift without the other Wailers.

As Nash had scored a few Top 10 UK hits in the late 1960s, he was understandably much more of a priority for CBS than Marley, whose success had been limited to the far smaller Jamaican market. Marley did not end up with credited instrumental or vocal contributions on *I Can See Clearly Now*, the album Nash recorded in London (though, according to a *Rolling Stone* review, he "was involved as a session musician and assistant producer"). But the LP did a great deal for Marley's career, as it included three Marley compositions and one Nash and Marley wrote together.

One of Marley's songs, "Stir It Up"—first recorded by the Wailers back in 1967—became a big hit for Nash, reaching the Top 15 in both the US and UK. The album sold reasonably well too, doing a great deal to increase Marley's global profile and royalty stream. A couple years later, Barbra Streisand even covered "Guava Jelly." At this point, Marley's future might have been judged more promising as a songwriter than a performer. "All his songs make magical use of an indescribable interplay between the peculiar rhythms of reggae and haunting tunes," wrote Charlie Gillett in his *Rolling Stone* review of *I Can See Clearly Now*. "But they still need Johnny's sympathetic singing to prevent the simple lyrics from becoming banal."

Some reggae purists might accuse Nash of watering down Marley's reggae or, even worse, exploiting him by gaining the success that should have gone to reggae's originators. "Johnny Nash wasn't altering or changing his voice to sing Bob's songs, but it was working," commented Livingston in *Before the Legend: The Rise of Bob Marley*. "And Johnny Nash, in reality, sounded very much like Johnny

ABOVE: "Reggae on Broadway" was a flop British single in May 1972. In 1981 WEA reissued it as the first single from the posthumous *Chances Are* compilation.

RIGHT: In March 1972, Nash and Marley performed a free concert for teenagers in the gym at a southeast London school, playing acoustic guitars with no PA system.

Mathis, when Bob only sounded like Bob. If I was made to choose in a purchase of both artists, I would take Bob Marley—even if he was talking." Marley himself expressed dissatisfaction with Nash's production of Marley's CBS sessions, telling *Melody Maker*, "He's a hard worker, but he didn't know my music. I don't want to put him down, but reggae isn't really his bag."

There's no question, however, that Nash did a great deal for Marley's career (and for reggae itself), and not just by covering his songs with respect and taste. He also helped introduce Marley to the British press and musical community, living (along with Sims and Bundrick) with Marley in a central London flat for which Sims was paying. Nor did Nash claim to be an authentic standard-bearer for reggae music, telling *Rolling Stone* that he didn't consider himself a reggae artist: "Somebody else started that rumor. Being a reggae singer for me is something new that somebody has suggested. I would like for them to explain it to me and just explain what it really is and maybe I can consider it."

In March, he and Marley even performed a free concert for teenagers in the gym at a southeast London school, playing acoustic guitars with no PA system. "Bob was saying that he desperately wanted to get back to the West Indies, but financially there was no opportunity, because he had no money at all," Keith Baugh, the teacher who'd arranged the show, remembered in *MOJO* almost forty years later. "I guess he saw that through Johnny Nash, he could make it as a songwriter."

Nash also wanted Marley to perform with him on UK touring dates, which led to the other Wailers—including Livingston, Tosh, and the Barretts—getting flown to London to join Marley later that year. If the Wailers, Bob included, were hoping this would mean an extensive series of concerts with a soul star that would introduce them to the British public, it didn't quite work out that way. When Marley performed, it was usually a short set with Nash's band, the Sons of Jungle (including Bundrick), not with the Wailers. The Wailers traveled with Nash and Marley, but were literally just along for the ride.

It's been reported this gave them an opportunity to watch and learn from the shows, but as they were seasoned performers by this point, it's not clear how much they stood to gain by standing in the wings for such an extended period. They did actually play at one show, and Marley and Tosh performed a benefit at a London school to raise money for a new swimming pool, but that was probably hardly the gig they had in mind when they left Jamaica. Danny Sims did arrange for the Wailers to record five tracks at CBS (including "Stir It Up" and four other songs that they'd re-record for *Catch a Fire*), but those weren't issued.

The spring *had* been productive for Marley in a nonmusical sense, though not one he was prepared to publicly acknowledge. In May, two sons were born to him by women to whom he wasn't married, Pat Williams and Janet Dunn (whose surname might have been Hunt). In April, his legal wife Rita had given birth to Bob's son Stephen in Delaware. Their marriage would never dissolve, but certainly both his prolonged absences and his extramarital affairs were putting quite a strain on it.

CHRIS BLACKWELL AND ISLAND RECORDS

Growing impatient with their lack of progress, the Wailers' frustration increased when their passports were inaccessible for an extended period after their arrival in London. Sims had taken them with the purpose of getting them work permits, and though they were eventually retrieved, it added to their general dissatisfaction with their career prospects abroad. With nothing coming out of his CBS association besides a failed single, Marley arranged for a meeting with another record label.

With the help of Brent Clarke, who did some record promotion for Sims, Marley was put in contact with Chris Blackwell, head of Island Records. Although it had started as a ska-oriented company in the early 1960s, by the late 1960s and early 1970s, it was one of the most successful British rock labels, issuing hit albums by Traffic; Jethro Tull; Free; King Crimson; Fairport Convention; Emerson, Lake and Palmer; Cat Stevens; Roxy Music; and other acts. Blackwell had not forgotten his roots in Jamaican music, however, and Island had recently landed a Top 10 UK single with Jimmy Cliff, who'd been one of the first reggae artists to get hits in the States as well.

Island Records founder Chris Blackwell had a huge hit licensing Jamaican singer Millie Small's ska single "My Boy Lollipop" (below) in the UK and US in 1964. In 1972, no one was more eager to bring reggae to a rock audience. BRIAN COOKE/REDFERNS/GETTY IMAGES

In 1972, Cliff was hot property after starring as the outlaw reggae singer in the cult film hit *The Harder They Come*, in which Blackwell was an investor. Its soundtrack featured recordings by Cliff and several other top reggae performers (though, oddly, not the Wailers), and it's been speculated that Blackwell hoped to break Jimmy into the rock album market in its wake. If so, those hopes were dashed when Cliff left Island for a bigger label. That in turn has generated retrospective speculation that when the Wailers walked in his door shortly after Cliff cut his ties with Island, Blackwell seized upon them as his chance to break reggae into the rock market.

"By that time, I was almost entirely engrossed in rock," Blackwell recalled in Christopher John Farley's *Before the Legend: The Rise of Bob Marley*. "The only person I had been working with really in Jamaican music at that time was Jimmy Cliff, and the week before I met Bob Marley, Jimmy Cliff had left Island, which was devastating to me. Because I was very tight with him, I put a lot of energy, love, and everything into it. And he left. He left because he felt I hadn't really done for him as much as I said I would do. He hadn't earned as much as I'd told him he would earn. He was offered a deal by EMI and he took it.

"I can understand it from his point of view. But I was devastated by it. Because I knew exactly how to break reggae at that time. I knew exactly how to break Jimmy Cliff at that time. The next record, I was going to have him in the T-shirt he was in in *The Harder They Come* and promote him as that."

Marley, remembered Blackwell in Chris Salewicz's *Bob Marley: The Untold Story*, "came in right at the time when in my head there was the idea that this rebel type of character could really emerge. And that I could break such an artist. I was dealing with rock music, which was really rebel music. I felt that would really be the way to break Jamaican music. But you needed somebody who could be that image. When Bob walked in, he really was that image, the real one that Jimmy had created in the movie."

If Blackwell was opportunistically sliding the Wailers into the slot originally intended for Cliff, it must also be noted that the group could not possibly have found a better record executive to advance their career. Not only did Blackwell have extensive experience issuing ska and reggae records—he *was* Jamaican, or nearly so, having been raised there for much of his boyhood. Family money enabled him to found Island Records when he was still based on the island in the late 1950s, and though he didn't record ska exclusively, he was in on the music almost from its inception. After moving both himself and his label to London in the early 1960s, he built Island's business on licensing Jamaican records for the UK market, selling plenty of copies to Britain's large Jamaican population. He'd even issued Marley's 1962 debut single, "Judge Not," in the United Kingdom, though it didn't sell much in that edition.

Licensed from Blackwell to a bigger label, Jamaican singer Millie Small's ska single "My Boy Lollipop" was a huge hit in both the United Kingdom and the United States in 1964. It was also vital in enabling Blackwell to get more hits in the pop market with artists he worked with personally, most notably the Spencer Davis Group, with a young Steve Winwood on vocals. The Spencer Davis hits, in turn, propelled Blackwell into the

Jimmy Cliff was one of the first reggae artists to get hits in the US. In 1972, he was hot property after starring as the outlaw reggae singer in the cult hit *The Harder They Come*, in which Blackwell was an investor. PICTORIAL PRESS LTD/ALAMY STOCK PHOTO

burgeoning progressive rock world with Winwood's next band, Traffic, and for the next few years, rock was Island's focus. There was nonetheless probably no other executive at a big British label as well schooled in reggae as Blackwell—and, just as importantly, no one else as eager to bring reggae to a rock audience.

In an extraordinary act of faith, before even signing a contract with the Wailers, Blackwell advanced the band money to record an album for Island. The amount usually cited is four thousand pounds, although it seems likely, as some sources report, that an additional four thousand pounds was to be paid when he received satisfactory tapes. It wasn't a huge sum, but it was by far the biggest budget the Wailers had been given to record in the studio. They would also be able to cut the tracks in Kingston after returning to Jamaica around the beginning of fall 1972.

Blackwell also spent another four thousand pounds to buy the Wailers out of their CBS contract. Danny Sims, who had to be bought out as well, was paid a similar sum and a small percentage of the band's sales on Island. Sims, however, kept Marley's publishing—an asset that would become more lucrative than anyone expected, especially after one of his songs became a chart-topper for another artist. For all of his erratic attempts to make a star out of his client, Sims had done a lot to bring Marley into the international arena, though it's doubtful he could have done nearly as much as Blackwell and Island Records would in just a few months.

THE *CATCH A FIRE* SESSIONS

The Wailers "had a reputation of being very hard to deal with," noted Blackwell in the documentary on their first album for Island, *Catch a Fire*. "And I felt that the only way to establish a relationship with them was to show some trust to them. So . . . I gave them the money to go and make the record."

Added Bunny Livingston in the same film, "Blackwell was sitting down, wondering if we were ever gonna turn in an album. So it was a challenge for us to prove to him different from what he thought. . . . So the album was done in like record time." It helped, too, that while the Wailers had barely been able to perform on their UK visit, they'd spent a lot of time rehearsing *Catch a Fire* material in a London basement studio, enabling them to record it quickly and efficiently in Kingston. Helping the Wailers out on a couple tracks was teenaged bassist Robbie Shakespeare, who would soon team up with percussionist Sly Dunbar to form the most renowned rhythm section/production team in all of reggae.

Teenaged bassist Robbie Shakespeare helped out the Wailers on a couple *Catch a Fire* tracks. Shakespeare would later team up with percussionist Sly Dunbar to form reggae's most renowned rhythm section/production team. DAVID CORIO/REDFERNS/GETTY IMAGES

As swift as the sessions went, the Island advance nevertheless allowed the Wailers more time in the studio than they'd ever previously enjoyed. Asked by Carl Gayle of *Let It Rock* what influenced the band "to do something so progressive," Marley responded, "There wasn't really an influence, it was just that this time we got the money from Chris Blackwell to go into the studio and spend as much time as we needed. You see musicians in JA have to work to a time limit so they have to come out of the studio when their time runs out whether they are satisfied or not."

Four of the nine tracks from the sessions eventually selected for the LP had already been released by the Wailers in different versions. This, of course, was nothing new for them or for the reggae world in general, where remakes were common. In any case, very few listeners outside of Jamaica would have known that "Concrete Jungle," "400 Years," "Stop That Train," and "Stir It Up" had previously appeared in different guises. Since Johnny Nash had just made "Stir It Up" into a hit, it was natural for the Wailers to include their own updated version, if only to help draw attention to an LP by an act still unknown to most of the world.

With the addition of five songs that would be appearing on record for the first time, the Wailers had a strong set of material for their first album to be made widely available throughout the United Kingdom and United States. While "Stir It Up" was the most accessible tune, "Baby We've Got a Date (Rock It Baby)" was also catchy romantic reggae, with harmonies that alternately soared and cooed. "Kinky Reggae" gave the album an anthem of sorts for the band's brand of music. And while Marley was the band's dominant writer and singer—as he had been for much of their lifespan—Peter Tosh got his say on the remakes of "400 Years" and the spiritual-flavored "Stop That Train." Both were up to the standards of Marley's compositions and gave the album some welcome diversity in much the same way George Harrison's songs functioned for the Beatles.

There was also room for the sort of sociopolitical commentary that had become a Wailers trademark. "Concrete Jungle" documented the Trench Town ghetto environment, while the previously unheard "Slave Driver" reflected the suffering of their Trench

Catch a Fire's "Baby We've Got a Date (Rock It Baby)" was catchy romantic reggae also made available in Jamaica with a different mix as "Rock It Babe." "Craven Choke Puppy" was another Tuff Gong single from 1972.

Town brethren and could have been a subtle indictment of the record industry, in which the Wailers had toiled for years without much reward. One phrase from the song was selected by Blackwell as the album's title: *Catch a Fire.*

"When the Wailers came with songs like 'Slave Driver,' it was a call to revolution within the music itself, the industry," confirmed Bunny Livingston in the *Catch a Fire* documentary. "The people needed that revolution because there were things that had to be dealt with, that singing about love could not deal with."

Added Bunny in the same interview, "Between myself, Bob, and Peter, we had to find a formula that would be acceptable. So what we did was lay down a hard, driving rhythm that suggests the basic reggae principles. And then we would put little bits and colorings here and there that would not take away from the basic principle, but would attract the international marketplace."

When Blackwell traveled to Jamaica to hear the results of the sessions, he was both relieved and excited to have his hopes not just met, but exceeded. "I was thrilled about it—because they at least had recorded something; so already all the nay-saying motherfuckers were wrong, you know," he told Timothy White in *Billboard* in 1991. "So I went in the studio and they played me all the tracks and I was just totally blown away by the musical quality of 'Slave Driver' and 'Concrete Jungle.' You know, 'Concrete Jungle' was just so far ahead of anything that had ever been made in Jamaica before—that one particular track, the structure of it, the whole thing. It was just unbelievable.

"This LP, *Catch a Fire*, was the first reggae record conceived as an album. Leslie Kong had previously put out that so-called *Best of the Wailers*, which was drawn from a series of late rock steady sessions that took place in a concentrated period of time. But *Catch a Fire* was conceived by the group as a cohesive project, and they went ahead and executed it. It was unprecedented in reggae."

As Blackwell elaborated in Vivien Goldman's *The Book of Exodus*, Marley had to make some adjustments. "Early on after I signed Bob, I took him to a couple of shows on a tour with John Martyn, Traffic, and Free, and he could see how all those shows were sold out, and Traffic had never had a single," he recalled. "In his experience of what music was all about, you needed to have a single and then go on and do shows."

Yet the tracks weren't quite finished. At Island's Basing Street Studios in London, overdubs were added by musicians who were neither in the Wailers nor Jamaican. Rabbit Bundrick,

American guitarist Wayne Perkins, seen here performing with Smith Perkins Smith at London's Roundhouse in May 1972, was brought in to adapt his bluesy rock chops to the reggae of *Catch a Fire*.
MICHAEL PUTLAND/GETTY IMAGES

by now a familiar face in Marley's world, contributed some clavinet, an instrument whose brittle funky tone had recently been popularized by Stevie Wonder on "Superstition." Another UK-based American rock musician, Wayne Perkins (who a few years later would unsuccessfully vie to replace Mick Taylor in the Rolling Stones), added guitar. Both musicians needed a bit of guidance to adapt their rock chops to reggae, but their contributions were undeniable, Perkins's bluesy guitar and Bundrick's clavinet making themselves known at the beginning of *Catch a Fire*'s opening track, "Concrete Jungle."

CATCH A FIRE

Review by Richie Unterberger

Catch a Fire is often hailed as the Wailers' international breakthrough, and in a marketing sense, it was. It was their first album made widely available to listeners outside of Jamaica, and the first Wailers release to receive significant media attention in the United Kingdom and United States. Artistically, however, it wasn't so much a breakthrough as a consolidation of their strengths and a subtle refinement of their sound in an effort to win crossover appeal among a rock audience.

The sense that the Wailers were molding what was already there for a new listenership was reinforced by the presence of four remakes of songs first released on late-1960s and early-1970s singles heard almost exclusively by Jamaicans. The originals of "Stir It Up," "400 Years," "Concrete Jungle," and "Stop That Train" were perkier and rougher. The do-overs were slicker and slower, verging on languid. Some reggae purists strongly prefer the earlier versions, and there's certainly room to argue the superiority of the first passes at these tunes. At the very least, they're markedly different approaches to the same material.

But the remakes are hardly sellouts. "400 Years," haunting to the point of gloominess in its first appearance, reemerges with a different, more somber gravity in this more deliberately paced arrangement, spiced by ethereal, almost classically flavored chiming keyboards near the ends of the verses. "Stop That Train" is transformed from an upbeat rock-steady tune into something weightier and far more spiritual.

The other two remakes are more obvious rearrangements (some would say concessions) to what some of the Wailers and their associates have euphemistically termed a more "international" sound. "Concrete Jungle" was more ominous in its original state, and the addition of bluesy rock guitar licks (from Wayne Perkins) and clavinet might be the most frequently cited examples of how Chris Blackwell reshaped the Wailers' raw material for rock radio airplay. "Stir It Up" underwent the most dramatic makeover, changing from the basic rock-steady exercise of the rather repetitious 1967 single to something immensely more sensual, loping, and languorous, heightened by washes of swooping, sometimes wah-wahing guitar.

These songs alone would ensure *Catch a Fire*'s status as a major release. Yet the other five tracks also illustrated the evolution of the Wailers' reggae to a more fully rounded sound incorporating growing heaps of rock and soul. "Slave Driver" is perhaps the most effective, its agreeably moody melody and

"The experiment was for Chris Blackwell to help Bob break in America," offered Bundrick in the *Catch a Fire* documentary. "So we needed to add a little bit of something that Americans were used to, like clavinets and things. So Bob was ready for that. But the thing that we were trying to do by bridging the gap between purist reggae and Americanized reggae, which Americans could palate, was not purist. My parts on *Catch a Fire* are nowhere near purist. They are an imitation at what Bob Marley taught me to do."

Catch a Fire, confirmed Blackwell in the same source, was "I don't say softened, but more, say, enhanced, to try and reach a rock market. Because this was the first record. And they

typically eerie Wailers harmonies coating a lyric drawing parallels between slavery's brutality and today's illiteracy and poverty. "No More Trouble" might be the grimmest song in popular music to urge listeners to make love, not war. "Midnight Ravers" is lyrically slighter than these tunes, but also affectingly downbeat in its interplay between Bob's lead vocal and the backup singers.

As a balance to the more serious statements, there is not only "Stir It Up" but also the anthemic "Kinky Reggae," foregrounding the chink-a-chink-a guitar rhythm the Wailers did much to popularize. Coming amid all these riches, "Baby We've Got a Date (Rock It Baby)" seems almost deliberately lightweight, as if to remind us the Wailers liked a good time as much as anyone. Chris Blackwell didn't seem to want *too* much of a good time to leak into the final product, vetoing the inclusion of two romantic-minded outtakes, "High Tide or Low Tide" and "All Day All Night," later made available on *Catch a Fire*'s deluxe edition.

If there's any regrettable imbalance to *Catch a Fire*, it's the lack of original compositions or lead vocals by Bunny Livingston. Peter Tosh gets to sing two of his own songs—"400 Years" and "Stop That Train"—but is also underrepresented. A greater diversity of material that drew from all three writers and singers in the Wailers could have mightily benefited the proceedings. However, that would have necessitated a double

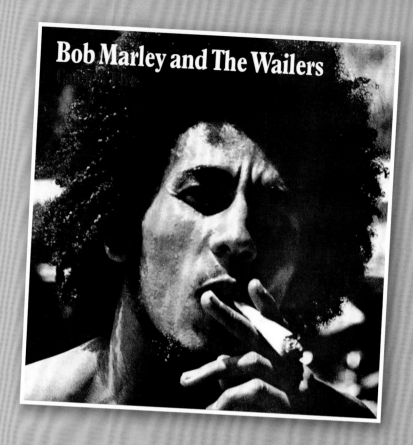

album, a format no major label would have approved as an act's first release for a company.

As it is, *Catch a Fire* is one of the Wailers' essential releases, even without factoring in its huge historical significance. It contains some of their most essential songs, has little filler, and expands the band's sound in interesting, accessible ways without diluting their messages, whether personal or political.

wanted to reach into that market." By way of illustration, "With 'Stir It Up,' what I was trying to merge it into was more of a sort of a hypnotic type feel. It's the kind of wah-wah feel and a different sort of guitar going all the way through it, and make it much less of a reggae rhythm, and more of a sort of a drifting feel." He also made it more of an early-1970s "rock" album by extending the length of tracks past the reggae norm (in a couple cases exceeding five minutes), claiming in *Before the Legend* to triple the length of "Stir It Up." He also decided not to use a couple of the more standard romantic numbers, "High Tide or Low Tide" and "All Day All Night," later made available on *Catch a Fire*'s deluxe CD edition.

CATCH A FIRE CATCHES ON

Island made more nods to the rock market in how it packaged *Catch a Fire*. The LP was enclosed in a sleeve that mimicked a Zippo lighter—the same kind that plenty of rock fans in the counterculture might have used to fire up the kind of joints that were so heavily smoked in Jamaica. According to Blackwell in the *Rebel Music: The Bob Marley Story* documentary, the strategy to bill the band as the Wailers rather than Bob Marley and the Wailers, "really was to present them as like a black rock group."

In the media, the strategy paid immediate dividends. *Catch a Fire* was the first Wailers release widely reviewed in UK and US music publications, most of the evaluations ranging from positive to downright ecstatic. "It seems to me that this may be the most important reggae record ever made," gushed Richard Williams in *Melody Maker*. "It's equivalent of Sly [Stone's] *Dance To The Music*, or Marvin Gaye's *What's Going On*. It has that kind of potential: revitalizing the style from which it springs, and introducing it to an entirely new audience. A few years will need to have passed before we'll know for sure, but Marley may even be a genius."

In his *Rolling Stone* review of the LP, Rob Houghton was hardly less elated: "The result is a blend: Lilting tunes of hypnotic character headed by super-progressive lead guitar work, Motown variations, and cowboy nuances, all backed by the tricky Jamaican beat that serves to keep the decibel level in a moderate range, thereby forcing the audience to be seduced by the charms of the music, rather than overwhelmed by the relentless force of most rock.

"The result is a mature, fully realized sound with a beautiful lyric sensibility that turns well known stylistics into fresh, vibrant music. The reggae beat has the capacity to lend direction to the Wailers' music, and force limits on their sound. But it is not a mere gimmick, although it could develop into one should it become the rage. It is a valid impression of American mainstream rock and blues, altered with the originality that can only come from a fresh viewpoint. . . . They display fantastic breadth in what would seem to be a restrictive format."

The original 1973 release of *Catch a Fire*, designed by graphic artists Rod Dyer and Bob Weiner, was encased in a hinged sleeve depicting a Zippo lighter.

"This music knocks me out in a manner not that different from the way those first Beatle discs did back in 1964," declared Gene Sculatti in the US rock magazine *Fusion*. "There's these foreigners, Western Hemisphere black dudes singing movie English, oohing and wee-oohing in that odd distanced manner, bouncing around chunks of very pliable yet almost frictionless instrumental sound that, for all its alien tongue traits, is unquestionably rock 'n' roll of the purest universal strain. It has earmarks of American soul, New Orleans rock, the corner crooners of the '50s, bubblegum in big doses, even gentle touches of pop psychedelia, and parents, teachers and church leaders are probably jacked up over it somewhere already."

Now that *Catch a Fire* is often acknowledged as a classic, it can be easy to forget that it wasn't universally praised upon its first appearance. Some critics felt it was almost a sellout of sorts. "Reggae is a deep beat and melodies you can't forget, where *Catch a Fire* is a soft beat and guitar solos you heard before and were glad to have forgotten," grumbled Charlie Gillett (author of the first highly praised history of rock, *The Sound of the City*) in *Creem*.

"Early Wailers material, in the ska mold, were tight, funky expressions of frustration, raucous and rude-boy lauding," complained *International Times*. "This set is slick production; over refined backbeats admonishing each number; and the once outstanding vocalizing of Marley has been incorporated into the central sound." (For those who found the production too glossy, the mix of the tapes as Blackwell first heard them in Jamaica is now available as a bonus CD on *Catch a Fire*'s deluxe edition.)

Island Records promotional display for *Catch a Fire*. ROGER STEFFENS' REGGAE ARCHIVE

Even by cult standards, *Catch a Fire* was slow to build momentum. It sold just fourteen thousand copies in its first year of release, though it would by the late 1990s (according to Blackwell) sell well over a million copies. Those fourteen thousand copies were still a lot more than the Wailers had previously sold outside of Jamaica, and gave them something to promote when they embarked on their first proper British tour in spring 1973. Just as key to upping their profile was an appearance on BBC television's *Old Grey Whistle Test* music program, on which the Wailers performed "Stir It Up" and "Concrete Jungle" to pre-recorded backing tracks, with live vocals. A fuller sampling of the band's repertoire was broadcast on BBC Radio One's *In Concert* program on May 24, featuring most of the songs from *Catch a Fire* and previews of a couple from their next LP.

"It was the first time the Wailers had played gigs like these, with a proper road crew and a proper PA system," wrote Dennis Morris, a then-fourteen-year-old photographer whom the group had invited onto the tour, in his book *Bob Marley: A Rebel Life*. "At the same time, they didn't yet have their own sound engineer, and they were trying to develop their own sound. There wasn't really any major dispute, but the road crew were used to miking up the drum kit for a rock band: four toms, a snare and a floor tom, whereas a reggae kit would have a bass drum, a snare, a hi-hat and a couple of toms. For a reggae drummer you need to mike up the snare and the hi-hat, but the hi-hat wasn't that important in rock music. Both sides were learning from each other."

SUNDOWN, EDMONTON

Whit Sunday, 27th May, 1973, 2 p.m.-10 p.m.

GRAND BANK HOLIDAY REGGAE REVUE

featuring

DESMOND DEKKER
NICKY THOMAS
THE CYMARONS   THE MARVELS
ERASMUS CHORUM
TONY MORGAN'S MUSSEL POWER BAND
Special Guests
BOB MARLEY and the WAILERS
+ OTHER STARS

Tickets available from: 30 Bancroft, Hitchin, Herts. or Sundown, Edmonton and ususal ticket agents.

The Wailers hit London in spring 1973. From left: Earl Lindo, "Family Man" Barrett, Bob Marley, Peter Tosh, Carlton Barrett, and Bunny Livingston.
MICHAEL OCHS ARCHIVES/GETTY IMAGES; INSET ROGER STEFFENS' REGGAE ARCHIVE

THE *BURNIN'* SESSIONS

Even before coming back to England, the Wailers had recorded the rhythm tracks for their next album at Harry J's studio in Kingston, adding some overdubs at Basing Street Studios after the tour. Like *Catch a Fire*, the *Burnin'* LP mixed new material with more polished remakes of songs already heard on previous Wailers discs. Indeed, "Put It On" dated back to their ska days in the mid-1960s, while "Small Axe" and "Duppy Conqueror" were among the highlights of their early-1970s recordings with Lee Perry. Reaching back yet further in a sense was "Rastaman Chant," an adaptation of a traditional nyabinghi hymn.

The Wailers had remade some of their songs for different releases before signing with Island and would continue to do so at the label, both on group and solo releases. "Early on when Bob was concerned about the early records he'd done for Coxsone, Scratch, and Danny Sims, those famous masters everyone releases because everybody claims them, I said I thought the best way to deal with it was to re-record some of the old songs," noted Blackwell in *The Book of Exodus*. "So every record had three or four classic songs that he'd recorded before, like on [the 1977 album] *Exodus*, ['One Love'] had been recorded before. Bob always picked the songs, all I did was say to him that it was a good idea."

Bob continued to sing and write the lion's share of material, but the spread was more democratic this time around. Bunny penned a couple songs and Peter another, as well as cowriting the classic "Get Up, Stand Up" with Marley. Yet when surplus tracks had to be squeezed off, both Livingston and Tosh lost out, with Tosh's "No Sympathy" and Livingston's "The Oppressed Song" and "Reincarnated Souls" failing to make the final cut (though the latter track, which the album had originally been titled after, did appear on a B-side). All have been added to the deluxe CD edition. But at the time, the decision to bump them in favor of Marley's songs became another source of tension.

Melody Maker ad for *Burnin'* shows an iconic image of Bob and lists 1973 UK dates.

While the rousing, anthemic fight-for-your-rights "Get Up, Stand Up" is one of the Wailers' most famous songs, another track on *Burnin'* became arguably Marley's most famous composition. As with "Stir It Up," however, it wouldn't be the Wailers who had the international hit with the song. "I Shot the Sheriff," which almost sounded like a Jamaican outlaw shootout set to music, was covered by Eric Clapton on his 1974 album, *461 Ocean Boulevard*. Although Clapton didn't change the arrangement a whole lot, it was he, not Marley, who reaped the big airplay and sales, his cover soaring to #1 in the United States.

When Clapton was recording *461 Ocean Boulevard* in Miami, local musician George Terry, as Clapton remembered in *Clapton: The Autobiography*, "came in with an album called *Burnin'* by Bob Marley and the Wailers, a band I'd never heard of. When he played it, I was mesmerized. He especially liked the track 'I Shot the Sheriff' and kept saying to me, 'You ought to cut this, you ought to cut this. We could make it sound great,' but it was hard-core reggae and I wasn't sure we could do it justice. We did a version of it anyway, and although I didn't say so at the time, I wasn't enamored with it. . . .

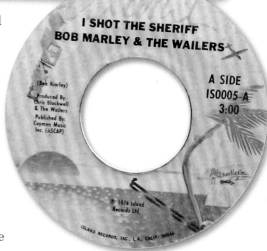

"I just knew we weren't doing it right. When we got to the end of the sessions and started to collate the songs we had, I told them I didn't think 'Sheriff' should be included, as it didn't do the Wailers' version justice. But everyone said, 'No, no. Honestly, this is a hit.' And sure enough, when the album was released and the record company chose it as a single, to my utter astonishment it went straight to number one. Though I didn't meet Bob Marley till much later, he did call me up when the single came out and seemed pretty happy with it. I tried to ask him what the song was all about, but couldn't understand much of his reply. I was just relieved that he liked what we had done."

Eric Clapton rode his cover of "I Shot the Sheriff" to #1 in the United States. Marley would, of course, be pressed to explain the lyric was purely metaphorical.

Marley gave a relatively straightforward explanation of the song to *Melody Maker* in 1975. "That message a kind of diplomatic statement," he divulged. "You have to kinda suss things out. I shot the sheriff is like I shot wickedness. That's not really a sheriff, it's just the elements of wickedness, you know. How wickedness can happen.

"But the elements of that song is people been judging you and you can't stand it no more and you explode, you just explode. So it really carry a message, you know. Clapton asked me about the song because when Clapton finished the song he didn't know the meaning of the song. Him like the kind of music and then him like the melody and then him make 'I Shot The Sheriff.'"

BURNIN'

Review by Gillian G. Gaar

The Wailers' second album for Island features what became some of Bob Marley's most recognizable songs: "Get Up, Stand Up" and "I Shot the Sheriff." Like the album's title, both reflected a strong, underlying desire for change.

After not releasing a studio album for two years, the Wailers seemed anxious to make up for lost time, dropping both *Catch a Fire* and *Burnin'* in 1973. The latter recycled some older numbers ("Put It On" from *The Wailing Wailers*, "Duppy Conqueror" from *Soul Revolution*, and "Small Axe" from the 1973 compilation *African Herbsman*) for what they hoped would be a broader audience now that they had the distribution muscle of Island Records behind them.

The differences are striking. The earlier version of "Put It On," for example, is faster and looser, with a more soft-spoken vocal, while the *Burnin'* version is sharper and tighter, with far better production values and a much more confident lead vocal. The Wailers had found their voice.

Certainly Marley was becoming a more sophisticated songwriter. "I Shot the Sheriff" was a metaphorical attack on an unjust system, with the sheriff representing a repressive government; recasting the incident in a personal narrative made the target less obvious. The song gave Marley his first #1, when Eric Clapton took his rock-influenced version to the top of the US charts in 1974.

"Get Up, Stand Up" was another rallying cry against injustice, cowritten by Marley and Peter Tosh, and partially inspired by the poverty Marley witnessed in Jamaica and on his travels. But the lyrics weren't tied to any one cause or nation, making the song a natural for just about any protest situation. Tosh and Bunny Wailer would later record their own versions; it was also the last song Marley would ever perform live, in Pittsburgh on September 23, 1980.

Other protest songs on *Burnin'* included "Burnin' and Lootin'" and "Small Axe," the latter about taking down the powerful David-and-Goliath style. But there are also songs of empowerment. "Pass It On" extols the virtues of doing the right thing, while the closing track on the original album (four bonus tracks were added to the 2001 reissue), "One Foundation," espouses a philosophy of building for the future, acknowledging that "we are all one people."

Burnin' marked the end of an era. After its release, both Tosh and Bunny Wailer left the group. But it was also the start of something new, laying the groundwork for Marley's future success in the US, becoming his first gold record and reaching #41 in the R & B charts. More change in Marley's fortunes was on the way.

Asked by *Billboard* how he could write such a song if he believed so strongly in peace, Marley replied, "Reggae reflects what goes on around us, right or wrong. We don't tell people to shoot anybody, we just say it happens."

Helping with the song's composition was one of Bob's girlfriends of the time, Esther Anderson, who has said the line about killing a seed before it grows refers to her use of contraception. Lee Jaffe, a young American filmmaker and harmonica player who had befriended Bob and introduced him to Anderson, remembered helping with some lyrics as well. "It was such a funny song," he said in *One Love: Life with Bob Marley and the Wailers*, remembering Marley playing it for the first time on a Jamaican beach. "The beach wasn't that crowded, but we had a whole bunch of people just dancing to that song."

1973 US TOURS

With a UK tour under the Wailers' belts and a second album in the can, the next step for Island was to break into the American market, then as now the most lucrative in the world. At this point, the first serious crack occurred in the Wailers' unity. Tested so often since the early 1960s, it was now beginning to fracture with the group on the brink of worldwide success. Bunny Livingston didn't want to tour and had never warmed to playing outside Jamaica, in part because the British climate wasn't as warm as in his native country. He was also put off when Blackwell told him the band would be playing "freak clubs." Perhaps he felt he'd be thrust into the heart of Babylon, though it's more likely the Island boss was attempting to build an American following in what might be more straightforwardly termed "underground venues."

When the Wailers played some US shows in summer 1973, Bunny was replaced by their old mentor Joe Higgs, though Bunny remained an official part of the group. With Earl "Wire" Lindo on keyboards, they played dates in Boston and New York, including a week in Manhattan at Max's Kansas City, sharing the bill with a similarly just-emerging Bruce Springsteen. According to Lee Jaffe, Bob got the gig after Jaffe played some of *Catch a Fire* to Max's booker Sam Hood, who heard in the Wailers "the Drifters with a raised consciousness."

"At last some genuine reggay [sic] has hit New York ears with the opening of the Wailers, one of the best-known and longest-lasting of the Jamaican groups," wrote the *New York Times* in its review of their Max's stint. "New York has seen Johnny Nash ironing out his reggay-rock appeal to a broader soul-oriented audience, endured the yearly—and much overblown—calypso-reggay spectacles, but with the Wailers it now has the real thing. On their first American tour, the Wailers came over as self-assured, primitive and metallically folksy."

Michael Watts of *Melody Maker* was less positive, finding the Wailers "rather stiff for most of their set. In fact, Bob Marley sounded somewhat thin and unconvincing on lead vocals. In all truth, they didn't appear to be enjoying themselves, and this reserve held back their music, which if anything relies heavily on its infectiousness." As he also noted, the audience featured "with virtually no exception, white ears." The lack of African-American fans at their US concerts would vex Marley for the remainder of his life.

"At first the audience showed mixed emotions," Higgs remembered of those early American shows in Stephen Davis's *Bob Marley* biography. "It was something they weren't ready to accept immediately. It was like reminding them of something. And we noticed it was a 95 percent white audience most of the way. Even though we were playing for capacity, we were concerned with the composition of the audience we had seen on tour."

In October, *Burnin'* was released, its appearance coinciding almost exactly with the Wailers' next (and brief) US tour. With the novelty of a reggae band forging into the rock album market worn off, there wasn't quite the flurry of media coverage as there had been for *Catch a Fire*, but reviews remained positive. "Music like this is Bob Marley's forte; soft, supremely sensual, and making its point through understatement," Richard Williams reported to *Melody Maker* when he sat in on some *Burnin'* sessions. "It doesn't shout at you; rather it insinuates, suffusing the brain like a heady wine."

ABOVE: In July 1973, the Wailers shared a six-night residency at New York's legendary Max's Kansas City club with another emerging musical talent.

RIGHT: In 1973, Blackwell and Island released a ten-track reggae sampler that included the Wailers' "Concrete Jungle."

"*Burnin'* offers a rather more representative sampling of the Wailers' unique wares than *Catch a Fire*," *Rolling Stone*'s Jim Miller opined. "The album sticks more closely to the ensemble's live sound, minus too many psyche-delicate embellishments. . . . On most of these songs Marley's singular vision of a gentle yet unsparing justice prevails, shaping the band's melodic and lyric attack."

The oft-staid *Billboard*, the leading American music trade magazine, gave the record an unusually passionate thumbs-up: "This LP is a significant venture into the folklore of the Jamaican people. The songs in reggae format kindle lights ablaze with images of shanty towns and the sadness of life for the destitute. It is the Jamaican version of the blues."

In its comparison of reggae to the blues, *Billboard* echoed Marley's own comments to the magazine, which featured two separate articles on the Wailers in November. "My music gets my message across," Marley told the publication, "so we are touring for more than commercial reasons. As for the harshness of my material, I compare it to the old American blues. It tells the truth from the people's viewpoint. But reggae is more free form than the blues. But most important, reggae is for everyone and we hope we can help everyone with our music."

Soviet bootleg flexidiscs. ROGER STEFFENS' REGGAE ARCHIVE

With his patois likely modified by print media into syntax more understandable to non-Jamaicans, Marley was becoming a spokesperson not just for the Wailers but for reggae in general. "To me," Marley declared in *Billboard*, "reggae is the people's music. It deals with reality more than many other forms of music and in a much starker way. Nobody plays a leading role in the music, and perhaps this is because a lot of Jamaicans haven't had much musical schooling. There are no superstars. We just try to put it together with what we know. The rhythm is the important part, not a lead instrument."

Even at this early stage in his exposure to American audiences, Marley realized it would be a long slog to break through in the United States, especially to black listeners. "The people in the US are showing more interest, but they still don't know a great deal about reggae," he fretted. "The sound just hasn't been exposed enough here, but there are other reasons. A lot of Americans don't understand the full meaning of the lyrics. . . .

"A lot of people ask me why I come to America when I can do very well in Jamaica. My answer is that I do want to spread peace and help others. We want to show that the world can get along very well without war, that humans must appreciate others as humans, not by race or religion." Asked a couple weeks later in a second

Billboard article whether reggae should be accepted by African Americans, he responded, "Yeah, man. It's a black people's music. But I prefer *all* people to like our music . . . I think as soon as the people in America find out what the *real* reggae is it will be around for a long, long while."

The month *Burnin'* came out, the Wailers played some more US shows, again without Bunny. The plan was to tour as a support act for Sly and the Family Stone, which seemed like an ideal vehicle for exposure to both white and black audiences. Like many such things that seem good on paper, in real life it didn't work out, the Wailers leaving the tour in Las Vegas after just four shows. According to some reports, they were thrown off because the headliners found them too good to function as an opening band. It seems just as likely, however, that they were dumped because Sly's audiences were, like most Americans, unfamiliar with reggae and unresponsive to the Wailers' set.

The Wailers made the most of the situation by doing some hastily arranged gigs in San Francisco, where "they played to two packed houses at Broadway's Matrix [club] including internationally famous rock musicians," reported Joel Selvin in the *San Francisco Chronicle*. "Marley, songwriter, bandleader and lead singer, bobs up and down, wavering in front of the microphone—very high and stoned—completely oblivious to the mike. He breaks all the rules of microphone technique—looking away and down at the same time even—yet his pitch is pure and unfaltering. . . .

After leaving their tour with Sly and the Family Stone after just four shows, the Wailers played some hastily arranged gigs in San Francisco. Management at the Matrix club seemed eager to defend the change of lineup.

"An extraordinary, hypnotic performer, Marley chants his couplet-based songs as if they were dirges, freely improvising versions when the feeling is right (or his guitar string broken). The sound of his high, fragile voice holds a measure of pain. When Marley sings 'we don't need no more trouble,' it is the voice—not the words—that tell how much trouble there has already been. Yet somehow the cumulative effect is not depressing, but oddly uplifting. In a world of sham, the Wailers are real."

It would be in these hip rock venues, rather than as a support for superstars like Sly and the Family Stone, that Marley would develop a cult American fan base. Album-oriented FM stations would also be key to finding listeners, and while in San Francisco, the Wailers broadcast a live, in-studio set (in Sausalito's Record Plant) on the city's most popular FM rock station, KSAN. Tracks from the show, issued nearly two decades later as part of *Talkin' Blues*, testify to the band's tightness, even with Joe Higgs in place of Bunny Livingston.

THE ORIGINAL WAILERS BREAK UP

After returning to Jamaica for a brief break, the Wailers began a UK tour in November 1973 without either Livingston or Higgs. Although they sound fine on a tape of a November 23 show at Leeds (now available as a bonus disc on the deluxe edition of *Burnin'*), the tour stopped almost as soon as it started and acted as the nail in the coffin of the original Wailers. Just a couple weeks into the tour, Peter Tosh left and the remaining dates were canceled.

Explanations for the tour's termination vary. Tosh was ill with bronchitis and generally indisposed to touring in cold weather. Snow at the final concert, in Northampton on November 30, seemed to be the last straw. While there was no official breakup at the time, with the exception of a few one-off shows in Jamaica over the next couple years, Marley, Tosh, and Livingston would never again perform as the Wailers.

There was probably more at work than dislike of touring and aversion to cold weather. "I left because I need recognition and respect," Tosh declared in a 1983 interview used as part of the *Marley* documentary. "The way [Chris Blackwell] intend to handle us was like we were unprofessional, or we were just beginners, which I did not appreciate." In an interview used in the *Behind the Music* documentary on Tosh, he elaborated, "I was [Marley's] background vocal, background decorator of his music for all these years. Well, the time came after twelve years, [to] see what was inside of me . . . because I did not come on this Earth to be a background vocal."

Livingston was more philosophical than bitter in an interview included in the *Marley* documentary's DVD edition: "Every Wailer is qualified to go solo. But we needed to . . . mold ourselves into that kind of a position by being a group. After that, everyone was strong enough. 'Cause, like, the band got too small."

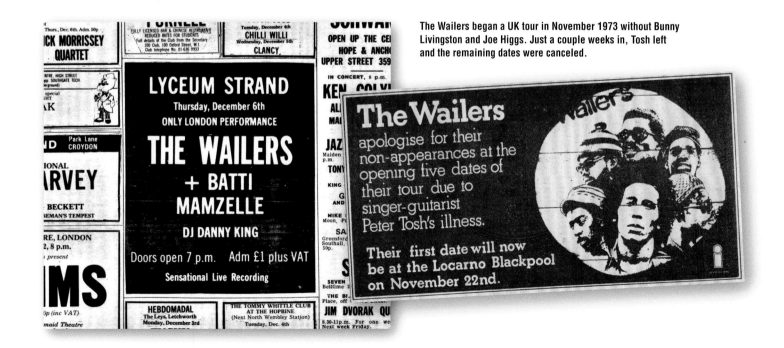

The Wailers began a UK tour in November 1973 without Bunny Livingston and Joe Higgs. Just a couple weeks in, Tosh left and the remaining dates were canceled.

In the same film, Blackwell intimated that Tosh and Livingston's reluctance to play the usual rock game of building up momentum through grueling touring was a drawback: "I was trying to get across that this is a black rock act, that's how I wanted it to be perceived. My sense is that Bob was willing to give it a try, and that the others weren't that keen . . . I had no doubt that it would succeed. The only thing that could stop it succeeding is if I couldn't get them to tour. That was my only fear."

More crucially, Peter and Bunny obviously had more to offer as songwriters and lead singers than the bits they'd been allowed on *Catch a Fire* and *Burnin'*. Both promptly embarked on solo careers that allowed them to flex their muscles. If their records and concerts didn't have nearly as much impact as Marley's over the next seven years, they were nevertheless highly successful, placing among the upper echelon of international reggae stars.

Dennis Morris, who'd gotten to know the Wailers as a British tour photographer, wrote in *Bob Marley: A Rebel Life*, "To me, Bunny was what Brian Jones had been to the early Rolling Stones. You never really saw him, but he was the one who was putting it all together, creating the sound. When Jones didn't like the direction the band was going in, then, like Bunny, he left. If Bunny had continued with the Wailers, it would have been completely different. More harmonies with all three voices. Bob had become the lead vocalist, with Peter and Bunny backing him, whereas before that it was three-way vocal harmonies.

"But I don't think Bob took over—it was just a natural progression. With the tour abandoned, it seemed like the group was finished. But for Island, it worked out perfectly. No one tried to stop it."

Some believe that Chris Blackwell was angling to position Marley as the focal point all along, or at least favor him as their principal singer. "He has a great voice for recording," Blackwell observed in the *Catch a Fire* documentary. "Because it's in the frequencies which you need to cut through. You can surround it with instruments at a high level." Theories that Blackwell was looking to make Marley a solo artist and sideline the others, however, are not supported by Blackwell's decision to bill them as the Wailers, rather than Bob Marley and the Wailers (as they had been on some of their pre-Island discs). As he's emphasized numerous times, he wanted to position them as something of a black rock group, not a star backed by other guys.

After leaving the Wailers, both Tosh (some 1972–1974 singles pictured here) and Livingston immediately embarked on solo careers.

In hindsight, had the core trio of the Wailers managed to stay together, it had the potential to be bigger than any one of them were on their own—even Marley. Had space been allotted for Tosh and Livingston's songs, one could even envision them cranking out two or three quality-packed albums a year, such was their wealth of original material. These records would have featured a rare blend of diverse yet complementary compositions and voices, much in the same way bands like the Beatles deployed the talents of three major singer-songwriters.

Yet, also in hindsight, there was just too much individual talent in one band to coexist indefinitely, and not enough space for every singer-songwriter to express himself as each grew more distinct from the others (factors that had also played a major role in the breakup of the Beatles, as it happened). Going forward, Wailers would be the name for whatever group of musicians was playing with Marley. Also from this point on, the billing on their records and concerts would change to Bob Marley and the Wailers.

THE *NATTY DREAD* SESSIONS

Without Tosh or Livingston, Marley began working on another Island album, again using Harry J's in Kingston. While the Barretts were still aboard, there were some major shifts in the backup crew. Tosh and Livingston's harmonies would not be so easy to replace. To his credit, Marley didn't try to replicate them with other male singers. Instead, he used three woman vocalists who were all talented reggae solo artists themselves.

One was Marcia Griffiths, who'd been recording since the 1960s, even cutting a duet with Marley back in the mid-1960s ("Oh My Darling"); as half of a duo with Bob Andy, she'd had a #5 UK hit in 1970 with "Young, Gifted and Black." Also on harmony were Judy Mowatt, who'd put out records as part of the Gaylettes, and Marley's wife, Rita, who'd returned to Jamaica shortly after the birth of her second son with Bob in 1972. As the I-Threes, they'd be part of Marley's records and concerts for the rest of his life, adding a different flavor to his music with their accomplished singing, and adding much to his stage show with their graceful presence and colorful outfits.

Melody Maker ad for *Natty Dread* also promotes the Wailers' back catalog.
INSET ROGER STEFFENS' REGGAE ARCHIVE

As Bob had fathered yet another child in London in 1973 (a daughter, with Janet Bowen) outside his marriage, and also started a serious affair with actress Esther Anderson that year, it might have seemed awkward for him and his wife to share the stage and studio time. But Rita (who'd give birth to a daughter, Stephanie, in August 1974), though sidelined to some degree in Bob's personal life through his numerous affairs and occasional children with other women, remained devoted to his musical career. "We were on a mission," she stated in the *Marley* documentary. "It was like an evangelist's campaign to bring people closer to Jah." *Melody Maker* even erroneously reported in 1973 that "Rita Marley is known as Bob's wife, but they aren't actually married—it was just an idea to get some publicity for one of her records."

For his upcoming LP, Bob again updated some old Wailers standbys, though the emphasis of the record that would be titled *Natty Dread* was on new material. "Bend Down Low" had been their first single on their Wail'N Soul'M label back in the 1960s, and the first version of "Lively Up Yourself" had been cut in the early 1970s. As the opening track, it got the LP off to as upbeat a start as could have possibly been hoped for, and had it been issued when Marley's stardom was in much greater ascension a couple of years later, it could well have been a hit single. It and the song that followed on side one, "No Woman, No Cry" (whose composition was credited to his friend Vincent Ford), quickly became two of his most popular numbers.

To replace Tosh and Livingston's harmonies, Marley enlisted three talented vocalists who were all reggae solo artists themselves: Judy Mowatt, Rita Marley, and Marcia Griffiths (pictured). As the I-Threes, they'd be part of Marley's records and concerts for the rest of his life. Bob even credited them on the label of Tuff Gong's 1974 issue of "Notty Dread" [*sic*]. MICHAEL PUTLAND/GETTY IMAGES

Elsewhere on the album, however, he often took a more socially conscious and rebellious tone, as heard on "Them Belly Full (But We Hungry)," "Rebel Music," "Revolution," and the title track, which took pride in Rasta dreadlocks. "*Natty Dread* was a special album for us, the feelin' of it," Marley told *Smash Hits*. "Sayin' children get your culture, won't win no battle if you just sit there."

"Lively Up Yourself" and "No Woman, No Cry" benefited from the licks of guitarist Al Anderson, yet another UK-based American who'd play a notable role in the Wailers' history. Much as Wayne Perkins had done for *Catch a Fire*, Anderson added parts to *Natty Dread* while the album was finalized in London, after which Marley invited him to become a Wailer. (According to Anderson, the job of playing guitar overdubs was first offered to Paul Kossoff, guitarist in Island's blues-rock band Free, after which Kossoff, then struggling with drug addiction, suggested Anderson do it instead.)

Anderson's guitar naturally steered the Wailers a little more toward rock, but not so much that Marley could possibly be mistaken for a rock artist. A *Rolling Stone* review of a Chicago 1975 Wailers show made special note of Anderson's "cathedral-volume wah wah" on "Slave Driver."

NATTY DREAD'S RELEASE AND ORIGINAL WAILERS REUNIONS

With much of his time occupied by reorganizing the Wailers and working on *Natty Dread*, Marley barely played any concerts in 1974. When he wasn't recording, he was often hanging out with other musicians, friends, and general hangers-on at a house Chris Blackwell had bought in an upscale section of Kingston at 56 Hope Road, Marley arranging to own the house himself by the mid-1970s. (Rita and their children were living separately in a two-bedroom home near the beach, though Bob was a frequent visitor.) Plans for him to contribute to an album by bluesman Taj Mahal (with whom Earl Lindo was now playing) didn't work out, as Mahal had finished recording the LP by the time Marley and Family Man Barrett flew to New York.

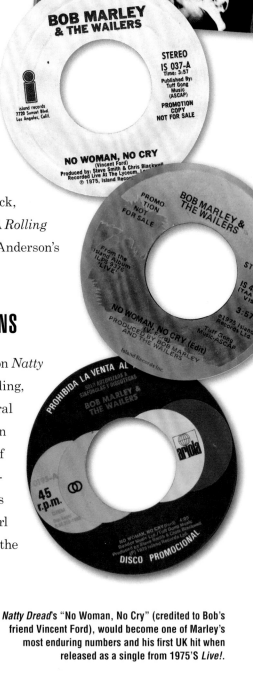

Natty Dread's "No Woman, No Cry" (credited to Bob's friend Vincent Ford), would become one of Marley's most enduring numbers and his first UK hit when released as a single from 1975'S *Live!*.

NATTY DREAD

Review by Pat Gilbert

If a single moment marked Bob Marley's emergence on the world stage, it was the release in October 1974 of *Natty Dread*, the first album to bear the singer's name *and* that of his group. The demotion of the Wailers to Bob's backing band was no accident: by the time the record was made the original harmony trio were no more, Peter Tosh waylaid by a personal feud with Island Records boss Chris Blackwell, and the trenchantly Rastafarian Bunny Livingston no longer interested in participating in a "corrupt" mainstream music industry.

Yet while the Wailers' disintegration on the brink of international success created a headache for Marley, it also allowed their leader's voice, music, and message to be heard for the first time in an unalloyed form. Throughout the first half of 1974, Bob worked on new material almost daily. One song, "Rebel Music (3 O'Clock Roadblock)," arrived in his head one night while dodging police checkpoints in his new BMW, while the hymnal "No Woman, No Cry," recalling the hardships of life in Trench Town, reportedly reduced old friends from the ghetto to tears when he played it to them.

As with Bob's other Island albums, *Natty Dread* recycled earlier material, including "Lively Up Yourself," "Bend Down Low," and "Them Belly Full (But We Hungry)," the latter's overtly political slant sitting comfortably alongside Marley's increasingly militant lyrical direction. After weeks of intensive rehearsals at Hope Road, the album was taped at Harry J's studio, with a band built around Aston and Carly Barrett's rhythm section, and mellifluous harmonies from newly formed all-female unit, the I-Threes: Marcia Griffiths, Judy Mowatt, and Marley's wife, Rita. Sylvan Morris, a gifted engineer who shared

Marley's Rastafarian beliefs, worked with him to create a sparser, harder-edged sound, suiting the album's uncompromising roots stance.

By the time American session guitarist Al Anderson had added some subtle licks to "Lively Up Yourself" and "No Woman, No Cry" in London, Marley was heading for the #1 spot on the *Billboard* charts—not from a Wailers release, but via Eric Clapton's cover of the *Burnin'* track "I Shot the Sheriff." It gave Bob's profile an immeasurable boost, but also influenced his decision to credit his new songs to Rita and other friends, apparently in a bid to divert royalties from Cayman Music, the publishing company set up by his controversial former manager Danny Sims.

Natty Dread—patois for "knotty dreadlocks"—only reached #43 in the UK and #92 in the US, but it was the foundational work of the spiritual and political superstar to come—now the undisputed master of his own music.

Marley barely played any shows in 1974, often hanging out with other musicians, friends, and general hangers-on at a house Chris Blackwell had bought at upscale 56 Hope Road in Kingston. DAVID CORIO/ REDFERNS/GETTY IMAGES

Marley did, however, play a couple charity shows in Kingston in late May, joined by Peter Tosh and Bunny Livingston. At both events, they opened for soul superstar Marvin Gaye, whose tour manager, Don Taylor, was a Jamaican who'd immigrated to the United States. Taylor soon would be Marley's manager, working in that capacity until near the end of Bob's life.

Under different circumstances, Marley could have found himself managed by someone much more prominent in the music business. According to Lee Jaffe, the Grateful Dead wanted the Wailers to tour with them and flew Marley and Jaffe to San Francisco to watch a week of Dead gigs. (This might have occurred in mid-October 1974, when the Grateful Dead played five straight nights in San Francisco's Winterland; though Jaffe wrote that the shows were at the Fillmore, that venue had closed its operations a few years earlier.) Jaffe wrote that, had this come to pass, the Wailers would have been managed by Bill Graham, the most powerful music promoter in the world, and with whom they watched the Dead's shows.

But Marley "backed out because they were called the Grateful Dead," Jaffe stated in *One Love.* "There wasn't really any other reason. . . . We were about life. They were about death. So how could the Wailers be touring with the Grateful Dead, we were the grateful living." It's hard to say how close this came to happening or whether there weren't other considerations, and it should also be noted that these were farewell Dead shows of a sort, the band then taking a break from touring until mid-1976. It's also hard to say if the mercurial Graham's management would have helped or hurt Marley's career, or made little ultimate difference in the scale of his global success.

Released in October of 1974, *Natty Dread* was a little more blatant in its revolutionary Rasta sentiments than the previous Island albums, and there's some indication the label tried to soften the more controversial corners of Marley's image when they readied it for release. The title was changed from *Knotty Dread* to *Natty Dread,* perhaps to make the references to dreadlocks less explicit, though it's doubtful that would have impacted sales. Taking more liberties, the cover painting of Marley somehow omitted his beard.

But the music wasn't tampered with, and its message couldn't be obscured by mere alterations of the title and artwork. *Natty Dread,* wrote future Marley biographer Stephen Davis in *Rolling Stone,* was "the culmination of Marley's political art to this point. With every album he's been rocking a little harder and reaching further out to produce the stunning effect of a successful spell. *Natty Dread* deals with rebellion and personal liberation, using tough and sensual reggae to slam home Marley's bold and dead-serious opinions on exactly what is right and what is wrong."

Even in the absence of Tosh and Livingston, *Natty Dread* became Marley's first album to dent the US Top 100, helped by FM radio-friendly cuts such as "Lively Up Yourself." (In its wake, both *Burnin'* and *Catch a Fire* made belated appearances near the bottom of the Top 200 at the end of 1975.) It also became his first British Top 50 entry, and even made #44 on *Billboard*'s R & B charts, indicating that at least a few African Americans must have been picking up on it. In truth, relatively few listeners would have noticed Peter and Bunny were missing, since many were hearing Marley for the first time, unaware of his long history with his former bandmates.

In 1975, the three Wailers would reunite as a support act for two Jamaican concerts by visiting American soul superstars. On March 8, they opened for the Jackson 5, with the I-Threes also in the lineup. On October 4, Bob, Peter, and Bunny were again in the Wailers when the group opened for Stevie Wonder at Kingston's National Stadium. Around this time, however, the official ties between the three were dissolved, with Peter and Bunny getting a settlement from Island of forty-five thousand dollars each. In the second half of the 1970s, Marley would complete his rise to worldwide superstardom on his own.

In 1975, Bob, Bunny, and Peter reunited as a support act at two Jamaican concerts by visiting American superstars: the Jackson 5 on March 8 and Stevie Wonder on October 4. The Wailers hang out in a tree with the J5. FIN COSTELLO/GETTY IMAGES

THE FIRST THIRD-WORLD SUPERSTAR 1975–1979

In the last half of the 1970s, Bob Marley became a bigger star by every standard used to measure artist popularity. His records sold a lot more copies. His concerts drew larger and, by the end of the decade, massive audiences. He was often covered in the media.

In some respects his status was growing in ways that couldn't be measured by numbers. Many fans looked up to him as a champion of rights and justice. He was hailed as the first true popular music superstar to emerge from the Third World. He was the leading ambassador for Jamaica's primary form of popular music, reggae.

Particularly in his homeland, Marley was also increasingly becoming regarded as a political figure, culminating in an attempt on his life at the end of 1976. Just over a year later, he brought together the leaders of the nation's feuding political parties in a dramatic gesture of peaceful unity. It's unlikely anyone else could have pulled off such a feat, even if the reconciliation was only temporary.

1975 TOURS AND LIVE ALBUM

At the beginning of 1975, Marley's goals were not just political, but also practical. For all the critical buzz the Wailers' Island albums had received, they were still a long way from becoming one of the label's most

Rainbow Theatre, London, June 1, 1977.
ESTATE OF KEITH MORRIS/REDFERNS/GETTY IMAGES

profitable acts. Island wanted them to tour and break the American market, where their following was fervid but small. A tour and concert album would bring them a lot closer to their goal, even if that live LP was not recorded in the States.

Aside from the March 8 Kingston concert opening for the Jackson 5 (where only a small audience saw the Wailers), Marley didn't play any shows in the first five months of the year. Nor did he record, though in the spring he spent a few weeks producing, with help from Lee Perry and Craig Leon, a rather unimpressive album by American singer Martha Veléz, *Escape from Babylon*. As much a reggae-influenced soul-pop record as a reggae project, it included the odd "Disco Night," cowritten by Veléz and Marley, and the first indication that Bob was aware of the disco trend then overwhelming the United States.

From early June through mid-July, Marley did his first American tour without either of the original Wailers (and with just two of the I-Threes, as Marcia Griffiths was in the final stages of a pregnancy). Although reviews of the shows were excellent, his itinerary was still one of an emerging figure, not a major moneymaker. With the exception of a few engagements at big venues such as the Spectrum in Philadelphia (where WMMR, in common with some other American FM stations, had given Marley heavy airplay right from *Catch a Fire*'s release), he was still usually playing clubs, albeit hip ones apt to attract committed listeners and enthusiastic reviewers. Most of the concerts, too, were concentrated on the East Coast and California. His East Coast swing was highlighted by a June 18 gig in New York's Central Park, soon followed by a weeklong residency in Boston's Pall Mall club, where he played two shows a night.

RIGHT and FOLLOWING PAGE: Marley's first American tour without Tosh or Livingston was highlighted by a June 18 gig at the Schaefer Festival in New York City's Central Park. BOTH WARING ABBOTT/GETTY IMAGES

"What we have here is a whole new high in politico good-time boogie music, like if Jefferson Airplane suddenly found fresh brains and started to dig their own potatoes," exulted Patrick Carr in his *Village Voice* review of the Central Park concert. "Marley works his crowd, too, moving sinuously around the mike, his face a mime with the lyrics, his pearly teeth (cleaned with natural tree bark, no toothpaste here) flashing from the smile of the permanently stoned. Brother Bob, a natural showman. Unlike Jimmy Cliff, whose show has all the sensuality of your standard R & B lounge act, pirouettes and all, Brother Bob is most definitely funky. Very sexy, too. See it now: Marley is the Jagger of reggae, without decadence, which doesn't apply."

A couple weeks later, his July 4 show merited the headline "Strange Night at Boarding House" in a review in the *San Francisco Chronicle*. "His face is cadaverous; fleshless skin drawn over bones; his 'dread-locks' hair sprouts out like a giant tarantula plopped on his head and movements are more reflexive than choreographed," wrote John L. Wasserman of Marley's performance in the city's Boarding House club. "Particularly during the last song, 'I Shot the Sheriff,' he seemed almost in a fervor-trance; leaping about, shaking his locks, posing, posturing like a rooster; a pantomime of defiance, a witch-doctor's voodoo suite. Indeed, on Friday night, so abandoned did he become at that point in the show that he lost his equilibrium and crashed to the floor. It was not, as I said [in the headline], a night like any other at the Boarding House."

In Los Angeles, the Wailers taped their first US television appearance on the short-lived program *The Manhattan Transfer Show*, performing "Kinky Reggae" live before a studio audience (and introduced, oddly, as "the big bad boss sound from Princetown, Jamaica"). At LA's Roxy Theatre, which often functioned as much as a showcase for the music industry as it did a venue for the typical fan, the audience included George Harrison, Ringo Starr, Herbie Hancock, and Joni Mitchell. Marley, Harrison told *Melody Maker*, was the "best thing I've seen in ten years. Marley reminds me so much of Dylan in the early days, playing guitar as if he's so new to it. And his rhythm is so simple yet so beautiful. I could watch the Wailers all night."

His most significant concert of the year, however, would take place during his short visit to England in July. It included just one show in Manchester, one in Birmingham, and two shows at London's Lyceum, Island recording both at the latter venue. Performances from the July 18 Lyceum show were selected for the *Live!* album, which became his most popular album to date after its release later in 1975. Initially available only in Europe, it came out in the United States after strong import sales pressured Island to make it available there.

Five-night residency, Roxy Theatre, Los Angeles, July 1975. George Harrison told *Melody Maker* Marley was the "best thing I've seen in ten years." MICHAEL OCHS ARCHIVES/GETTY IMAGES

"That was the tipping point," reckoned Blackwell of the Lyceum shows in the *Marley* documentary. "After that, everybody knew his name. There was that sense that he's about to be massive." It was probably shows such as this, and the *Live!* album, that *Rolling Stone* had in mind when giving the Wailers their Band of the Year award for 1975 "for their spunky music and their early-Stones, street-fighting spirit."

"The slow bass, the slow drum, the unrepentant idleness, the matronly figures [of the I-Threes] stepping and gliding—all are visitations from a world which whites in the audience, bobbing ardently but fitfully, cannot hope to comprehend," wrote Philip Norman in his review of one of the Lyceum shows in the *Times* of London. "Through them black music is, once more, triumphantly private."

The even mix of black and white listeners at the concerts was noted in the *New Musical Express* by Charles Shaar Murray, who also detected the kind of difference between Marley's live and studio music that made recordings from the Lyceum worth issuing on LP: "The band are solid and unified, gliding more than steamrollering, and they keep coming; never more so than on 'Lively Up Yourself,' which was so powerful that it made the recorded version seem positively Mickey Mouse by comparison."

"No Woman, No Cry" was getting especially wild audience response, and the version on *Live!* gave Bob his first hit in the United Kingdom, where it peaked just outside of the Top 20. Concentrating on his most popular songs from the Wailers' Island albums (and throwing in "Trench Town Rock" as well), the album featured lively, convivial versions of "Lively Up Yourself," "No Woman, No Cry," "I Shot the Sheriff," and "Get Up, Stand Up" that were in some ways more accessible and radio-friendly than their studio counterparts. Some of the studio originals, unlike the renditions on *Live!*, had not used the I-Threes' backup harmonies, further differentiating the live recordings from their previous incarnations. (Although a deluxe edition featuring recordings of both the July 17 and July 18 shows at the Lyceum was planned to appear in 2006, its release was canceled.)

The Wailers performed just twice more in 1975, both times in Kingston. Just days before the first of these dates, Marley and much of Jamaica were shaken by the news that Haile Selassie, regarded as an invincible and perhaps immortal messiah-like savior by many Rastafari, had died in Ethiopia. His death shook the foundations of their very faith. Some elected to believe or at least state that Selassie had simply disappeared or taken another form, and his death did not appear to weaken Marley's staunch advocacy of Rastafari principles. As a sort of response, Bob recorded the single "Jah Live" as an upbeat affirmation of a continued holy presence.

Wailers arrive at the Birmingham, England, Odeon, July 19, 1975. The band played four English dates that month. IAN DICKSON; INSET GAB ARCHIVE BOTH REDFERNS/GETTY IMAGES

The track (now available on *Rastaman Vibration*'s deluxe edition) was coproduced by Lee Perry, who made his return to the Wailers after the estrangement that followed their early-1970s recordings together.

The second Wailers show, in support of Stevie Wonder on October 4, reunited Bob Marley, Peter Tosh, and Bunny Livingston, marking their final concert together. In Jamaica at least, Tosh and Livingston had remained active. Peter was recording for his own label, Intel Diplo. Bunny also had a label of his own, Solomonic, for which he was cutting tracks.

At the October show, Tosh took the opportunity to do a few of his own songs, including the most notorious of the tracks he'd include on his early solo releases, "Legalize It." He made sure everyone knew what "it" was by lighting a spliff onstage, something he'd never done at other Wailers gigs.

Just a month after the concert, on November 11, Peter was at the wheel during a car accident in which his girlfriend, Yvonne Whittingham, was gravely injured. She fell into a coma and died a few months later. Tosh survived, but bore permanent facial scars from the crash and, in the eyes of many, deeper psychological scars of grief and guilt.

THE *RASTAMAN VIBRATION* SESSIONS

In the last half of 1975, Marley began to record his next studio album, *Rastaman Vibration*—the record that, more than any other, would elevate him outside Jamaica from cult figure to star. While most of the same Wailers who'd played and sang on *Natty Dread* remained on board, a few personnel changes were in store. Tyrone Downie, who'd been touring with them for a while (and appears on *Live!*), was on keyboards, his synthesizer in particular adding a more modern sheen to the arrangements.

Al Anderson, though credited for lead guitar on one track ("Crazy Baldhead"), was replaced by Jamaican session musician Earl "Chinna" Smith, who contributed lead and rhythm guitar (he had also played, along with several Wailers, on the Marley-produced Martha Veléz album). Playing some lead guitar was Donald Kinsey who, like Anderson, was an American with little reggae background.

A young but experienced Chicago blues guitarist, Kinsey had recently moved in a rockier direction with the band White Lightning. He'd also done some recording and touring with Peter Tosh before being invited to play on *Rastaman Vibration*. Cynics might see his enlistment as a move on Bob's part to make his sound more palatable to an international audience, but it was in keeping with Marley's constant and growing eagerness to expand the parameters of his music.

"When I first got with those guys," remembered Kinsey in *Option* magazine, "the reviews that were coming out! 'Donald Kinsey bringing blues to reggae.' Some would write about it as if it was a positive thing, and others would write about it as if it was a negative thing. But I knew it was a positive thing and Bob and Peter knew it was a positive thing, too. It helped give the music a different type of flavor. The guitar players in Jamaica weren't into string bendings and the blues type of style. They were more into just a rhythm type of thing."

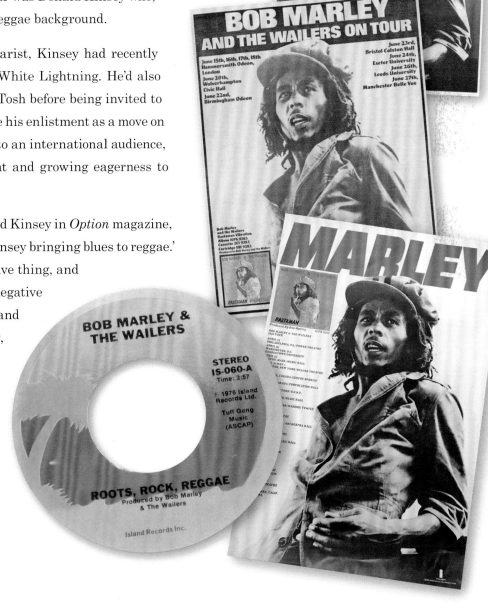

Rastaman Vibration was indeed closer to mainstream rock than Bob's previous records, though it was still very much a reggae album, if one with some very catchy songs. "Roots, Rock, Reggae" was a joyous paean to the music.

Rastaman Vibration was hardly mainstream rock, but was indeed *closer* to mainstream rock than Bob's previous records. It was still very much a reggae album, if one with some very catchy songs. That was in evidence from the first lines of the opening track, the simple but memorable chorus of "Positive Vibration." Right behind it, both in track sequence and in singability, was "Roots, Rock, Reggae," a joyous paean to the music with saxophone by Skatalite Tommy McCook, who'd played on Wailers ska sides going back to "Simmer Down." It included several veiled pleas to play reggae, specifically Bob's ("play I on the R & B"), on American radio.

Some of the tracks, in keeping with other Wailers albums, were remakes. "Cry to Me" had been on a mid-1960s 45; "Night Shift" reworked "It's Alright" (from *Soul Rebels*); and "Who the Cap Fit" did the same for the early-1970s "Man to Man" single. Those who wanted something more up-to-the-minute and militant, however, could sink their teeth into tracks about a death in the ghetto ("Johnny Was"), greed ("Want More"), and the "Rat Race." Most unusual of all was "War," a musical adaptation of a speech given by Selassie to the United Nations in October 1963.

In *Bob Marley: The Untold Story*, Chris Blackwell said Lee Perry "produced some tracks on *Rastaman Vibration*—the good ones, the groove ones, but Bob didn't give him any credit. I don't know if it was a rivalry or what. There was some unease about the relationship. . . .

"The one person I would say I met who Bob was wary of, or had a lot of respect for, was Scratch. Bob was like a master in the studio, but not as far as Scratch was concerned. Scratch would push him a lot more. I think the best tracks of Bob are the ones that Lee Perry produced. He was always important. But certainly when I was working with Bob, he and Bob never really got on that well."

Although it is not the most famous Bob Marley album, *Rastaman Vibration* was the one that finally made him an across-the-board, across-the-borders star. It made #8 in the United States (where "Roots, Rock, Reggae" also gave him a small hit single), and was the only Marley record to make the American Top 10 during his lifetime. In the United Kingdom it made #15, and it also did well in parts of continental Europe, proving his music carried a powerful message, even in countries where English wasn't the first language.

"This is a very uncluttered album—the rhythms are spare, Marley's voice is totally dominant and the support is suppliant—voices and keyboards responding like a gospel group, the guitars played blue," wrote renowned British critic Simon Frith in his review

the LPs

RASTAMAN VIBRATION

Review by Chris Salewicz

Arguably Bob Marley's finest ever long-player, *Rastaman Vibration* was also his first album to make the US Top 10. Released on April 30 1976, it reached the #8 slot.

By the time *Rastaman Vibration* was recorded at Harry J's and Joe Gibbs's studios in Kingston in late 1975 and early 1976, a larger, riper sound was developing, broader than the sparse feel of the previous *Natty Dread*. "Chinna" Smith, the king of Kingston session guitarists, was brought in, adding a warm, organic sound. "Maybe something in the scene was changing," ventured Sylvan Morris, who engineered the sessions along with Errol Thompson. "But certainly the consciousness had started to settle within the whole scene: where the Rasta thing was sort of blossoming. So in the lyrical content that is starting to be expressed as well: the maturing within the Rasta scene."

It's all there in the first song, "Positive Vibration," a powerful, sinuous statement of intent that extends into track two, "Roots, Rock, Reggae," expressing the very essence of what Bob Marley was mining. But then it's the stark, heartfelt truth of "Johnny Was," a ghetto youth gunned down in the street—everyday Kingston life in 1976.

Scratch Perry was present at some *Rastaman Vibration* sessions, offering creative input on the structure of both songs and the entire record. A pair of tunes included were do-overs, first recorded with Scratch: "Night Shift," inspired by Bob's grinding work at the Delaware auto plant, was a new version of "It's Alright" from *Soul Rebels*; "Who the Cap Fit" was originally titled "Man to Man." Scratch also arranged "Rat Race."

Sylvan Morris recalled the recording of the inspirational tune "War," which acts like the album's philosophical fulcrum, its lyrics the text of a United Nations speech by Ethiopian Emperor Haile Selassie. Allan "Skill" Cole, Bob's footballer friend, had urged him to turn it into a song. "It hit me very strong with that particular tune," said Morris. "It was the first time I was hearing statements like that: 'I'm a Rastaman, this is me, I'm going to put out as much as I can in terms of how I feel.' They handled everything in that vein. My personal remembrance of Bob is that he wasn't a very laughing character. If he smiled, he would smile very briefly. He always seemed to be so disciplined."

in *Street Life.* "*Rastaman Vibration* is a religious album, its purpose and power come from a set of beliefs which have been stripped here of their normal trappings and mysticism and ganja good will. They are beliefs of a black culture and of black pride. Bob Marley, entertaining and exciting as he is, expresses something further, a quality he'd think of as righteousness. It gives his music, this album, a quality that is inspiring even when it's played for dancing and chatting and drinking as it mostly will be."

Island promoted the record aggressively to ensure its success, even advertising the LP with a large billboard on Sunset Strip. "*Rastaman Vibration* was very much more geared to America," Blackwell admitted in Vivien Goldman's *The Book of Exodus,* adding that *Live!* "had already done very well in England, I was more in America at the time, and Bob was happy there because it was starting to wake up, there was a vibe happening. We did a great marketing job and took a big advertisement out in the *New York Times.*"

1976 US TOUR AND AMERICAN STARDOM

When Marley toured the US in spring 1976, he usually played much larger venues than he was booked into during his previous visits. Besides his usual strongholds on the coasts, he played some shows in cities such as Houston, Denver, Saint Louis, and Montreal, spreading his word into the North American interior. At the Tower Theater near Philadelphia, his mother saw him perform for the first time—a surprisingly long wait, even considering she'd left Jamaica before the Wailers' first record.

Broadcast at the time on the Los Angeles radio station KMET, the May 26 show at West Hollywood's Roxy was issued in 2003 as *Live at the Roxy* (most of whose tracks are also on the bonus disc of *Rastaman Vibration*'s deluxe edition). In common with many acts past and present, Marley used the concert setting to draw out the length of many of his songs. "Rat Race," for instance, was almost three times as long as the studio version. The set concluded with a marathon twenty-four-minute medley of "Get Up, Stand Up," "No More Trouble," and "War," as did some other shows of the period. The vibrations radiating out of the speakers were so intense during the tour, Family Man Barrett claimed in *Wailing Blues: The Story of Bob Marley's Wailers,* that "at some of the concerts we did, you'd see people being carried out on stretchers after the sound had hit them. The sound of the bass and drums would knock them out."

Hammersmith Odeon, London, June, 1976.
ERICA ECHENBERG/REDFERNS/GETTY IMAGES

Marley was also getting major American media coverage. "Marley is Jamaica's superstar," enthused *Time*. "He rivals the government as a political force. The mythical hero of his last album, *Natty Dread*, has already become a national symbol. Marley is a cynosure both in Jamaican society and in the Trench Town ghetto where he grew up."

A more unlikely source of praise was *Playboy*, which gushed, "Bob Marley & the Wailers seem to have finally emerged as the finest rock 'n' roll band of the '70s and what's more, they're as heavy a group as we've heard in the 22-year history of the music. They're right up there with any of the giants you care to name, from Chuck Berry, through to Sly Stone. And that includes the Beatles, Otis Redding, and the Stones, all of them. That's how good they are. . . .

"When these people sing about Jah and hunger and burning and injustice, they aren't kidding. They don't sound slick and dumb nor, thanks to the ganja-informed beauty of Marley's lyrics, are they stridently didactic. Because the music speaks of real and present dangers, of righteous religious faith, of not giving up the fight, it has the power to play upon an audience's emotions as no music has in years."

More controversially, Bob also gave an extensive Q&A to *High Times,* in which he waxed poetic on marijuana at greater length than would have been possible in any other publication. Virtually all other celebrities would have dodged questions such as "What was the best weed you ever smoked?" In this *High Times* cover story, Marley embraced them, detailing one spliff in particular as "de bes' herb I ever smoke."

PETER TOSH AND BUNNY WAILER GO SOLO

If interviewing with *High Times* could be considered an endorsement of herb-smoking, it was subtle compared to the cover of Peter Tosh's 1976 debut album. Lee Jaffe's cover photo showed the dreadlocked singer smoking a pipe—presumably filled with ganja—in a marijuana field. The title track, "Legalize It," lobbied for the legalization of what he and other Jamaicans so often smoked. Despite the controversy, it was released by a major label, Columbia, in the United States. Tosh wasn't nearly as well-known as Marley, even when both were in the Wailers during their early Island albums, but the industry saw he also had the potential to cross over to the rock audience.

LEFT: Toward the end of 1976 Bob gave an extensive Q&A to *High Times,* in which he waxed poetic on marijuana.

OPPOSITE: Peter Tosh sits in a field of marijuana in Westmoreland, Jamaica. Marley's endorsement of marijuana was subtle compared to Tosh's. The title track of his 1976 debut album, *Legalize It*, lobbied for decriminalization of ganja. LEE JAFFE/GETTY IMAGES

INTEL
H.I.M.

LEGALIZE
IT

(P. Tosh)
Peter Tosh

45 RPM

Dist. by:
Talent Corp. Ltd.,
1c Oxford Rd.,
Kingston 5

o.11 Music
B.M.I.

(C) 1975

PETER TOSH
DIPLO

(P) 1975

PETER TOSH
LEGALIZE IT

OUT NOW—RUSH RELEASED ON VIRGIN RECORDS. V2061 SINGLE VS14.0

Bunny Wailer's 1976 solo debut *Blackheart Man* won as much rabid critical acclaim among reggae fans as Marley or Tosh's higher-profile releases. In addition to his Island releases, Bunny issued a number of seven-inch sides in Jamaica on his own Solomonic label.
HULTON ARCHIVE/GETTY IMAGES

Far from ducking responsibility for encouraging the activities pictured on the album cover, Tosh eagerly claimed it. "They made up the sleeve from my ideas," he boasted in *Sounds*. "My idea was LEGALIZE IT! and the whole package must be dealing with 'erb. People must know what I'm dealing with when I say legalize it."

In common with albums that Marley had done with the Wailers and on his own, *Legalize It* combined previously unheard material with remakes of songs from the Wailers' deep catalog, though naturally Peter picked items that had featured him in the original versions. "No Sympathy" and "Brand New Second Hand," for instance, had first been cut by the group back in the early 1970s during their sessions with Lee Perry. Quite a few Wailers associates helped out with the LP, including Rita Marley, Al Anderson, and Donald Kinsey. While it barely made the American charts, it set Tosh on the way to establishing himself as a solo performer abroad, and he toured the United States in late 1976.

Also contributing to *Legalize It* was Bunny Wailer. Bunny had been considered the least viable solo act of the original Wailers, perhaps in part because of his distaste for touring, but also possibly because he'd taken fewer lead vocals and written fewer songs than Marley or Tosh. Blackwell nonetheless signed him to a deal with Island, Bunny not quite as suspicious of the record executive as Peter, though both would sometimes disparage Blackwell and complain about their financial returns from Island in subsequent years.

Wailer was not destined to get nearly as wide an audience as Tosh, let alone Marley. This wasn't solely because he wrote less and was more reclusive. His solo records were less commercially accessible to the non-Jamaican listener and less incendiary in tone than either Tosh's or Marley's. Yet he surprised some of his doubters by writing all of the songs on his 1976 debut *Blackheart Man*, which won as much rabid critical acclaim among reggae fans as Marley or Tosh's higher-profile releases. Like his former bandmates, Bunny dealt with oppression, mysticism, Rasta, and the struggle for justice, but with a humbler and at times eerie aura.

The other Wailers had made a practice of remaking some of their stronger songs, and Bunny proved no exception, reviving "Dreamland" and doing another adaptation of "This Train." Like *Legalize It*, *Blackheart Man* benefited from the presence of several musicians who'd played in the Wailers, most notably Tosh, but also the Barretts, Chinna Smith, and Marley himself (on backing vocals). It was still firmly Bunny's record. Blackwell called it "the best album ever to come out of Jamaica" in *Sounds*, and while the record executive might have had a stake in praising it to the press, writer Vivien Goldman, in the same article, hailed it as "an album that contains a wisdom and a healing power that becomes stronger the longer you live with it."

Peter Tosh's and Bunny Wailer's solo careers never approached Bob Marley's in magnitude. Wailer seldom even made the charts. Nor was either revered nearly as much as Marley as a spokesperson or symbol. But their post-Wailers activities were not mere footnotes to their time in the band. Each did much to spread reggae's popularity and, in their distinctively different ways, perpetuate and embody many of the qualities that first crystallized in the music made during the Wailers' first decade. Wailer is still doing so, though Tosh's life was, like Marley's, cruelly shortened. "We're still functioning towards the same work, which is Rastafari, so we're together," Bunny stressed to *Sounds* shortly after *Blackheart Man*'s release. "We might not be together physically, but we're working at the same goal, teaching the same things."

1976 EUROPEAN AND UK TOURS

If Bunny and Peter's prospects as solo artists took great leaps forward in 1976, Bob's fortunes continued to outpace theirs and those of every other reggae star. In June, Marley played some shows in Germany, Sweden, and Holland before a more extensive swing through Great Britain. As one index of his burgeoning popularity, he did concerts for several nights running at London's four thousand-seat Hammersmith Odeon, though the first was marred by some muggings and petty crime in the audience.

Legendarily acerbic British critic Mick Farren was nonetheless moved to tears by one of the Hammersmith shows. "Nothing had prepared me for the sheer power that Marley is able to generate," he confessed in *NME*. "By power, I don't mean sodding great amplifiers either.

"Marley's simple, direct, unselfconscious propagation of his message brought me to me feet, exalted, and once or twice almost had me reaching for a Kleenex. It's one hell of a long time since a rock 'n' roll show did anything approaching that to me."

Bob was now drawing crowds out of proportion to his respectable but hardly monumental record sales. "Rather like the Rolling Stones, Bob never sold colossal amounts of records," admitted Mick Cater, the Island Records employee who booked the Hammersmith Odeon shows, in *Bob Marley: The Untold Story*. "But he sold concert tickets by the wheelbarrow-load."

Marley's romance with Cindy Breakspeare (center) became much more public when she was crowned Miss World in 1976. CENTRAL PRESS/GETTY IMAGES

Bob was busy with some other residents of foreign countries in the mid-1970s, though the relationships didn't receive publicity at the time, and still aren't too widely documented. He fathered two more sons, the first of whom, Julian, was born to Lucy Pounder of Barbados in June 1975. The second was born to Anita Belnavis, a Bermudan table tennis champion, the following February. The romance that grew between Marley and a Jamaican woman, Cindy Breakspeare, would be much more serious, and much more public, especially after Breakspeare was crowned Miss World in November 1976.

The following month, an event would put Marley in the headlines more than ever before, though not for his personal affairs or his music.

The Wailers taped a television appearance and enjoyed some downtime in Amsterdam in summer 1976. ALL LAURENS VAN HOUTEN/ FRANK WHITE PHOTO AGENCY

SMILE JAMAICA CONCERT

In his many interviews, Marley had usually declined to comment at much length on specific political issues, preferring to espouse a general philosophy of peace, justice, and Rasta. "Me don't deal wit' no politics," he'd declared in *High Times*. "Me deal wit' de truth." Likewise, he'd told *Essence*, "Me no take no part in the government because me no interested in power. If me was, me would try to become a politician. But me is a Rasta man, and me talk bout things the way me see them."

Marley was nonetheless seen as a political force, and not just by the Jamaicans in power. "I believe that politics wasn't #1 for him," reiterated Al Anderson in *Rebel Music*. "But it was #1 for him to make an explanation to people who didn't understand what was going on politically . . . all the ghetto people from Trench Town. . . . He could explain it to them better than any politician." And Bob would get caught up in a political storm that would almost cost him his life soon after he returned to Jamaica after his successful mid-1976 tours.

Jamaica had never been too calm or stable in Bob's lifetime, but 1976 was an especially tense year for the country. There were about two hundred politically motivated killings in the country in 1976; unemployment was nearing 25 percent; tourism was down 35 percent; and tens of thousands of middle-class Jamaicans were leaving the island (often resettling in Miami), draining the nation of vital medical and professional services. Two entrenched political parties, the People's National Party (PNP) and Jamaica Labour Party (JLP), were engaged in a power struggle that spilled into the poorest parts of Trench Town. Violence often erupted between supporters of different parties, sometimes spurred by henchmen throwing their weight around in the ghetto's neighborhoods.

The PNP, led by then–Prime Minister Michael Manley, had a democratic socialist platform and hoped to build stronger ties with nearby Cuba. The more conservative JLP, led by Edward Seaga, wanted to build stronger ties with the United States, whose CIA was sometimes accused of trying to undermine the PNP. (Incidentally, in the late 1950s and early 1960s, Seaga had produced some of the first ska records, issuing discs by the likes of Joe Higgs on his WIRL label.) The country was in such turmoil that a nationwide state of emergency was called on June 19.

While popular music usually doesn't exert significant influence on the government, Jamaica wasn't like most countries in that regard. "I think the politicians used reggae," Dudley Thompson, Jamaica's minister of foreign affairs in the mid-1970s, stated in *Rebel Music*. "Reggae, especially through people like Bob Marley, expressed the wishes and the sentiments of the people. The protests came through music and through the song."

Manley himself acknowledged his awareness of Marley's impact in the same documentary, stating "Bob was not by temperament or mind the kind of person who would ever become, say, a part of a party. Political, yes, in that he was one of the most articulate troubadours of the ghetto—its suffering, its pressures—that I have ever, ever heard."

Careful to avoid aligning himself with one political party, Marley nonetheless worked with the PNP to arrange the free Smile Jamaica concert in Kingston, even writing a song for the event—one of his most innocuous, lightweight compositions.

Seaga also made his awareness of the music's significance evident in that film, observing, "The songs reflect what happenings are taking place in political life. You wouldn't be able to separate politics and music in terms of the extent to which [they're] interwoven as a form of message."

Manley expressed similar sentiments in *Time* magazine's March 22, 1976, issue: "Reggae is much more accurate than a political machine when it comes to gauging mass reaction. I listen attentively. At a time when the Establishment cries halt, these songs provide a wonderful counterweight."

While Bob could generally be expected to be more sympathetic to the PNP than the JLP, he avoided aligning himself closely with one party or candidate. He did, however, work with the PNP to arrange a free concert in Kingston to be billed as a "Smile Jamaica" concert. Manley even asked Marley if he could write a "Smile Jamaica" song for the event. One of Marley's most innocuous, lightweight compositions (cocredited to Lee Perry), it was released as a Jamaican single on the Tuff Gong label (and, much later, as a bonus track on the deluxe edition of *Rastaman Vibration*). The song, Bob commented in *Sounds* magazine, "is supposed to be what's happening now . . . Jamaica need to smile, because in Jamaica everyone really vex too much."

Presented, as the poster announced, "by Bob Marley in association with the Cultural Department of the Government of Jamaica," the concert was planned for December 5, 1976. A week after the show was announced, however, Manley announced that elections would be held just ten days afterward, on December 15. Marley was then seen or even accused by many as endorsing the PNP in the upcoming elections by playing a PNP-connected event so close to voting day. This wasn't Bob's intention, but in the fraught atmosphere of Kingston in late 1976, that's how many interpreted it.

"Bob rang me up about the fact he'd been asked by Manley to do a show," Blackwell remembered in *The Book of Exodus*. "There was some talk about an election coming up, and I said, 'It depends when the election is. Are you doing it for the party in government, or are you doing it for the country? Because if you play at election time, it could look as if you're doing it for the party. Check out when the election is.'

"Anyway, Bob couldn't get one response or the other. He announced he was doing the show, then almost right after that, Prime Minister Manley announced the election. So it really looked like he was doing a show for the PNP, and he'd always tried very hard to stay clear of politics, even though he was probably closer to the PNP, as most musicians are on the left. But he was not really into either of the parties."

ASSASSINATION ATTEMPT

"Once word got out that he was going to do a free concert, it seemed like everything just went haywire, just out of control," Donald Kinsey told Chris Heim of *Option* magazine almost a dozen years later. "People in the band were getting nervous. Some of the girls left the island, said that something ain't right and they weren't going to do it."

Despite general unease about whether the situation could rile the JLP or others, rehearsals for the concert went ahead. After a rehearsal at Bob's house at 56 Hope Road on December 3, he was getting something to eat in the kitchen when a gunman entered and began shooting.

"We were rehearsing at his house about nine o'clock two nights before the concert," Kinsey continued. "We had just taken a break, so people were moving around. Good thing, because if everybody had been in the same room, it would have been a real massacre. I was in the kitchen getting something to drink. Bob was in the kitchen and his manager was in the kitchen, and we started hearing gunshots go off. I didn't know what was happening. There was a back door to go outside and as soon as I thought about going out that door, this gun came up inside and started shooting. We couldn't go anywhere."

Miraculously, Marley was not seriously wounded. The only bullet that hit him grazed his chest and left arm. Kinsey, also in the room, managed to avoid getting hit by any shots. Bob's manager, Don Taylor, wasn't so lucky. He took several bullets in his midsection. Had Chris Blackwell not been elsewhere waiting around for Lee Perry to finish a mix, he might have been caught in the gunfire too, as he was planning to visit the house that night.

The would-be assassin in the kitchen wasn't the only gunman who'd barged into the premises. A couple others took aim at Rita Marley as she started up her Volkswagen outside. As she drove off, a couple

Bob outside the X-ray department of Kingston's University Hospital after being shot by a gunman who invaded his home on December 3, 1976. Marley went on to play National Heroes Park two nights later, performing ninety minutes for nearly one hundred thousand fans at the Smile Jamaica event. BETTMANN/GETTY IMAGES

Island Records' 1976 Bob Marley yearbook. Indeed, it had been a momentous year for Bob. According to Rita Marley, writing in her memoir, "He'd become more important than the prime minister." GAB ARCHIVE/GETTY IMAGES

bullets entered the car, one of them grazing the top of her head. Bleeding from her wound, Rita might have been finished off had she not stopped the car and played dead.

After the gunmen fled, Bob, Rita, Don Taylor, and a friend of the Wailers who had also been wounded were sped to the hospital. Incredibly, the bullet that had caused Rita's bleeding had lodged between her scalp and skull without seriously endangering her. Taylor had lost a lot of blood, however, and nearly died before surgery. It now seemed uncertain whether the Smile Jamaica concert would take place, or whether Bob would even stay in the country.

No one could have blamed Marley for canceling his appearance, or for leaving Jamaica altogether, with worries that another attempt on his life might take place. The next day, however, PNP housing minister Tony Spaulding urged Bob to play, as a demonstration that Marley wouldn't be cowed into reclusion. Despite understandable reservations, Rita confirmed she'd support Bob if he decided to go ahead with the event.

Courageously, Marley went to National Heroes Park to perform in front of nearly one hundred thousand fans, playing for ninety minutes. Rita Marley was onstage singing with him, still in her hospital gown. At one point, Bob even pulled up his sleeve to show the crowd his wound, declaring "Bang-bang—I'm okay." More than two hundred people surrounded Bob onstage, helping to ensure that shots weren't fired. "When I decided to do this concert two and a half months ago, there were no politicians involved," he told the crowd. "I just wanted to play for the love of the people."

"I talked to Bob by walkie-talkie the night of the concert [because people feared phone lines might be tapped]," Kinsey told *Option*. "All the rest of the acts said they weren't going to do nothing if we didn't show up. He asked me if I would do it. I just felt God was with us because we survived that night, so I said, 'Yeah, I'll do it.' Boy, we did it! You talk about a mystic night, ooh, it was mystic."

Doing his full set at Smile Jamaica was an important symbolic gesture for Bob, one that let the world know he wouldn't be intimidated for singing and speaking his mind, even at risk of his life. He wasn't so foolish or heedless, however, to tempt fate by sticking around longer than necessary. Right after the show, he flew on a chartered Learjet to the Bahamas, where he stayed at a Nassau house owned by Blackwell and was joined by other family, friends, and Wailers. Blackwell also paid for Taylor to be flown to Miami where an operation was performed. Marley didn't return to Jamaica for more than a year.

As in many successful or attempted assassinations, much mystery remains as to who shot Marley and their motivations. The gunmen have never been publicly identified, let alone brought to trial or imprisoned. Many felt the JLP had something to do with it, angered by Marley's perceived support of the rival PNP. Some feel the CIA was behind the attempt, a theory that gained more believers when it emerged that a cameraman for the unreleased film of the event was the son of a former director of the agency. There's also been speculation that it was retribution for a supposed botched fix of a horse race by one of Bob's associates at a nearby track.

Even a major Jamaican newspaper, the *Gleaner*, viewed the shooting as politically motivated. "Whether he chooses to think so or not, Marley is a powerful political voice in Jamaica," it pronounced. "And it's this, together with his Rastafarian beliefs and his criticism of his country that instigated 'the incident' last December."

Keeping an open house for help and handouts was also putting Bob into contact with dangerous characters from several sides of the political spectrum. "At home he was seen as 'the voice of the people,' and the ghetto youth were very aware of this," noted Rita Marley in her memoir. "Despite his move uptown, they still regarded him very highly. The biggest murderers, the biggest gunmen, would come to him for help. Hope Road became a welfare center—there was no night there, 24 hours a day they'd arrive demanding to see him.

"He'd become more important than the prime minister. It began to seem as if he had to live *for* them. Added to this, he was subjected to certain pressures from one party or the other, and it was risky to be in the middle. He was living a very dangerous life, simply because he had brought all this attention to the island of Jamaica through his music."

THE *EXODUS* SESSIONS

Whatever was behind the shooting, it wasn't considered safe for Marley to be in Jamaica. After the break in Nassau, where he'd managed to do some writing of songs that would appear on his next two albums, he and the Wailers rented a house in London's Chelsea district. By early 1977, he was recording a wealth of material at Island's Basing Street Studios, much of which would be culled for his next album, *Exodus*. Replacing Donald

Print ad for *Exodus* as well as Marley's back catalog.

Kinsey (who'd gone back to Peter Tosh) was guitarist Junior Marvin, who would remain in the Wailers for the rest of Bob's life.

In London, the Wailers recorded enough tracks for two albums. In a move that's since confused many fans who followed the group's evolution, Marley decided to issue the more forceful, grittier songs on *Exodus*; the remainder were saved for the mellower, more romantic *Kaya* in 1978. *Kaya*'s reputation has suffered some as a result, many fans not realizing that both albums were recorded at the same time and finding *Kaya* to be something of a retreat from the harder realities of *Exodus*.

Even within *Exodus*, there was a split between the socially conscious and the romantic. The more sober tunes were on side one, which ended with the horn-driven, nearly eight-minute title track, depicting the exodus of "Jah people" from Babylon to their fatherland. Whether intentionally or not, "So Much Things to Say," "Guiltiness," and "The Heathen" seemed to reflect a disquiet Marley might have felt after the December shooting, the last of these noting that those who "run away live to fight another day."

In Junior Marvin, Marley had found another rock-influenced guitarist, as can be heard on Marvin's biting responsive licks on the opening "Natural Mystic." At the mixing stage, Blackwell pulled out one of his tricks from the *Catch a Fire* days, tripling the length of the song's intro to heighten the drama. As for the song itself, "to me 'Natural Mystic' is who he was," Cindy Breakspeare remarked in *The Book of Exodus*. "Every time I hear it, I think, 'Little did you know you were singing about yourself.'"

Perhaps to dispel the gripping but somewhat downbeat grim wariness that pervades side one, side two lightened up with love songs and party tunes. "Jamming"—not a jam, but a taut if lyrically basic urge to keep on truckin'—is justifiably one of Marley's most popular compositions, both for the dynamic basic groove and the sparkling vocal interplay between Bob and the I-Threes.

"That song was very much loved by Stevie Wonder," recounted Family Man Barrett in *Wailing Blues*. "After we'd met with him in Jamaica, he said, 'Why don't you put this song on a 45 because that's a single!' But we wanted to keep the strength of the album, and after we tell him that, he said, 'OK, but if you don't do something about it, then I will.' And that's how come he wrote this song 'Master Blaster.'" Subtitled "Jammin'," it bore a heavy reggae influence and would be a #5 hit for Wonder in 1980.

"Waiting in Vain," "Turn Your Lights Down Low," and "Three Little Birds" were tender love odes, likely inspired by Bob's passionate affair with Cindy Breakspeare. The *Exodus* song most closely identified with Marley, however, might be his closing update of the mid-1960s Wailers classic "One Love." Slowed down and embellished with the I-Threes' backup vocals, it was more readily interpreted as a hopeful plea for love between people the world over. For this version, Bob changed the title to "One Love/People Get Ready"—though it's much more "One Love" than "People Get Ready," a big 1960s hit for the Impressions. Maybe Bob was simply acknowledging his debt to Curtis Mayfield (who was given a cowriting credit), the Wailers' biggest musical inspiration.

For those who found his love songs too soppy, Bob had a reply at the ready. "People are gonna like ['Three Little Birds'], people that don't even know about Rasta, and it will make them want to find out more," he told *Sounds*. "Like with that song, 'Waiting in Vain.' That nice tune, mon, that from long time back. It's for people who never dig the Wailers from long time, 'cos dem just couldn't relate. So, what I do now is a tune like 'Waiting in Vain' so dem might like it and wonder what a go on. A different light. It's movement time."

"One of the things they were trying to do was have something that was not just totally roots, because they knew that totally roots was at its peak," Karl Pitterson, an engineer on the album, acknowledged in *The Book of Exodus*. "It wasn't just the band. Chris [Blackwell] had a lot to do with it at that point. He had this thing where they could get into the wider market—and it worked." As part of the move away from the earthier reggae "roots" sound, a drum machine was used on "Waiting in Vain" and a vocoder on the title track. There were also modifications to the guitar sounds by electronics wizard Roger Mayer, who'd devised effects used by Jimi Hendrix on early Hendrix classics.

"Both Junior and Bob's guitars were sent to me for rebuilding and had all the frets and bridge perfectly set up with all the correct fret profiles and alignments to ensure that the guitars now produced the perfect tone with no fret buzz and more sustain," Mayer explained to the *Bob Marley Magazine* website. "I also supplied Junior

with some modified [wah-wah] pedals and custom effect overdrive and distortion pedals for solo work. I basically gave them guitars with all the [modifications] I did for Jimi on them, both mechanical and electrical. I think if you listen carefully you can hear the change in tone of both Bob and Junior's guitars as compared to the tone used on previous albums. They are in perfect harmony."

Rock-influenced guitarist Junior Marvin replaced Donald Kinsey on the *Exodus* sessions and would remain in the Wailers for the rest of Bob's life. ED PERLSTEIN/REDFERNS/ GETTY IMAGES

These modifications were, Mayer explained in *Wailing Blues*, implemented after Marley told him the Wailers "wanted to sound international. He said it with a smile, but I understood what he was saying, because I'd been working with black bands to help break them into different markets and had the sound remained like it was before Junior came aboard, the band wouldn't have sounded so international. It would have sounded like a Jamaican band and it couldn't have been marketed internationally like it was. That's the way I saw it and it was the same thing with Stevie Wonder and the Isley Brothers, because they changed what they were doing from a mainly black sound into something more international. The music can travel after that, but if you haven't got the quality in the recordings, then it's not going to happen."

Exodus has since come to be regarded as one of Marley's core classics. Its selection at the end of 1999 by *Time* magazine as the album of the century is one of the most quoted factoids in overviews of Marley's career. "Every song is a classic, from the messages of love to the anthem of revolution," *Time* declared. "But more than that, the album is a political and cultural nexus, drawing inspiration from the Third World and then giving voice to it the world over."

At the time of its release, *Exodus* was fairly successful, but not quite the leap into the top tier of record-sellers for which Marley and Blackwell were probably hoping. It was most successful in the United Kingdom, where it made #8. "Exodus," "Waiting in Vain," and "Jamming" were all hit singles, the last of these hitting the Top 10. In the United States, the album didn't do quite as well as *Rastaman Vibration*, stalling at #20, though Blackwell hoped the next tour would push it higher.

"Karl Pitterson's usual crisp, clean sound is calculated to be springy enough for rock fans while staying punchy enough to keep the roots fans just about satisfied," surmised Vivien Goldman in her review for *Sounds* magazine. Goldman's enthusiasm for the album resulted in an entire book about the record nearly thirty years later. "It's a dangerous tightrope, and Marley's treading it," she wrote in *Sounds*. "While Marley's songwriting abilities remain as powerful as they are, [and] while he continues to surround himself with musicians as excellent as the Barrett brothers . . . Bob Marley will continue to remain King of Reggae in the eyes of the world."

"Exodus," "Waiting in Vain," and "Jamming" were all hit singles. Produced by Lee Perry, "Punky Reggae Party" served as the B-side of "Jamming" and name-checked fellow reggae stars the Maytals, as well as British punk bands the Clash, the Damned, and the Jam.

EXODUS

Review by Gillian G. Gaar

Exodus was an apt title for the first studio album Bob Marley recorded outside of Jamaica. In the wake of the assassination attempt on his life on December 3, 1976, and the Smile Jamaica concert at which he appeared two days later, Marley quickly relocated to Nassau, where he remained a few weeks before flying to London. Marley wouldn't return to Jamaica for two years.

The album's title track referenced his self-imposed exile, also giving a nod to another famous exodus in its lines about "Brother Moses." "Jamming" was likewise inspired by Marley's recent ordeal, a seemingly laid-back, jaunty number that nonetheless defiantly proclaims, "No bullet can stop us now." There's also a richer feel to the music; it was the first time Marley and his musicians had worked in a twenty-four-track studio.

The listener is immediately drawn by the fade-in on the opening track, "Natural Mystic" (which *Rolling Stone*'s Greil Marcus compared to Bob Dylan's "Blowin' in the Wind"). Marley offers no explanation for why people have to suffer, but casts a hopeful eye toward the future. The album goes on to mix the personal and the political. "Guiltiness" disparages the "big fish" who trample over others in their determination to get their way—possibly a veiled allusion to the men who tried to kill Marley. On a more conciliatory note, a newly recorded version of "One Love" (which the Wailers first recorded in 1965 and which incorporates Curtis Mayfield's "People Get Ready") celebrated that which unites humanity: one love, one heart, and faith.

As much a lover as a fighter, Marley also displayed his romantic side, most prominently on "Turn Your Lights Down Low," a sweet plea to rekindle a relationship. Musically, it's closer to pop than reggae. "Three Little Birds" also exudes optimism, a committed belief that things will work out, tied to a musical backing that moves like a gently rolling wave.

Though not charting as highly in the United States, *Exodus* still reached gold status on its release, and climbed to #20—the last Top 40 album of Marley's lifetime. It was a different story in the United Kingdom, where *Exodus*, "Waiting in Vain," "Jamming," "One Love/People Get Ready," and the title track all hit the Top 40 and bolstered Marley's crossover appeal. Ultimately, *Exodus* went on to be Marley's biggest-selling album and remains one of the mostly highly regarded works in his catalog.

Before *Exodus* came out, Marley preceded an American tour with a few weeks of shows in northern Europe. The dates climaxed with a few nights at London's Rainbow Theatre at the start of June 1977. GRAHAM WILTSHIRE (MAIN) AND VINCENT MCEVOY (INSET) BOTH /REDFERNS/GETTY IMAGES

1977 EUROPEAN TOUR AND CANCER SCARE

As Marley awaited the release of *Exodus*, he continued to make headlines, but not in the way he would have chosen. In London, cannabis had been found in the car in which he and Family Man Barrett were riding on the way back from a recording session. On April 6, he was fined fifty pounds (and Barrett twenty pounds)—a far lighter penalty than they could have suffered, avoiding jail or deportation. "Whatever the approach or attitude in your own country you must really appreciate that here it is still an offense," the judge gently chided. "While you are here it would be very unwise to use or have possession of cannabis."

Bob was also generating media coverage, not all of it flattering, for his now-public extramarital affair with Breakspeare. "Beauty and the beast" was the politically incorrect tone of some of the tawdry articles, which hardly dampened their relationship, as Breakspeare became pregnant by Bob later that year.

Putting the focus back on his music, Marley prepared to promote his latest work. Even before *Exodus* came out, Marley preceded an anticipated American tour with a few weeks of shows in northern Europe, where he was steadily gaining in popularity. Including gigs in Belgium, France, Holland, Germany, and Scandinavia, it climaxed with a few nights at London's Rainbow Theatre at the start of June 1977. (A film of the June 4 show is on the DVD *Live! At the Rainbow*; some audio performances from the same concert are on the bonus disc of the *Exodus* deluxe edition.) Marley, announced J. Bradshaw in the *New York Times Magazine* after witnessing the final Rainbow show, "has become the Third World's first real superstar." Yet the US tour would not take place,

due to an incident that, though it seemed like more of an annoyance than a calamity at the time, would have more far-reaching implications than any of his albums or mild tabloid scandals.

Bob was a fanatical soccer (or, as it's called in Jamaica and most of the rest of the world, football) player, fitting in games wherever he could, at home and on tour. During a contest in Paris with the Wailers and local journalists the day before the start of the European tour, he hurt his right foot badly enough that the toenail needed to be removed from his big toe. He'd already hurt the foot badly on several prior occasions, both playing football and in other ways, as a child and an adult. Although a Paris doctor instructed him to stay off his feet, he went ahead with the tour, sometimes taking the stage in sandals and a visible bandage. He even continued playing soccer and dancing onstage with the customary verve he brought to live performances.

The toe wasn't healing, and worse, his shoe was filled with blood after some shows. Eventually he saw a specialist in London, who told him the toe was afflicted with melanoma cancer. It was recommended that the toe be amputated, and noted that the foot was at risk, too, if the cancer had spread. Bob was due to start an American tour in August, but on July 20 promoters were informed it would be delayed until fall.

ABOVE: A fanatical soccer player, Bob suffered a foot injury while playing the sport that eventually alerted physicians to cancerous melanoma in his toe. Marley's seen here after playing with Toots and the Maytals. GAB ARCHIVE/GETTY IMAGES

BELOW: The cancer discovery led to the postponement of Marley's fall US tour. The Portland show was the band's only live American appearance that year.

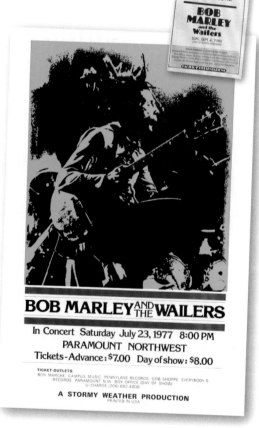

In *Bob Marley, My Son*, Cedella Marley emphasized Bob "did not want his toe cut off. He loved to play football; he loved to dance on the stage when he was performing. He thought he would be able to do none of these things if his toe was amputated."

Wanting to avoid an amputation at all costs, even after a second London doctor advised the same, Marley consulted William Bacon, the Miami doctor who'd successfully operated on Don Taylor's spine after the previous year's shooting. Bacon removed the cancerous parts of the toe and performed a skin graft. The hope was that this would remove cancer from his body for good. Bob remained in Miami, where he'd bought a home for his mother (her American husband, Edward Booker, had recently died), for a few months, canceling the American tour.

PUNKY REGGAE PARTY

For obvious reasons, Marley didn't record much in the last half of 1977. As a lighthearted break from the gloomy prognosis on his health, he did find time over the summer to record one of the most offbeat records of his career. Produced by Lee Perry, "Punky Reggae Party" exhorted everyone to have a—what else—punky reggae party, listing the Wailers, fellow reggae stars the Maytals, and early British punk bands the Clash, the Damned, and the Jam as attendees.

As unlikely an alliance as it seemed, punk and reggae did share some common ground. Musicians from both camps viewed themselves as outsiders, at least in the early phases of their careers, when both punk and reggae were considered fringe underground styles that rebelled against the musical and social status quo. Many punk musicians were big reggae fans, and a few of them (such as the Clash, Sex Pistols singer John Lydon, and the Slits) would incorporate reggae influences into some of their records.

"The punks are the outcasts from society," Marley declared in *Sounds*. "So are the Rastas. So they are bound to defend what we defend. In a way, me like see them safety pins and 'ting. Me no like do it myself, y'understand, but me like see a man can suffer pain without crying."

With Marley and the Wailers' US tour on the rocks, Don Kirshner's *Rock Concert* aired a taped performance from England in October 1977.

In fact, most reggae musicians were not even that aware of punk, let alone of punk fans who were enthusiastic for reggae. And even some punk rock stars who were avid reggae listeners weren't big fans of the ideology. "Reggae, punk, it's not like most of the stuff you hear on the radio," said Clash bassist Paul Simonon in the same *Sounds* story. "It's something you can relate to, kids your own age—they've got their battles, we've got ours. Black people are still being suppressed, we are being suppressed, so we've got something in common.

"But personally, all that about Rastafari bores me. Kids can relate to us singing about social things, like some reggae does, because they're living it. If we started singing about God, it would be fantasy, like it's all green when you die because you've been good. I don't think there ever would be a God-music punk band, because punks want to tear down everything that's establishment, like church and police."

BOB'S LES PAUL

Dave Hunter

Perhaps Bob Marley didn't set out to take reggae to the masses, but that's certainly the way it ended up. The genre existed before Marley became a household name, but by the time the Jamaican artist was done transforming that loping rhythm into something entirely his own, he had made it into one of the most universal forms of music the world has ever known. Bob Marley has been gone for nearly four decades, but close your eyes and you can still see it and hear it: the Wailers, chunking out that big, potent groove while Marley skanks along in front of the mic, road-worn Les Paul Special in his arms, dreadlocks flying.

Marley played a Fender Stratocaster before acquiring his 1957 Gibson Les Paul Special in London in 1973, but the Gibson is far and away the guitar identified with him, and it accompanied him through his best-known hits and worldwide tours. Through the course of the 1970s the Gibson underwent several modifications, on top of the mods it received before landing in the reggae star's hands. It came to him with small pearloid block inlays on the neck in place of the original dot position markers, the holly headstock veneer and pearloid logo replaced by a simple Gibson logo decal, a nonstock brass nut, and white binding added to the edges of the headstock. After Marley purchased the guitar, he added a large white plastic ring around the pickup selector switch

to disguise damage to the wood. He also removed the one-piece wrap-over bridge, filling the large holes for its stud mounts with wooden dowels and adding a Tune-O-Matic bridge and stop-bar tailpiece, as found on Gibson's Les Paul Standard.

This is the way the Les Paul Special appeared through most of the guitar's tenure in Marley's hands, although a few further modifications were undertaken in 1979 by acoustical engineer and guitar effects pedal innovator Roger Mayer, who replaced the original black plastic pickguard with an aluminum one and swapped out the large white plastic switch ring for an eyeball-shaped aluminum ring held in place with two screws.

Mayer had also set up the guitars of both Marley and Wailers guitarist Junior Marvin, dressing their frets and setting their intonation prior to the recording of *Exodus* in 1977. "If you listen to *Exodus* and compare it with previous albums, you can hear that both Bob's and Junior's guitars resonate and sustain better and are in perfect harmony with each other," Mayer told this writer in 2004. Despite these modifications, Marley's Les Paul Special retained its formative parts—namely its original P-90 pickups and solid mahogany body and neck—and, therefore, its thick, juicy tone, as can be heard driving almost every tune the star recorded on electric guitar from 1973 onward.

Marley's Les Paul Special is now on display, in its final form, in the Bob Marley Museum in Kingston, Jamaica.

Gibson's Custom Shop replica of Bob's Les Paul Special. The real guitar resides in the Bob Marley Museum in Kingston. GIBSON BRANDS, INC

"Punky Reggae Party" was still an admirable show of solidarity between the movements. Alas, "Punky Reggae Party" was only a mildly entertaining diversion from Marley's main course, with nothing "punk" about it, save the punk acts named in the lyrics. It nonetheless was used on the B-side of the hit single "Jamming."

KAYA RELEASE AND RECEPTION

Marley had recorded little else since the sessions that produced *Exodus*, but had a stockpile of outtakes to fill what could have been a lengthy gap between releases. These were used for his next LP, *Kaya*, which came out at the beginning of spring 1978. Here and there, some critics who'd followed the Wailers for a long time had accused Marley of selling out, or at least going soft, at various points in his Island career. With *Kaya*, such complaints for the first time became commonplace, as the record was lighter, sunnier, and indeed softer in tone than any of his previous albums. Lester Bangs panned the LP as "quite possibly the blandest set of reggae music I have ever heard" in *Rolling Stone*, and the first sentence of *Creem*'s review wasn't much more encouraging: "The fire hasn't gone out, but it is on low flame and being used more for warmth than for arson."

The same review, however, was actually quite positive overall, writer Wayne Robins clarifying in the next paragraph that "the politics of intimidation haven't totally been abandoned in Bob Marley's rebel music—there's still a warning voice, and sneakily smoldering technique—but *Kaya* takes on a conciliatory tone as Marley's inner world competes for attention with the gathering storm. His singing is relaxed, passionate and playful, closer than ever in spirit to such American soul sources as Curtis Mayfield, Smokey Robinson and Ray Charles (and sometimes the fatigued, druggy Sly Stone of [his album *There's a Riot Goin' On*]), and the album's mood and musical surface makes it his most instantly enjoyable studio album since the landmark *Natty Dread*."

"What they said about *Kaya* is true, but you can't show aggression all the while," said Marley in *Melody Maker* the year after its release.

A stockpile of outtakes would come to comprise *Kaya*, which came out at the beginning of spring 1978.

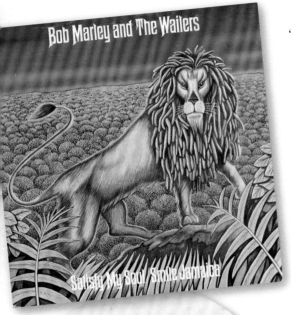

"Me always militant, you know. Me *too* militant. That's why me did things like *Kaya*, to cool off the pace." Along the same lines, he told the *New York Times*, "People say, 'Oh Bob, you gone from politics, we want to hear some more politics.' But we use *Kaya* to feel them out, so everybody keep their ears open. And me write about freedom, not about politics."

It wasn't universally known that *Kaya*'s tracks had been cut at the same time as the harder stuff at the *Exodus* sessions, and thus seemed to some that Bob was going pop, or at least poppier. In the first edition of *The Rolling Stone Record Guide*, Dave Marsh went as far as to find it symbolic of a general decline in Marley's importance, writing that "by the time of 1978's *Kaya*, he seemed more like a popularizer of the [reggae] form, much as Cream was for blues rock, than one of its elder statesmen."

Kaya nonetheless featured some songs that were beloved by Marley fans, many of whom didn't take critics' carps as gospel. The title track was one, and like a couple other cuts on the LP ("Satisfy My Soul" and "Sun Is Shining"), had first been done with Lee Perry back in the early 1970s. "Satisfy My Soul" even became a UK hit, as did one of Bob's most straightforward love tunes, "Is This Love," which went into the British Top 10 (and for which he filmed a promo video). The *Kaya* album itself became Bob's biggest UK hit so far when it peaked at #4, though it only made #50 in the United States, where his momentum was slipping.

Family Man Barrett defended the remakes—not that the practice was anything new or unusual—in *Wailing Blues*: "We wanted to give them that progressive Island sound. Those versions we did with Scratch [Lee Perry] represented an early stage, and by the time we did *Exodus* and *Kaya* we had better equipment, use of a better studio and better knowledge too. We knew we could record them so they would have more impact and take on that international sound."

Despite critical pans, *Kaya* featured some songs that were beloved by Marley fans. "Satisfy My Soul" even became a UK hit, as did Bob's straightforward love tune, "Is This Love," seen here in its Portuguese and white-label promo pressings.

KAYA

Review by Gillian G. Gaar

Bob Marley's tenth album might almost be called *Exodus II*, since a number of its songs came to life during the *Exodus* sessions. But the focus here is less on militancy than on enjoying the good life. This is evident in both the album's back cover, which features an illustration of a well-packed joint, and in the opening line of the first song, "Easy Skanking," which has Marley singing, "Excuse me while I light my spliff." The title track (let's not forget that *kaya* is Jamaican slang for ganja) also celebrates watching your life go up in sweet smoke: "I got to have kaya now," Marley insists in the song.

But love—both romantic and spiritual—is also on the menu, most notably on the buoyant "Is This Love," a Top 10 hit in the United Kingdom, Australia, and New Zealand and one of Marley's best-known numbers. It's a simple, charming song about nothing more than being together with your beloved, as is "Satisfy My Soul," which reworks an earlier Marley song called "Don't Rock My Boat" (see the 1992 *Songs of Freedom* box set). The earlier version has a slower, funkier groove; the *Kaya* version gently boosts the tempo, adds a horn section for a little snap, and has a brighter feel overall. Marley was by now a more confident musician, accompanied by other equally talented musicians. Working in a modern studio only helped give his music a more professional, streamlined sound.

On *Kaya* Marley also expresses more vulnerability, particularly on songs like "She's Gone" and "Misty Morning." The former touches on a time when Rita had briefly left him, though the song's tone is more matter-of-fact than sorrowful. There's a real unhappiness evident in the more mournful "Misty Morning," which finds Marley at home in the gloom while his erstwhile partner is off having fun.

Marley told journalist Chris Salewicz that he played down political commentary on *Kaya* out of fears for his safety in the wake of the attempt on his life. But a song like "Crisis" nonetheless addressed the fact that life was hard for many who have only their faith in Jah to pull them through. The closing track, "Time Will Tell," is a surprisingly melancholy number expressing hope for a better future.

Kaya didn't chart as high in the United States as *Exodus*, reaching #50, while in the United Kingdom it peaked at #4. (It did achieve gold status in both countries, however.) It served as something of a break between the more outspoken political sentiments of *Exodus* and subsequent albums like *Survival* and *Uprising*.

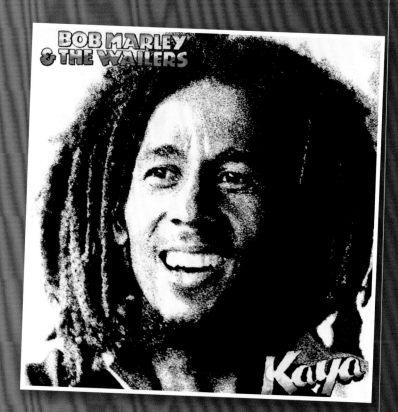

ONE LOVE PEACE CONCERT

About a month before *Kaya* came out, Marley returned to Jamaica for the first time since the attempt on his life. The month after *Kaya*'s release, he was at the forefront of a concert that, both at the time and in retrospect, overshadowed the album. At his One Love Peace Concert in Kingston on April 22, 1978, Bob didn't just reaffirm his presence in Jamaica—he also pulled off one of the most effective public acts for the cause of peace that any entertainer has managed.

After Michael Manley won the election he called for in late 1976, severe problems continued in Jamaica, and not just between the rival parties. A shortage of basic goods in the country's stores hit the poor the hardest. The One Love Peace Concert was organized to bring much-needed good vibes to the scene. To ensure its humanitarian goals, profits from ticket sales went to community projects. Marley himself funded the event with fifty thousand dollars.

While the concert is most remembered for Marley's concluding set, it was more like an all-star reggae festival. Among the day's dozen-plus acts were some of the biggest reggae stars of the 1970s, including Culture, Dennis Brown, Jacob Miller, Big Youth, and Ras Michael. Also on the bill was Peter Tosh, who put the proceedings on edge with spoken harangues against police abuse and in favor of marijuana use, lighting up a spliff onstage to underscore his point. However valid his points, Tosh risked no small payback, especially as he was addressing his remarks to Manley and JLP leader Edward Seaga, both of whom were in the audience.

By contrast, Marley was all good cheer during his set, which mixed such crowd-pleasing favorites as "Positive Vibration" with more serious stuff, such as "War" and "Trench Town Rock." At one point, he engaged in a rap that, like so many of his interviews, rambled through his general philosophies without saying anything too specific: "To make everything come true, we've got to be together, yeah, yeah. And to the spirit of the most high, His Imperial Majesty Emperor Haile Selassie I, run lightning, leading the people of the slaves to shake hands. . . . To show the people that you love them right, to show the people that you gonna unite, show the people that you're over bright, show the people that everything is all right. Watch, watch, what you're doing, because. . .

"I'm not so good at talking, but I hope you understand what I'm trying to say," he allowed. And then his talk took a turn that no one expected. "I'm trying to say, could we have, could we have, up here onstage here the presence of Mr. Michael Manley and Mr. Edward Seaga?" he asked. "I just want to shake hands and show the people that we're gonna unite . . . we're gonna unite . . . we've got to unite."

To some degree, Bob might have felt cornered into an apparent Manley/PNP endorsement at the Smile Jamaica concert. Now Manley and Seaga were put into a spot that would be impossible to refuse without losing face. Both politicians gingerly mounted the stage, taking positions on either side of Bob. The singer then took hands from each party leader, raised them over his head, and joined them together.

At his One Love Peace Concert in Kingston on April 22, 1978, Bob pulled off one of the most effective acts for the cause of peace that any entertainer has managed when he pressed fierce political rivals Michael Manley (far left) and Edward Seaga (third from left) into joining hands on stage. ECHOES/REDFERNS/GETTY IMAGES; PRESS PASS ROGER STEFFENS' REGGAE ARCHIVES

PRESS PASS

ONE LOVE CONCERT FOR PEACE
APRIL 22, 1978
National Stadium
Kingston, Jamaica

ONE LOVE
GET YOUR TICKETS AT THE
NATIONAL STADIUM
ALL DAY TODAY
FROM 10 a.m.
TOGETHERNESS SECTION — $2.00   LOVE SECTION — $5.00
PEACE SECTION — $8.00
SHOWTIME 5 P.M.
GATES OPEN 2 P.M.

While neither Manley nor Seaga looked too happy about it, they were linked in a show of unity before tens of thousands of concertgoers. The filmed concert eventually reached millions of viewers who never set foot in Jamaica. It was a public truce between two warring factions that seemed as unimaginable as the Camp David Accords between Israel and Egypt had before they took place later that same year. And it could probably have never been effected by anyone other than Bob Marley.

Although it was a great feat of unofficial statesmanship, the clasp between Manley and Seaga did not result in lasting cooperation between Jamaican factions (much as the Camp David Accords hardly guaranteed peace in the Middle East). Violence, poverty, and sociopolitical volatility continued to plague Jamaica over the next few years, whether Manley or Seaga (who was prime minister for most of the 1980s) was in power. Nevertheless, it demonstrated the unlikely meetings musicians could enable for peaceful purposes. Long after Marley's death and Manley and Seaga's reigns as prime minister, the event continues to touch uncounted people thanks to the filmed sequence that has been excerpted in several documentaries.

"In Jamaica," Marley summarized a couple months later in the *New York Times*, "the political parties and the peoples at war. Them never love Rasta, but Rasta bring them politicians to shake hands together. I feel like that must really touch some people."

1978 TOURS

If there were major health complications from Marley's toe operation, none were apparent to the public through the rest of 1978. Marley launched his most extensive tour to date in mid-May, playing for about a month in the United States before swinging to Europe for a few weeks, then returning to the States for another few weeks before wrapping up in early August. The ever-fluctuating Wailers lineup had a new wrinkle with the return of Al Anderson to the fold to share lead guitar duties with Junior Marvin. Twin lead guitars were uncommon in rock, and perhaps unprecedented in reggae, though Al and Junior's experiences in rock bands had prepared them well for the job.

Marley launched his most extensive tour to date in mid-May 1978, playing for about a month in the US, swinging to Europe for a few weeks, then returning to the States before wrapping up in early August. Bob adjusts his mic stand at Chicago's Uptown Theater on **May 27, 1978.** PAUL NATKIN/GETTY IMAGES

The American shows were ill-timed in the sense that *Exodus* would have been more effectively promoted by the tour than *Kaya*, the less zealously received current release. If his record sales weren't zooming, his popularity as a live act was. He was playing bigger venues; appearing in secondary markets such as Buffalo, Pittsburgh, and Austin, as well as his usual coastal strongholds; and selling out New York's Madison Square Garden, one of the most famous concert venues anywhere. Recordings from his shows at Boston's Music Hall on June 8, 1978, were compiled for the 2015 CD *Easy Skanking in Boston '78*.

On June 15, Bob received an honor that might have meant more to him than a sold-out theater. At New York's Waldorf Astoria Hotel, he was given the United Nations' Peace Medal of the Third World, presented on behalf of five hundred million Africans by Senegalese Youth Ambassador Mohmmadu "Johnny" Seka in recognition of Marley's efforts for disenfranchised blacks the world over.

Asked at the event's press conference how he felt being "a Third World hero," Bob modestly demurred, "Third World hero? No mon. Me don't deal with hero. Really . . . no hero. True, true . . . no hero."

A reporter attempted to draw Marley out by stating, "It seems that in recent years there have been attempts to subdue reggae's revolutionary message by making it more of an 'I love you, you love me' thing."

"Long time you fight revolution and when you fight revolution you use guns," Bob replied. "You don't really want talk about revolution until you have guns, right? So me don't want ever to talk 'bout revolution because me no never get gun. Me mek music. Music a deh biggest gun."

After noting that the Madison Square Garden audience had many West Indians in attendance, *New York Times* reviewer John Rockwell added that "the concert was a triumph . . . for reggae in general but Mr. Marley in particular. There were plenty of non–West Indians on hand for one thing. And for another, after a slightly slow start, the concert built to a climax that was really wonderful in its fervor and exultation . . .

"Mr. Marley is both a fine composer and a superbly professional showman, a master of the sort of theatricality that attains its highest art by looking abandoned and natural. As a vocalist, he is decent but unexceptional— compared, for instance, to the golden-throated but erratic Jimmy Cliff. But he phrases well, his songs are remarkably high in quality, his Wailers band is a skillful one and his personal image compelling. The result had the Garden in swaying, singing rapture by the end of Saturday's show, the kind of celebration that justifies large-arena concerts all by itself. . . . Who would have believed Madison Square Garden would have swayed en masse to a speech by Haile Selassie, the words of which Mr. Marley incorporates verbatim into 'War'?"

Concluded Rockwell, "Marley's images of exodus, resistance and paradise on earth aren't just Jamaican or even confined to underdeveloped parts of the world; they can speak to everyone through the power of his music as a modern day Utopian vision."

But not everyone was as enamored with Marley's concerts of the period, or enthused about the slightly revised Wailers. "Marley has now taken the best of his material to the absolute limits of interpretation," Eric Fuller wrote in *Sounds*, in a mixed critique of Bob's Bingley, England, show. "The Wailers are much concerned with showy and extended instrumental workouts within the framework of each song to give them some feeling of freshness and supply the extra thrills demanded by live performance. Given that Marley's melodies are his finest moment, the value of this style of execution is a matter of debate—but certainly lead guitarist Junior Marvin's exaggerated stage showmanship and US-soul-revue fashion histrionics seem headed in precisely the wrong direction."

Near the end of the tour, two of Bob Marley's closest associates figured in a couple of his more momentous occasions of the year. On July 21, Cindy Breakspeare gave birth to Bob's latest son, Damian. As a sign of how serious the relationship had become, Marley bought her a house in a nice area of Kingston and gave her one hundred thousand dollars to set up an Ital Craft store. She was probably the most important love of his life aside from his wife, Rita. But Breakspeare would not be his last affair, nor Damian his last child.

On June 15, at New York's Waldorf Astoria Hotel, Bob received the United Nations' Peace Medal of the Third World. Asked at the press conference how he felt being "a Third World hero," Bob demurred, "Third World hero? No mon. Me don't deal with hero. Really . . . no hero."
LYNN GOLDSMITH/CORBIS/VCG VIA GETTY IMAGES

PETER TOSH AND ROLLING STONES RECORDS

The day after Damian's birth, Mick Jagger watched from the wings as Peter Tosh joined Marley onstage at Burbank's Starlight Bowl to sing "Get Up, Stand Up," one of the most famous songs they'd performed (and, in this case, written) together in the Wailers. It would be the last time they performed together in public. Not that either's career was suffering from the other's absence—Tosh's own star was rising in the United States, especially with the patronage of the world's biggest rock band.

Tosh had followed his debut album with the equally well-received *Equal Rights* in 1977. If side one leaned a little heavily on remakes of Wailers classics—including, as it happened, "Get Up, Stand Up," along with "Downpressor Man" and "Steppin' Razor"—side two showed him capable of summoning quality new material. Like Marley, Tosh was becoming more interested in writing about Africa, as he did in "African" and, more notably, "Apartheid," one of the few songs of the day to address the South African practice. Like *Legalize It*, the new album came out on Columbia. But it would be his last LP for the label, due in part to the unexpected interest of a rock band that sometimes visited and recorded in Jamaica.

The Rolling Stones had taken an interest in reggae and Jamaica at least a half-decade prior. Most of their 1973 album, *Goats Head Soup*, was recorded at Kingston's Dynamic Sound Studio, and while there wasn't a noticeable reggae influence on that LP, they'd since tried their hands at the style on the mid-1970s tracks "Luxury" and "Cherry Oh Baby." It's been reported that the band asked the Wailers to open for the West Coast dates of their 1975 tour, though that didn't happen, Marley perhaps feeling he was moving beyond opening-act status. Now the Stones were interested in signing Tosh to their Atlantic-distributed label, Rolling Stones Records.

Stones guitarists Keith Richards and Ron Wood went to Jamaica's Island Music Festival to see Tosh perform in February 1978, and Tosh met with their label manager, Earl McGrath, that month, although he wasn't yet beside himself with excitement. When American reggae promoter Michael Epstein called Tosh to relay the group's interest, Tosh responded, as Epstein remembered in John Masouri's *Steppin' Razor: The Life of Peter Tosh*, "I man don't need no Rolling Stone. I don't play rock 'n' roll. I'm a reggae artist." Added Epstein in the same book, "I couldn't believe he didn't know or care about the Rolling Stones. I mean how can you *not* know who the Rolling Stones are? Peter was smart, but he wasn't what you'd call educated."

The Stones' interest in signing Tosh might have heightened when Mick Jagger attended the One Love Peace Concert. According to McGrath, there was more at work than their admiration for Tosh's music. "The reason I signed Peter was because Keith was in a bad state," he told Tosh's biographer. "He wasn't interested in anything and I thought if we can get Peter's thing up and running, then he'd get interested because he was such a big reggae fan and that's just what happened. Keith got involved and felt stimulated by it, and it was something he and Mick could share. Peter Tosh helped keep the Rolling Stones together at that time, frankly."

Whether or not the Rolling Stones would have broken up if Tosh hadn't signed to their label, their enthusiasm for him was sincere. "If anybody can bring reggae music to the rest of the world, especially America, then Peter's the one to do it along with Bob Marley," Keith Richards told his biographer, Barbara Charone, in *Creem*. "After all, we were second to the Beatles. You need a door opener and then you need the serious stuff. I'm not saying Marley isn't serious. It's just that Peter has chosen his scene, his band and his music very carefully. And he's done an amazing job putting it all together."

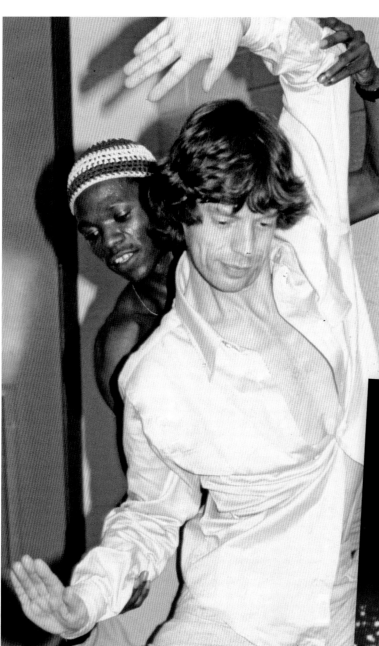

Tosh signed with Rolling Stones Records in May 1978. Joining its roster was hardly an automatic guarantee of success. Launched in 1971, the label had functioned almost exclusively as an outlet for records by the Rolling Stones themselves, as well as scattered solo releases by members of the band. At the deal's outset, Peter seemed pleased with the association, telling *Oui*, "Finding Mick and Keith to spread the word, and deal with the music—knowing they not only are *interested* in the music,

In May 1978, Tosh signed with Rolling Stones records. His first LP for the label, *Bush Doctor*, featured a cover of the Temptations' "(You Gotta Walk) Don't Look Back" with Mick Jagger sharing vocals. LYNN GOLDSMITH/CORBIS/VCG VIA GETTY IMAGES

but love and respect the music—is a great, great blessing." Tosh would be the only other artist the label promoted much, issuing three of his albums in the late 1970s and early 1980s.

On the first of these, 1978's *Bush Doctor*, Richards helped out with guitar on a couple of tracks. Harder to miss was the remake of "(You Gotta Walk) Don't Look Back," a Temptations cover Tosh had first recorded with the Wailers back in 1966. Sharing vocals with Peter on the remake was Jagger, who himself sang lead on a couple Stones covers of Temptations classics in the 1970s. Bassist Robbie Shakespeare, who with drummer Sly Dunbar comprised the album's rhythm section, remembered suggesting Mick and Peter do a song together, and Temptations material made for a logical shared influence.

"All the people who know Mick Jagger don't know me," was how Tosh explained in *Creem* his decision to duet with Jagger. "And the people who know me don't know Mick Jagger. It's a new era for reggae which breaks down certain barriers. It's a way of getting music over to people who would otherwise bias their minds." As for the choice of "Don't Look Back" in particular, he added, "I recorded that song because it is very symbolistic to the progressive move. It's got the power and a very militant, up feel. I only deal with progress. It is commercial but people will realize they are listening to reggae. The public will easily latch onto it. It's not worthwhile making music just for you and your friends to dance to."

Like many of the Wailers' late-1970s records, *Bush Doctor* moved away from Jamaican roots reggae toward a more internationally accessible sound with rock, pop, and funk influences.

A selection of Peter Tosh singles for Rolling Stones Records.

At times, this could work to the music's detriment. Compared to the genuine toughness of Tosh's original 1966 recording, *Bush Doctor*'s remake of "The Toughest" (retitled "I'm the Toughest") sounded wimpy, or at least like an attempt to sand off the edges to attract late-1970s commercial radio airplay. "Soon Come" was another Wailers classic remade for *Bush Doctor*, though Peter continued to offer new material with harder-hitting lyrics, such as "Stand Firm" (a quite blatant critique of organized religion) and the title track, another demand for marijuana legalization. The cover design once again made his stance on ganja clear, with a scratch and sniff sticker that got some publicity for supposedly emanating a ganja-like aroma.

The Stones also boosted Tosh's career by having him open some of the dates on their extensive mid-1978 American tour, such as a June 17 show in Philadelphia's JFK Stadium in front of about one hundred thousand fans. He and Jagger filmed a promo video for "Don't Look Back," and Mick sang it with Peter on the December 16 episode of *Saturday Night Live*. The program also featured "Bush Doctor," a daring move on the part of Peter, considering its lyrics quite plainly and repeatedly stated "legalize marijuana." In the late 1970s, *Saturday Night Live* was the only network television show giving national exposure to cutting-edge musical acts, and the appearance was quite a coup for Tosh, putting him on more American TV screens than even Bob Marley managed during his lifetime. The "Bush Doctor" lyrics were so controversial that one wonders how the performance was approved for airing, though *SNL*'s late-night slot might have helped.

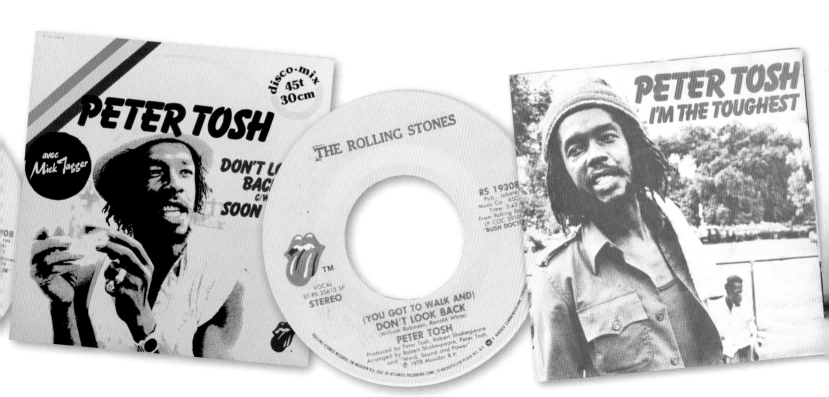

It wasn't all good news for Tosh in the final months of 1978. On September 11, he was viciously roughed up by police in Kingston after being arrested for a marijuana offense. Tosh and others speculated this might have been retribution for the confrontational comments he'd directed at the government a few months earlier at the One Love Peace Concert. With the help of Marley, who went to the police station where Tosh was beaten after learning of the arrest, Tosh was bailed out and charges were withdrawn.

Asked by *Oui* magazine why he was singled out for harassment, Tosh replied, "It was because of my militant act within the society, because I speak out against repression and the shitstem, seen? Yes mon! I know it is a *direct connection*. I have been threatened before in Kingston; the superintendent of customs *drew his gun*, and said he had wanted to kill me for *years*."

Combined with the Rolling Stones connection, all of the publicity surrounding the singer sparked hopes that Tosh could become an international star (indeed a symbol, especially in light of his recent struggles with authority) on the order of his old bandmate Bob Marley. That didn't quite happen, although the blaze of activity did help Peter become one of the most internationally successful reggae musicians over the last decade of his life. *Bush Doctor* fared better than Tosh's first two albums, but not by much, rising to #104. "Don't Look Back" only made it into the lower reaches of the Top 100. In the first edition of *The Rolling Stone Record Guide*, Dave Marsh worried that *Bush Doctor* marked "a softening of Tosh's raw musical and abrasive political posture. Not a sellout but enough to sow seeds of doubt."

For all of *Bush Doctor*'s mixed commercial and artistic results, there could be no doubt that Tosh was emerging as one of reggae's most successful ambassadors, save Marley himself. The same could not quite be said of Bunny Wailer, whose late-1970s releases did not attract even the limited notice that his solo debut *Blackheart Man* had. This might not have been due so much to a lack of effort to commercialize him as an attempt to commercialize him too much. His 1977 follow-up, *Protest*, even included a version of "Get Up, Stand Up," a song also remade by Peter Tosh on one of his early solo records, though Wailer (unlike Tosh) was not one of the song's writers. More troublingly, the production of Bunny's "Get Up, Stand Up" verged on disco.

Still, the "Get Up, Stand Up" arrangement wasn't typical of the *Protest* album, which emphasized Bunny's compositions. The front-cover collage of newspaper headlines on subjects

Bunny Wailer's late-1970s releases did not attract even the limited notice that his solo debut had. This might have been due to an attempt to commercialize him too much. His 1977 LP, *Protest*, even included a version of "Get Up, Stand Up."

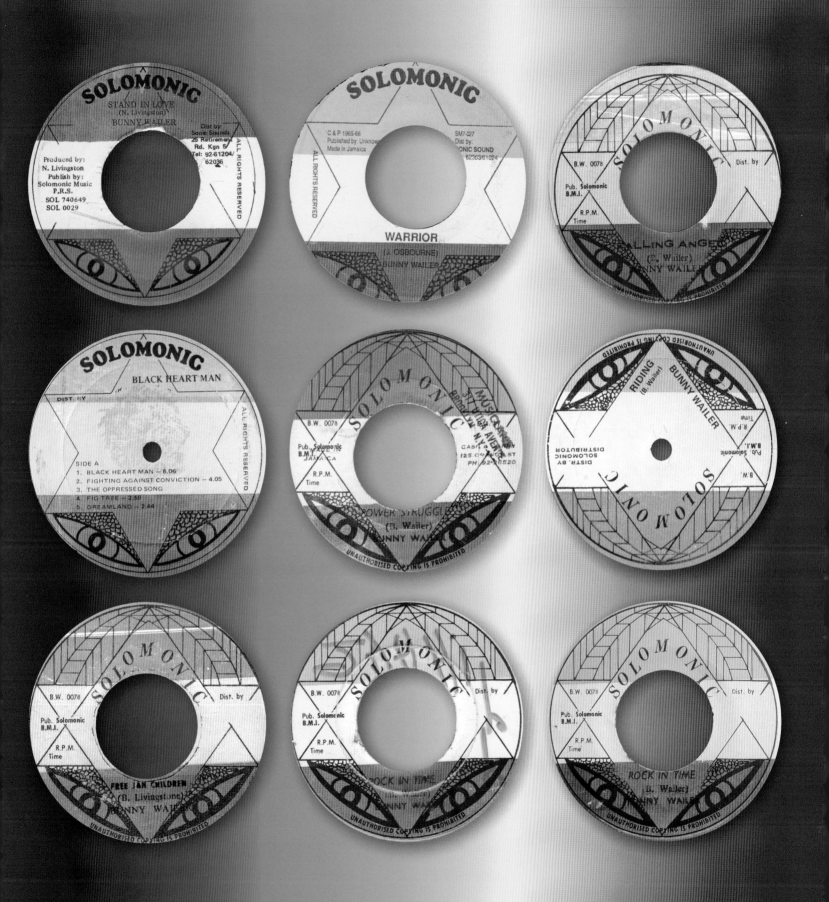

African and Rastafarian announced that political observations were still a priority. Nevertheless, *Village Voice* critic Robert Christgau griped in his *Christgau's Record Guide* review, "Neither Bunny's voice, strong by Jamaican standards but no soul shout, nor reggae's persuasive but rarely irrefutable rhythms, are suited to the more forceful (or is it just louder?) procedures of this follow-up." In contrast to Marley and Tosh, his international visibility would diminish through the rest of the 1970s, though, fortunately, the retreat wouldn't be permanent.

STOPGAP LIVE ALBUM

Having completed a successful but extremely long world tour, Bob took it easy, professionally at least, for the last half of 1978. As part of his on/off relationship with Lee Perry, he did some recordings at Perry's Black Ark Studio, though the pair would never again link up for a full album. Marley also made his first trip to Africa, a country he'd referenced in song and speech as a homeland for his people, briefly visiting Ethiopia. He didn't perform there, but it could have stoked his interest in doing shows on the continent, which he'd soon take steps to arrange.

In the meantime, Island filled the gap between Wailers studio LPs with a double live album, *Babylon by Bus*. Its title taken from a *New Musical Express* concert review headline, the live release was taken largely from concerts at the Pavillon de Paris in late June 1978. As it had been just three years since the *Live!* LP, *Babylon* drew some criticism—or at least some indifferent reviews—for milking a market that had relatively recently received live Marley material.

In *Babylon*'s defense, just one of its songs had also appeared (in a different, earlier version) on *Live!*, and by this time, Bob had a considerably more extensive repertoire from which to cherry-pick highlights. With decent concert renditions of staples such as "Exodus," "War," "Jamming," and "Positive Vibration"—as well as less exposed numbers such as "Rebel Music" and "Punky Reggae Party"—*Babylon by Bus* was a worthwhile addition to his catalog. It might be appreciated better in retrospect than at a time when the world was hungry for new Marley songs.

Island filled the gap between Wailers studio LPs with a double live album, *Babylon by Bus*, recorded largely at the Pavillon de Paris in late June 1978.

Roskilde Festival, Denmark, July 1, 1978.
JORGEN ANGEL/REDFERNS/GETTY IMAGES

SURVIVAL SESSIONS

In early 1979, for the first time in a couple years, Bob recorded an album featuring new material. Cut at Kingston's Tuff Gong Studio—another branch of his Tuff Gong company—*Survival* has been reported to be the first installment of a trilogy that also includes 1980's *Uprising* and a third record to be titled *Confrontation*. Its songs marked a decisive turn toward the socially conscious side of his songwriting. Coming after *Kaya*, it couldn't help but be interpreted as a reaction to criticisms of that previous album as lightweight. However, *Survival* could well have been a natural reflection of where Marley's head and music were going rather than a deliberate attempt to craft different songs, especially as *Kaya*'s tracks had been specially chosen to accent easygoing tunes.

Africa was very much on Marley's mind with *Survival*, as the LP cover made clear. Featuring flags of independent African countries, the design was topped by a drawing of slaves on the kind of ships that had brought some of Marley's ancestors to Jamaica. Neville Garrick (who also designed several other Marley LPs) played a part in shortening the title from the original *Black Survival*. "I always believed one-word titles were easier to promote," he explained to *MOJO*. "I also said [the original] could eliminate some of his fans, who might think it was only for black people. I wanted to say Black Survival without using the word 'black,' so I came up with the idea of using the flags of all the independent countries in Africa. After that I wanted to identify with the blacks in the diaspora in America, Jamaica, Trinidad, England, so I added the plan of a slave ship."

Two of the record's most well-known songs also paid homage to the continent. On "Africa Unite," Bob urged the unification of all Africans and "all Rastaman." Written during his visit to Ethiopia, "Zimbabwe" offered support for the liberation of the country (then still known as Rhodesia) as it moved toward independence. That wasn't an unusual position among progressive thinkers the world over, but Marley was the only major pop musician from outside Africa to address the subject in song. The following year, he would do much more, traveling to the country to give one of his most renowned concerts.

Coming after *Kaya*, *Survival* couldn't help but be interpreted as a reaction to criticisms of that previous album as lightweight. The Japanese ad may have been in advance of Wailers dates there in April 1979.

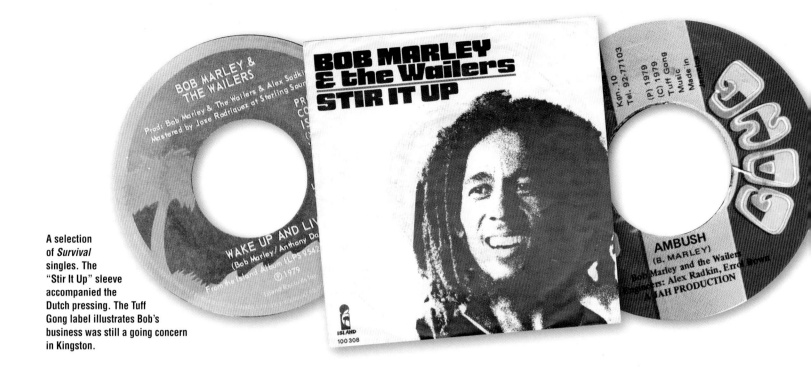

A selection of *Survival* singles. The "Stir It Up" sleeve accompanied the Dutch pressing. The Tuff Gong label illustrates Bob's business was still a going concern in Kingston.

Elsewhere on *Survival*, Bob attacked the "Babylon System" by advising rebellion and truth-telling; mixed references to the attempt on his life with cries against suppression of the poor in "Ambush in the Night"; and celebrated black survival on the title track. Opening with "So Much Trouble in the World," it might be logical to assume that the tone of the album was bitter and angry, in line with some of the early- to mid-1960s protest singer-songwriters of the folk revival. Yet the musical settings were upbeat and groove-grounded, somehow making for a mood far more jubilant and inspiring than might be expected from reading the words on paper. It helped that the songs were more calls to action than resigned complaints, asking listeners to, as the final track entreated, "Wake Up and Live."

"He was a fisherman baiting his hook with *Kaya* to reel in an audience," is how Neville Garrick put it to *MOJO* magazine. "He knew that when he had them hooked he could give them *Survival*, which was his most political, for want of a better word, and militant album. It was time to deliver the message."

As expected, Marley's return to a more militant posture was welcomed by critics. "*Survival* marks a surprising but welcome return to the frontline of political entertainment with a passion strengthened by reasoned analysis and the most beautiful singing I've heard in a long time," wrote Chris Bohn in *Melody Maker*. "With America conquered and success long since assured, it's doubly pleasing that Marley should again choose to speak out, now that his voice will be heard by thousands more people attracted to him by the softer focus of his two previous albums. And now that he avoids the self-defeating stridency of less articulate militants, people might actually listen to what he's singing.

"*Survival*'s firm grounding in the three Rs—Rasta, Rebellion and Rhythm—informs without preaching and entertains without condescension. It's a fiery mix and a potentially difficult one, but it's made possible by the Wailers' oozingly confident playing and the expressive simplicity of the songs. If the language is readily comprehensible, the songs themselves fall into a larger, complex framework which outlines the problems facing

the LPs

SURVIVAL

Review by
Garth Cartwright

The release of *Survival* in October 1979 marked a conscious shift in Bob Marley's sound and worldview toward a heavier sense of dread. The songs showed Marley embracing a more political, pan-Africanist stance: the album's working title was *Black Survival*, but Island convinced Bob to shorten it, fearful that such a title would alienate the now huge white fan base he commanded.

Ironically, *Survival* was coproduced by Marley and Alex Sadkin, a thirty-year-old white American sound engineer who would go on to produce huge hits for the likes of Duran Duran in the 1980s. Sadkin's studio skills had won the attention of Chris Blackwell, who began employing him as an engineer on various projects (including *Rastaman Vibration*). It's likely Blackwell handed Sadkin his first production job on *Survival* knowing the aspiring wonder-kid would give Marley a powerful, radio-friendly sound no matter how militant the songs.

Marley's previous studio album, *Kaya*, had been a commercial success, if drawing criticism from those who felt its subject matter (smoking marijuana, making love) showed the Jamaican icon selling out. Whether Marley paid any attention to such carping is debatable, the Bible being his main reading matter up to then, but at the start of a US tour in 1978, Bob entered a black bookshop in Ohio and purchased titles by Malcolm X, Angela Davis, and others. These tomes, which he now read on the bus, and news reports on the successful guerilla movement to overthrow white rule in Rhodesia, inspired Bob to write his most militant songs since *Burnin'*.

Recording in Kingston for the first time since 1976, Marley emerged with an almost-forty-minute-long album that finds guitarist Al Anderson and keyboardist Earl "Wire" Lindo both back in the Wailers alongside eight horns. The dense sound that resulted is filled with an urgency quite removed from *Kaya*'s more acoustic and laid-back feel. From opening track "So Much Trouble in the World" to the closing "Wake Up and Live," Marley sang with a preacher's conviction about war and righteousness. "Zimbabwe" is a hymn to the soon-to-be independent African nation where Marley and his Wailers were invited in 1980 to play independence celebrations. A cover assemblage of African flags (and the Papua New Guinea flag) further emphasized where Marley's head and heart were at.

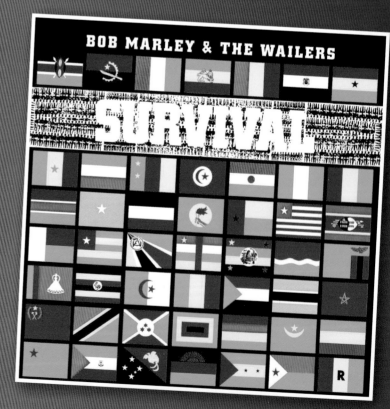

Africans both inside and outside Africa and the more subtle methods of oppression used against them. The album ends with an insistence on black pride and culture, which is both the core and method of resistance." Concluded Bohn, "I doubt if I'll hear a more provocative or worthwhile album of popular music for a long time to come."

1979 TOURS

Before *Survival*'s release, Marley took his music to territories that previously had seen few if any Jamaican reggae performers. In April he played shows in Japan, Australia, and New Zealand. Returning to the Western Hemisphere, he played a couple shows in Hawaii. For his final US show of the summer, he performed in support of African liberation at a Boston benefit, introduced by comedian and activist Dick Gregory. This marked the first public performance of "Zimbabwe," Bob exhorting from the stage, "We must come together for Zimbabwe . . . Zimbabwe must be free by 1983, Jah seh, Africa must be free!" (The show was filmed, but as yet has not been released on video.)

The summer's other main event was Marley's set at the second annual Reggae Sunsplash festival in Montego Bay on July 7. Including a preview of "Ambush in the Night" from the still-to-be-released *Survival*, his appearance helped ensure the continued staging of Reggae Sunsplash. Despite an interruption of almost a decade in the late 1990s, the festival endures as a major international tourist draw to this day.

One of summer 1979's main events was Marley and the Wailers' set at the second annual Reggae Sunsplash festival in Montego Bay, Jamaica, on July 7. MAIN DENIS O'REGAN/GETTY IMAGES; INSET BRIDGEMAN IMAGES

Marley signs copies of *Survival* at the Tower Records on L.A.'s Sunset Strip in November 1979. CHRIS WALTER/WIREIMAGE/GETTY IMAGES

Released at the beginning of the fall, *Survival* was not a big hit, though it did nothing to diminish Marley's stardom. On the US chart, it only reached #70; in the United Kingdom, where he'd almost always charted higher, it peaked at #20, the absence of a hit single probably limiting its commercial prospects. Bob still promoted *Survival* with a rigorous North American tour that lasted nearly two months in late 1979, his set including highlights of the new album, such as "Africa Unite," "Zimbabwe," and "Ambush in the Night." His filmed performance at the Santa Barbara County Bowl on November 25 joined the growing parade of Marley archival releases when issued on DVD as *The Legend Live!* in 2003.

With Haile Selassie looming in the background, the performance at the Santa Barbara County Bowl on November 25 was filmed and eventually joined the growing parade of Marley archival releases when issued on DVD as *The Legend Live!* in 2003.

CHRIS WALTER/WIREIMAGE/GETTY IMAGES

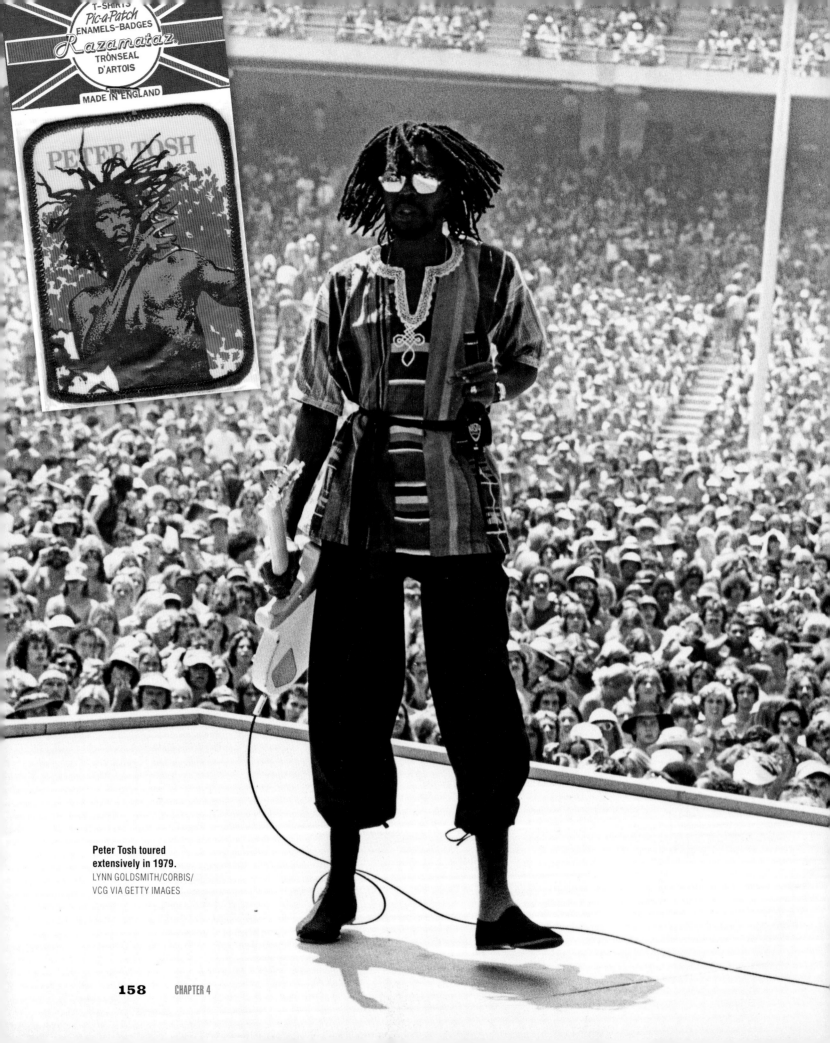

Peter Tosh toured extensively in 1979.
LYNN GOLDSMITH/CORBIS/
VCG VIA GETTY IMAGES

TOSH AND WAILER AT THE END OF THE 1970S

Peter Tosh was also touring the world in 1979, this time without the Rolling Stones. For the last half of the winter, he did numerous shows on his first extensive North American tour, mostly in the same East Coast and West Coast cities where the Wailers had first taken off. In the summer, he toured Europe, followed by a few shows in Canada and the East Coast in late summer. On September 22, he and many other artists played the No Nukes concert at Madison Square Garden, though he didn't make the cut for the accompanying album or film documentary.

"On his first solo tour here, Tosh brought along a bag of interesting songs but his performing style hadn't quite pulled together," the *New York Daily News*'s Patricia O'Haire wrote in a review of one of his shows at the Bottom Line club. "At that time he seemed to be working with his body only; his mind seemed to be off somewhere else and the two weren't connecting—and they weren't connecting with the audience either, not like now. This time, electricity sparkles like a Con Ed generator. Backed by a solid band with three backup singers, he weaves a powerful path from the slower, easier paced numbers which open his show to the strong, biting and bitter statements that bring the audience to its feet, cheering."

Robert Palmer was just as gung-ho in his *New York Times* review, calling it "the tightest, most powerful reggae show that has yet played in the United States . . . if any Jamaican star is going to explode in the United States, it will surely be Mr. Tosh."

Also in 1979, Tosh released his second album on the Rolling Stones label, *Mystic Man*. More than *Bush Doctor*, it dissatisfied some critics who'd grown attached to his rootsier sound, the arrangements sometimes employing synthesizers and fusing reggae with contemporary funk-soul. Those attributes also caught some flak in reviews of his European concerts. "Despite the grace afforded by the backing trio the Tamlins and the best rhythm section in the world, his live show is a letdown," wrote Adrian Thrills in *NME*. "Tosh is forsaking much of his militancy and spontaneity for the new holy trinity of compromise, accessibility and bland musical sophistication. Particularly disappointing in his current set is the bias towards orthodox rock guitar breaks and keyboard soloing, and the horrendously excessive use of synthesized disco percussion. They're unnecessary concessions to commercialism."

Tosh retorted to Thrills, "Now the music is more perfect. It is more beautiful. It is more properly decorated than it was because in those days there was no synthesizers and

Tosh's *Mystic Man* disappointed some who'd grown attached to his rootsier sound, the arrangements sometimes employing synths and fusing reggae with contemporary funk-soul.

clavinets and them bloodclaat [Jamaican slang word, roughly equivalent to "bloody" in Britain] t'ings! It takes more instruments to make reggae acceptable to the ears of people, and the best is yet to come man."

A review of an August 10 show at Montreal's Théâtre St.-Denis from the same year makes one wonder if Thrills was seeing the same performer. Tosh, speculated the *Montreal Star*, "will be recognized as the most important popular performer to emerge in this decade. Most superlatives would understate last night's event. Tosh cast a spell over the audience and held it spellbound for a good two hours. He is an explosive performer. His voice, honey-toned, soulful and exquisitely restrained, is a beguiling and accomplished instrument."

Tosh had another reason to be happy with the outcome of his late-1970s North American tours, where he met Melody Cunningham, with whom he'd have two children, daughter Niambe and son Jawara. Jawara eventually became one of several Wailers descendants to pursue a career in music, performing as Tosh1.

While Marley and Tosh were gaining in popularity overseas, Bunny Wailer was sinking farther under the radar. By the end of the 1970s, his new releases, issued on his Solomonic label, were seldom heard outside of Jamaica. Wailer's fortunes would rise in the decades to come, but as the 1980s dawned, he was overshadowed even more by the other Wailers than Tosh was by Marley, who had yet more ambitious plans on his agenda as 1979 wrapped up.

BOB MARLEY AT DECADE'S END

Some of the most notable shows of Bob's 1979 American tour took place at Harlem's Apollo Theater, America's premier venue for black acts since the 1930s. It was here that James Brown had recorded several of his live albums and where the Motortown Revue had given key early exposure to many Motown soul acts when that label was just becoming a powerhouse in the early 1960s. From October 24 to October 28, Marley gave seven concerts at the theater (supported by soul singer Betty Wright), in his most concentrated attempt yet to reach a specifically African-American audience.

"He thought, as an artist, that he might have the white market, but look at the oppressed black people in America: 12 percent of the American population, and 90 percent of its prison population," Island Records radio promo man Lister Hewan-Lowe pointed out in *The Book of Exodus.* "He had to mobilize those people and get them involved in the 'Movement of Jah people.' That is where Bob Marley felt his legitimacy lay. Make the connection, bring them all together under one roof, and then you have the great exodus."

"The tone of his new *Survival* album—deliberate, taken at a slower, more considered pace, but full of thought and purpose—was carried into the performance," Richard Grabel wrote in his *NME* review of one of the Apollo shows. "Marley played down the athletic display and instead emphasized the incredible expressiveness and control of his singing. He was less the impassioned shaman and more the eloquent preacher. He has serious things on his mind and now, more than ever, he wants to be sure we get the message.

"The setting of the Apollo Theatre, a Harlem landmark, is well chosen for Marley's return after a year and a half absence. It's small enough for his concentration on lyrical message and emotional subtleties to reach out and connect. The use of the stage set is effective, with three backdrops used during the show. The first is an Ethiopian flag, the second a portrait of Selassie I, the third a collage including images of Marcus Garvey, Selassie I and guerilla fighters. They don't distract, but unobtrusively encourage a little thought about the political context in which this music is made." Even with ten musicians, Grabel added, "the sound is still quite lean and spare, avoiding the pratfall of creating an overblown, big band version of what ought to be an essentially minimalist sound."

Although it's often repeated as gospel that few blacks in the United States knew or cared about Bob's music, it's curious that his albums continued to routinely chart, if modestly, on *Billboard*'s R & B listings. If that meant at least some African Americans were listening, Marley was still determined to reach more. He also made an effort to direct some of his profits to African Americans who needed them most. On November 27, he played a benefit at the Roxy in Los Angeles for the Sugar Ray Robinson Youth Foundation, which put on programs for inner-city youth in LA schools.

In a more private philanthropic gesture, he set up a Tuff Gong record store in the city's heavily African-American Crenshaw district, to be run by former road manager Tony Garnett. It might have been part of a plan to build Tuff Gong's US presence in preparation for a much more ambitious goal. He told Garnett he wanted to independently manufacture and distribute the Wailers' records in the United States. While artist-run labels have a harder time getting their

From October 24 to October 28, Marley gave seven concerts at Harlem's Apollo Theater, America's premier venue for black acts since the 1930s. ROGER STEFFENS' REGGAE ARCHIVE

Determined to reach more African Americans, Marley made efforts to direct some of his profits to African Americans who needed them most. On November 27, he played a benefit at the Roxy in Los Angeles for the Sugar Ray Robinson Youth Foundation. MICHAEL OCHS ARCHIVES/GETTY IMAGES; INSET ROGER STEFFENS' REGGAE ARCHIVE

BOB MARLEY
& THE WAILERS
Benefit for the
Sugar Ray's Foundation

Tues., Nov. 27, 1979
9:00 P.M.

$20.00

This ticket is not assignable and is not transferable. The proceeds from any resale are assigned to the Roxy Theatre Corp.

product into stores and into the charts than major labels, Marley and Tuff Gong were developing enough clout to at least consider such a proposition.

Tuff Gong showed signs of expanding its operation in other ways, too. Even after Bob became an international star, the label had issued Marley singles intended primarily or exclusively for the Jamaican market, such as "Smile Jamaica" and, in the late 1970s, the similarly easygoing "Blackman Redemption" and "Rastaman Live Up." By the end of the 1970s, Tuff Gong had a sixteen-track studio and label that were more actively recording and releasing product by other artists, including the I-Threes' Rita Marley and Judy Mowatt. There were hopes that Tuff Gong could grow into something like a Jamaican Motown, drawing on Kingston's incredible concentration of talent, to house a large roster of creative artists, producers, and session musicians. Bob Marley was the logical core of such an enterprise, and he could have been giving it greater consideration as the end of the contract he'd negotiated with Island in 1975 (remembered as a ten-album deal for one million dollars by Don Taylor in his memoir) drew closer.

Near the end of the tour, Marley expanded his reach in the Caribbean, doing shows in Trinidad and the Bahamas. His December 15 concert at Nassau's Queen Elizabeth Center was a free benefit for the UN's International Year of the Child. It was also his last with the Zap Pow horn section of saxophonist Glen DaCosta and trumpeter Dave Madden, who'd been along for the entire North American tour to give the shows a slightly different spice.

Bob also gave the International Year of the Child royalties from a song he'd written for some of his kids a few years earlier, and which had just been issued on a Tuff Gong single. Ziggy, Cedella, and Stephen Marley were the actual artists on the disc, singing "Children Playing in the Streets" under the name of the Melody Makers. Despite the youth of the singers, it was very much a depiction of the day-to-day realities of the ghetto, as seen through the eyes of the very young. Heard by few people at the time, it marked the first of many record releases by children of the Wailers.

Some observers remember Marley looking worn at points in late 1979. At the time, this was usually put down to his punishing tour schedule. In retrospect, the cancer he'd hope to eliminate with his toe operation might have been taking hold in other parts of his body. His pace would not decelerate, however, with the onset of the new decade, starting with his first concerts in Africa, the continent in which Bob was becoming a symbol of liberation from colonial rule.

Even after Bob became an international star, Tuff Gong issued Marley singles intended primarily or exclusively for the Jamaican market (above). Tuff Gong was also actively recording and releasing product by other artists, including Rita Marley and Judy Mowatt.

THE FINAL YEARS 1980–1981

6

Despite bumps in the road, Bob Marley experienced some of the highlights of his career during the first half of 1980. He played one of his most dramatic, legendary concerts in a newly independent African country. He drew some of his biggest audiences during a lengthy, successful European tour. And he put out the second LP in his planned *Survival/Uprising/Confrontation* trilogy, though no one knew it would be the last album he'd release in his lifetime.

AFRICAN CONCERTS

Marley had visited Africa for the first time when he made a trip to Ethiopia in 1978. Now, as 1980 began, he gave his first actual concerts on the continent. In the first week of January, he and the Wailers did a pair of shows in Libreville, the capital of the West African nation of Gabon. These were staged in a sports facility as part of the birthday celebrations for Gabonese president Omar Bongo and arranged after his two daughters expressed their interest in a Marley performance to Bob's manager, Don Taylor. "We didn't know he was a dictator when we went," admitted Al Anderson in the *Marley* documentary. "But we found out. And it was like, okay, we're here, it's too late. Let's just play."

The previous year had not been without its challenges, but Marley opened the new decade with several career highlights. EBET ROBERTS/ REDFERNS/GETTY IMAGES

Marley and the Wailers enjoyed their stay in Gabon for the most part, Bob starting an affair with one of the president's daughters, Pascaline Bongo. But not everything went as planned or hoped. They were disappointed that the concerts were done to small audiences of well-off Gabonese. More seriously, tensions boiled over between Marley and Taylor when the manager was suspected of pocketing twenty thousand dollars after telling Bob the fee for the show was forty thousand dollars, though Bob heard Taylor had been paid sixty thousand dollars. The lengthy argument that ensued in Gabon blew up into a physical conflict, Bob beating and berating his manager as more stories of similar discrepancies for other concerts emerged. Accounts vary, but several Marley associates remembered both the violent altercation and Taylor's generally dubious handling of Bob's finances. Soon after they left Africa, according to Taylor's memoir *Marley and Me*, Marley beckoned Taylor to Marley's mother's house in Miami. There, according to the manager, Marley and his close friend/associate Allan "Skill" Cole threatened to shoot Taylor if he didn't sign a document ending his professional agreements with Marley.

No shots were fired and the confrontation dissolved after Marley's mother told them to stop fighting, but Taylor's term as manager was over. "I always thought my son was far too lenient with Don Taylor," Cedella Booker wrote in *Bob Marley, My Son*. "As far as I'm concerned, whatever chastisement he gave to Don Taylor was richly deserved."

Taylor didn't entirely take his dismissal lying down, suing Marley for half a million dollars before agreeing on an undisclosed settlement with Rita Marley after Bob's death. Taylor's termination was no surprise, but his replacement was. After an absence of a half-dozen years, Danny Sims took on Marley's management, though at this point Marley could have had his pick of many top managers in the entertainment business.

Sims's earlier stint as Marley's manager had been mixed, to say the least. Sims had also done quite well from interest in the singer's publishing and the points he'd been awarded on Marley's Island releases. On the other hand, Sims had done much to lay the groundwork for the Wailers even making it to the early 1970s intact. Marley might have simply been inclined to work with someone he knew rather than risk being taken advantage of by a more powerful wheeler-dealer.

Marley's plans became more ambitious as the new decade got rolling. In March, he went to Rio de Janeiro for almost a week with Chris Blackwell and fellow reggae star Jacob Miller. Officially, the jaunt was a promotional trip, but Marley was also feeling out the possibilities for a South American tour as part of his ever-extending global reach. Such a venture couldn't take place, however, until he fulfilled his commitments to an upcoming European tour in the spring and early summer, followed by a US tour that would take him through much of the fall. A damper was put on the South America visit when Miller—a hugely popular figure in Jamaica both for his solo work and releases as part of the band Inner Circle, though his reputation was only beginning to spread beyond the island—died in a Kingston car accident a few days after returning from Brazil.

Marley only did a couple more concerts before beginning his European tour at the beginning of May, but they were among the most momentous of his life. As author of the song "Zimbabwe" and a Rasta who revered Africa as his rightful homeland, Marley could naturally have been expected to take a great interest when the nation formerly known as Rhodesia completed its transformation into the independent country of Zimbabwe on April 18, 1980. When he was invited to the independence ceremonies in Harare, he put his money where his mouth was, flying over the Wailers and the I-Threes at his own expense—which was considerable, estimated at about $250,000—to perform for free.

**"Three Little Birds" from 1977's *Exodus*
album was released as a single in
January 1980.**

Uprising would not be remembered as one of Marley's best records, but it did feature a couple tracks that are among his most famous, including "Could You Be Loved." The sleeves shown are the German, UK, and French pressings, as well as a twelve-inch reissue from 2005.

Like his Smile Jamaica and One Love Peace concerts, the Zimbabwe shows had their share of edgy unpredictability. Although new Zimbabwean president Robert Mugabe, Prince Charles, and Indira Gandhi were in the crowd, the concert was interrupted when fans crashed into Rufaro Stadium. Riotlike conflict between them, police, and soldiers interrupted the set as tear gas streamed over the premises, including the performers. Marley and his musicians retreated offstage for half an hour before returning to finish the concert, minus the I-Threes. The following day, they did a free second show at the stadium, attended by more than one hundred thousand people. "Zimbabwe," naturally, featured in the set, along with "Exodus," "Get Up, Stand Up," and less political favorites such as "Positive Vibration," "Lively Up Yourself," and "Roots, Rock, Reggae."

Marley and most of his entourage stayed in Zimbabwe to see more of the country for a few days, but the two shows would be Bob's last in Africa. When Zimbabwean officials pressured him to stay and perform more shows, he and his associates made a hastier exit than they might have liked. Still, the two concerts, along with Smile Jamaica and the One Love Peace events, marked rare intersections between politics and art where, despite some dangerous moments, Marley's music brought people together in celebration of triumph against the odds.

UPRISING SESSIONS

For much of the rest of early 1980, Marley was occupied with finishing his *Uprising* album. The title might have signified more political posturing, but *Uprising* didn't have rabble-rousing songs on the order of "Zimbabwe," "Exodus," or "War." There were still tracks that addressed justice and righteousness, such as "Bad Card" and "Real Situation," making an unusual turn into prostitution for "Pimper's Paradise." Spirituality and

The song for which *Uprising* is most remembered was added to the album late in production when Chris Blackwell pressed Marley for more songs.

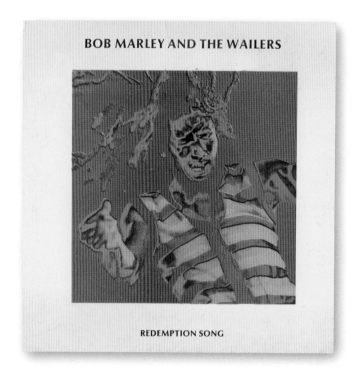

BOB MARLEY AND THE WAILERS

REDEMPTION SONG

religion got some space with "Zion Train" and "Forever Loving Jah." Musically, however, the Wailers were treading water somewhat, with a midlevel energy that delivered the kind of reggae Marley fans had come to expect, without major surprises.

Uprising would not be remembered as one of Marley's best records, but its status was enhanced by a couple tracks that are among his most famous. The gently pulsating "Could You Be Loved" evened reggae's jagged rhythms ever so slightly in the direction of disco, a nod accentuated even more heavily by a twelve-inch single version. If the hope was to get American radio airplay, it was no more successful in the United States than most of Marley's other singles, missing the pop charts and only hitting #56 on the R & B listings. In the United Kingdom, however, it was a different story, rising to #5 and becoming his biggest British hit in his lifetime. Buried in its lyrics were a couple paraphrases of words from his very first single, "Judge Not," which would have been known to very few listeners in 1980.

The song for which *Uprising* would be most remembered, however, was its least typical. Added to the album late in the production process when Chris Blackwell pressed Marley for more songs, "Redemption Song" was unlike almost anything the Wailers had released. Sung with no accompaniment other than acoustic guitar, it was not so much reggae as impassioned folk. It was also one of Bob's most personal compositions, acknowledging his ancestors' roots in slavery and urging listeners to help him sing "redemption songs"— songs of freedom that emancipate us, and him, from slavery both physical and mental. There's more than a touch of autobiography to his repeated lament that such songs are all he's ever had, even as his wealth and fame soared to unimaginable heights.

Much like "Dock of the Bay" was far more introspective and folky than anything soul great Otis Redding had previously written and recorded when he cut it just before his death in late 1967, "Redemption Song" marked an exciting, entirely new possible direction for Marley to pursue. He also tried a full-band version that came out as a B-side, but the song works better—and, despite the absence of electricity or additional instruments, is more powerful—as a stark acoustic ballad. Heard today, it sounds almost like a requiem by which Bob wanted to be remembered. It wasn't a hit single, but it's one of his most famous songs, and deservedly so.

Bob might not have been selling as many records as many fellow superstars, but he was tough to top as an audience draw, playing before more than one hundred thousand in Milan's San Siro Stadium on **June 27, 1980.** ADRIANO ALECCHI/MONDADORI PORTFOLIO VIA GETTY IMAGES; INSET ROGER STEFFENS' REGGAE ARCHIVE

MURATTI
MUSIC

ROBERTO CIOTTI
PINO DANIELE
con James Senese e Toni Esposito
AVERAGE WHITE BAND

RADIO
1 CITTÀ 2

BOB MARLEY
and The Wailers

STADIO SAN SIRO DI MILANO
Venerdì 27 Giugno '80 ore 16.00

INGRESSO
N° 4898

Il Concerto si terrà anche in caso di pioggia

Lo spettatore che da una verifica di controllo viene trovato sprovvisto del presente tagliando dovrà corrispondere di nuovo il prezzo del biglietto.

"Last year's *Survival* found Bob Marley close to his peak, boldly appraising global black unity from a Rastafarian viewpoint with his most biting and uncompromised music in some time," wrote Chris Morris in *Rolling Stone*. "*Uprising* is that landmark album's disquieting successor. The new record finds reggae's foremost poet-prophet in a contemplative and pessimistic mood, secure in his religious beliefs but concerned about a gloomy future. If *Uprising* doesn't snap one's head back (as *Survival* did), it certainly proves unnerving with its alternating moments of exaltation and introspection . . .

"Though Marley's vision on *Uprising* is fairly dark, the sound is full and bright, tinged with a lightness similar to the air-headed pleasures of *Kaya*," added Morris, who also singled out "Redemption Song" for special praise: "As the artist performs this folk ballad (with its aching cry of 'Won't you help to sing, these songs of freedom/'Cause all I ever had, redemption songs,' so reminiscent of the young Bob Dylan), one feels a man reaching out and grappling with the dreadful possibilities of liberation and disaster. Such a tour de force, like much of *Uprising*, is as moving as it is deeply troubling."

Longtime Marley chronicler Vivien Goldman also highlighted the differences between Bob's most recent two albums in her *New Musical Express* review. "*Survival* was a wardance," opened her assessment. "*Uprising* is a statement of consolidation, a tactical retreat from the front line to consider strategy. As such, it's a discussion, Marley proffering thoughts, observations, notes."

Goldman also took care to distinguish *Uprising*'s musical qualities from its immediate predecessors. "Musically, the Wailers make a return to the slow, sultry rock steady era, with Family Man's bass as sparse as it was in the days when he and his brother Carly first joined the (then) Wailers trio," she observed. "Though the melodies are beautiful, *Uprising* is in no way a pretty-pretty album à la *Kaya*. The Western rock 'n' roll influence (Junior Marvin's near heavy-metal live guitar breaks) has vanished; it's a return to strictly Jamaican basics."

Helped by "Could You Be Loved," *Uprising* became Marley's third UK Top 10 LP, though it continued his pattern of steady-but-unspectacular sales in the United States, where it peaked at #45. Just before it was released, he began a six-week European tour that solidified his position in the top rank of live attractions. He might not have been selling as many records as many of his fellow superstars, but he was becoming tough to top as an audience draw, playing before more than one hundred thousand in Milan's San Siro Stadium and one hundred thousand in Dublin's Dalymount Park. On a couple German

the LPs

UPRISING

Review by
Garth Cartwright

In January 1980, Bob Marley and the Wailers returned from playing in Gabon (for the nation's dictator, President Bongo) and entered Tuff Gong studios in Kingston to begin work on what would become the final studio album released in Marley's lifetime. If *Survival*'s ominous tone had helped Marley get many things off his chest, *Uprising* found him in a more upbeat if reflective mood.

Chris Blackwell was back as co-producer, likely offering tips on how to cut an album that would garner both pop and R & B radio play. *Uprising* certainly achieves this, being the slickest-sounding album Marley ever cut. Alongside several songs that are, essentially, Rastafarian hymns—"Zion Train," "Forever Loving Jah," "We and Dem," and "Work"—there's the social uplift of

"Coming in from the Cold" and the ominous foreboding of nuclear destruction in "Real Situation."

But *Uprising* gets more interesting. "Bad Card" employs a catchy skanking rhythm to help condemn Don Taylor (Marley's former manager, who he learned had been skimming huge sums from his earnings when the band was in Gabon), while "Pimper's Paradise" has an almost doo-wop flavor (recalling the younger Bob's love of American vocal groups), while its lyrics offer a moralistic, and rather chauvinistic, condemnation of women who like the high life of parties and drugs.

"Could You Be Loved," with its propulsive rhythm and big chorus, is Marley aiming to get onto the dance floor and pop radio (he succeeded with both—it reached #5 in the UK, the biggest hit of his lifetime, and charted strongly internationally).

And then there's "Redemption Song." The version on the album is just Bob playing his acoustic guitar, but he also recorded it with the band and released that version as the acoustic single version's B-side. "Redemption Song" was largely overlooked at the time of *Uprising*'s release. Some critics noted its stark sound, unlike anything Marley had released before. Few fans then bought Bob's LPs for acoustic introspection. It was after Bob died and fans began considering "Redemption Song" as a last testament of sorts, that it gained attention. Over the intervening decades "Redemption Song" has followed "No Woman No Cry" as Bob's most recorded song, with everyone from Macy Gray to the Specials performing it.

Released in June 1980, *Uprising* consolidated Bob as a global superstar. No one knew he had less than a year to live.

dates, he shared the bill with Fleetwood Mac, then arguably the most popular rock group in the world. The archival release *Uprising Live!* contains his June 13 concert at Westfalenhalle in Dortmund, Germany, in its entirety (along with the I-Threes' opening set) on both CD and DVD.

THE FINAL TOUR AND FATAL ILLNESS

Marley looks rather wan in the photo of the Wailers used on *Uprising*'s back cover, taken by Adrian Boot in a London elevator in April 1980, when the band was on the way back to Jamaica from Zimbabwe. It's often used as evidence that he was becoming seriously ill as the year progressed, though Junior Marvin has said Bob looked faded because he'd been up for several nights speaking with people in Zimbabwe. At the time, there was little suspicion that Marley's health was in jeopardy. He continued to play soccer and plan for his next tour, spending time in Miami before setting off on a round of US shows and serving as grand marshal for Brooklyn's West Indian Carnival Parade on Labor Day. It was probably around this break in Marley's schedule that an American named Yvette Crichton conceived his final child, Makeda Jahnesta, a daughter born on May 30 of the following year.

What was intended as a full American tour started in Boston in the middle of September. On September 19 and 20, Marley shared the bill at Madison Square Garden with the Commodores, the funk stars featuring Lionel Richie on lead vocals. At this point, the Wailers wouldn't ordinarily have

Brighton Leisure Centre, Brighton, England, July 1980. MIKE PRIOR/ REDFERNS/GETTY IMAGES

ABOVE: **Madison Square Garden, September 19, 1980.** FRANK WHITE PHOTO/FRANK WHITE PHOTO AGENCY

LEFT: **Ticket stub from the Madison Square Garden stand with the Commodores, and backstage pass for the final show at Pittsburgh's Stanley Theater.** ROGER STEFFENS' REGGAE ARCHIVE

played shows in which they weren't the headliners or only act, but Bob remained eager to somehow break into the American R & B market. Playing these kinds of gigs was a vehicle for doing that, and perhaps gaining some airplay on US R & B radio stations as well.

"The last concert in New York was to try to get African-American R & B airplay in America," commented Danny Sims in the *Marley* documentary. "Bob had a cult following in America, and when you'd go to a Bob Marley concert, it was sold out. But it was white. . . . So Frankie Crocker, the #1 DJ in the country [then working at New York radio station WBLS-FM], said, 'We'll guarantee you three months of airplay if Bob will open for the Commodores.'"

Market penetration, however, would take a backseat, as would everything else, after Marley collapsed while jogging in New York's Central Park. A neurologist delivered the worst news imaginable. Bob had a brain tumor, and was given just three more weeks to live.

Unbelievably, the tour did not stop. Marley, perhaps in denial, went on to the tour's next stop in Pittsburgh. He also wanted to get more medical opinions, though the tumor was so large that chances of a better diagnosis were remote. Somehow he and the Wailers got through a full set at Pittsburgh's Stanley Theater on September 23. Eventually issued on CD as *Live Forever* in 2011, it was the last show Marley gave.

Marley sounded a little hoarser than usual at the concert, but otherwise it seemed like just another Wailers performance, at least going only by the audio evidence. Several songs from *Uprising* were featured, including, as the finale, "Get Up, Stand Up." Rita Marley in particular, however, was adamant that Marley had to get off the road. The rest of the tour was canceled, a press release giving the official reason as "exhaustion."

Nearly fifty thousand attended Marley's last concert in France, at Le Bourget, near Paris, on July 3, 1980. JACQUES PAVLOVSKY/SYGMA VIA GETTY IMAGES

THE FINAL MONTHS

For a short while, Marley's illness was shielded from the public. Tests at New York's Memorial Sloan Kettering Cancer Center soon revealed he also had cancer in his lungs and stomach. He did have more than three weeks to live, though radiation treatments couldn't rid his body of his fatal disease. Nevertheless, he did not acknowledge this in public, taping a message in New York for radio stations that claimed, in part, "Ya t'ink anyt'ing can raas kill me? I understand that writers and people in the press are very interested and concerned about my health. I want to say thank you for your interest and that I'll be alright and I'll be back on the road again in 1981—really, performing for the fans we love."

Even more extraordinarily, *Rolling Stone* ran a misleading bulletin in its November 13 issue: "'There's nothing the fuck wrong with me,' says reggae star Bob Marley, denying rumors that he had been hospitalized for cancer. Marley *was* admitted to New York's Memorial Sloan Kettering Cancer Center on October 8, but he says he picked that facility only on the advice of a friend and was simply suffering from 'serious nervous exhaustion.' The singer, who was released after three days, is now in good spirits and plans to tour with Stevie Wonder in mid-November."

In reality, Marley's condition was rapidly worsening. After mulling over possible nonconventional cures, he decided to try the Sunshine House Cancer Clinic in Bad Wiessee, West Germany. Heading the clinic was controversial doctor Josef Issels.

Bob and his mother Cedella at the office of Dr. Josef Issels.
BRIDGEMAN IMAGES

By early 1981, Marley had outlived his initial prognosis by quite a few months as he underwent treatment at the clinic, out of the eyes of the media. His weight plummeted, however, even as he managed to spend time with visiting family and friends and engage in some modest exercise. On a relatively bright note, in early 1981 he was awarded the Jamaican Order of Merit—an honor that can't be shared by more than fifteen living persons, or given to more than two people in any year—by Edward Seaga, who had defeated Michael Manley in a recent election to become the country's prime minister. Bob hadn't been in Jamaica since leaving for his 1980 European tour, and in his absence the award was accepted by his son Ziggy.

By May, he'd deteriorated so badly that Issels gave him just a couple more weeks to live at the most. With the help of Chris Blackwell, a plane was chartered to take him back across the Atlantic, where he could at least be nearer to his mother in Florida, even if getting back to Jamaica wasn't in the cards. On May 11, he died in Cedars of Lebanon hospital in Miami.

FUNERAL IN JAMAICA AND FINAL TRIBUTES

The tone struck by British national newspaper the *Guardian* in its obituary was echoed in many others around the world: "The death of Bob Marley, aged 36, from cancer yesterday robs Jamaican music of its first ambassador, and popular music in general of one of its most eloquent powerful and conscientious voices. Over the past ten years Marley has been almost single-handedly responsible for introducing reggae music to an international audience, and with it, the first popular knowledge of the Rastafarian faith which he followed and always espoused in his music. Marley became a figure of incalculable influence and inspiration to the young.

"The beautifully melodic quality which surfaced in Marley's work, allied to the irresistible reggae rhythm and the potent conviction of his lyrical messages [was] to make Marley the first reggae artist to achieve recognition in the popular market. . . . Marley achieved the rare feat of being a popular figure, feted and lionized by the chic and the powerful, while remaining aloof to it all and without compromising his credibility as a spokesman for millions of young blacks."

Posters for canceled US shows.

Bob's music continued to see release on his Kingston-based Tuff Gong label.

In Nigeria, *Spear* magazine highlighted a side of Marley's legacy that resonated especially strongly in Africa and other regions of the world where blacks suffered oppression: "Bob Marley's music will be sung wherever men and women come together to demand justice and freedom. Bob Marley has left a legacy of hard work, a spirit of love and freedom for black people which will prove an inspiration to many as the crisis of the Babylonian system deepens."

After a memorial service primarily for family and friends in Miami, Bob's body was flown to Jamaica. On May 20, forty thousand filed past his coffin to pay tribute as he lay in state in Kingston's National Arena. At his state funeral in the same building the following day, the Wailers performed, Bob's sons Ziggy and Stevie dancing along with them on the stage. Bob's mother, Cedella, along with his stepsister Pearl Livingston, sang Cedella's composition "Hail," and the I-Threes sang "Rastaman Chant" and "Natural Mystic."

"His voice was an omnipresent cry in our electronic world, his sharp features, majestic locks, and prancing style a vivid etching on the landscape of our minds," said Seaga in his eulogy. "Most people do not command recollection. Bob Marley was never seen. He was an experience which left an indelible, mystical imprint with each encounter. Such a man cannot be erased from the mind. He is part of the collective consciousness of the nation . . . He was almost too much with us for there to come a time when he bid us farewell."

Marley was also paid official tribute from the Jamaica Council for Human Rights. "He audaciously used his immense talent to carry the message of the rights of the downtrodden and exploited into the chambers of the rich and the powerful," the organization noted in a written statement. "Despite the trenchant and even threatening quality of his message, these colossi were forced to acknowledge and applaud his works, if not actually enjoy them."

After the service concluded, Marley's body was transported fifty-five miles to his burial site near his birthplace in the village of Nine Mile. "Thousands of people left villages and factories in Jamaica's countryside to cluster at nearly every bend in the road and wave goodbye as Marley made the final four-hour journey," reported *Rolling Stone*. "The motorcade to Marley's birthplace suffered delays, including the breakdown of the hearse, a fancy pickup truck. So many people jammed the burial site—a natural amphitheater formed by a hill near the wooden cottage Marley grew up in—that the last rituals took place amid confusion and shoving. The bronze casket was put in its humble holding place (a concrete rectangle with the striped red, gold and green Rastafarian colors)."

The Bob Marley mausoleum, Nine Mile, Saint Ann Parish. FRANZ MARC FREI/LOOK DIE BILDAGENTUR DER FOTOGRAFEN GMBH/ALAMY STOCK PHOTO

Many couldn't help but note a couple absentees from the funeral: neither Peter Tosh nor Bunny Wailer was present. In Tosh's case, as he told *Black Echoes*, "for spiritual reasons I go to no funeral," noting he hadn't gone to his girlfriend Yvonne Whittingham's funeral either. Bunny opted to pay his tribute to the Wailers' legacy by often reinterpreting their songs on his solo releases, starting with 1980's *Bunny Wailer Sings the Wailers*. "You might hear a little bit of Tosh, and you might hear a little of Bob, and you will hear the I, as well as the harmonies," he wrote in the liner notes. "You will hear Wailers still, and that is as close as I can get."

Some of the most moving testaments to Marley, however, came from noncelebrity fans at the funeral. "We were living the situation he was talking about," Zimbabwean student Petronila Mutenda told the *New York Times*. "He was not against whites, but he wanted the other race to realize they are human beings and mustn't feel inferior." Added twenty-year-old Billy Boyle, to the same reporter, "I feel moaning till I can't stand it no more. I know him from down in the ghetto. He know his destiny. He live his destiny. He showed black people truth and light."

"As an orator, he wasn't much," acknowledged another fan, Faith Webley, in the same article. "But his music said it all."

EPILOGUE: LEGACY

Usually musicians with hit records fade from the forefront of popular consciousness after their death or after their bands break up. Bob Marley has traveled in the opposite direction. As famous as he was during his lifetime, Marley has become more iconic and revered in the three and a half decades since his death. He's certainly sold more records, especially with his greatest hits collection *Legend*, which is now among the top fifty best-selling albums of all time.

When artists die in their prime, their legacy is invariably propagated—and sometimes exploited—by their close musical, personal, and business associates. Marley's has been no exception. On the downside, this has sparked bitter squabbles over his estate and disreputable attempts to capitalize on his name. Some of his principal musical partners have met ends far grislier than his own, especially Peter Tosh.

On a much more positive note, with the emergence of numerous documentaries, concert DVDs, and previously unreleased live recordings, there's much more Marley for fans to enjoy than ever. Quite a few of his family members became respected reggae performers and recording artists in their own right, especially his son Ziggy, who achieved a level of stardom not far removed from his father's. Marley's life is celebrated by several memorials and museums, most in Jamaica, drawing more pilgrims to the island than anyone would have thought possible even after he'd reached international stardom.

Some of these pilgrims were in the crowd of more than twenty thousand in Montego Bay in August 1981 for the Fourth International Reggae

As famous as he was during his lifetime, Marley has become more revered in the decades since his death. INTERFOTO/ALAMY STOCK PHOTO

Sunsplash Festival, which was billed as a tribute to Bob Marley. Besides performances by the I-Threes and the Melody Makers, it was highlighted by an unannounced appearance by Stevie Wonder, who dueted with Rita Marley on "Redemption Song." Marley, pronounced Wonder at the event, "gave us so much of his life that will help us to be a stronger people. You see, I believe it's music that brings people together."

Not long after Marley's death, record labels began scouring their vaults for material to reissue, or issue for the first time. The month after his death, "No Woman, No Cry" entered the UK charts, where it peaked in the Top 10. Several months later, Cotillion Records' *Chances Are* album was drawn from recordings done for JAD in the late 1960s and early 1970s, sometimes with new overdubs. Poorly received despite some decent tracks, it was outshone by the more conscientiously assembled *Confrontation*, which came out on Island in 1983.

A POSTHUMOUS ALBUM

Confrontation was supposed to have been the title of the third part of a trilogy, preceded by *Survival* and *Uprising*, had Marley survived. It was a little misleading, however, to give this release the same title, as it wasn't the complete *Confrontation* album as originally intended, or even a *Confrontation*-in-progress. Instead, it gathered ten odds and ends from the last few years of Marley's life, including some outtakes and demos and a couple of tracks that (with different harmony vocals) had appeared

ABOVE: Seven Bob Marley and Wailers cuts were included on the soundtrack to the 1982 film *Countryman*, about a Jamaican fisherman who rescues two Americans from a plane wreck.

RIGHT: Stevie Wonder dueted with Rita Marley on "Redemption Song" at the August 1981 International Reggae Sunsplash Festival at Montego Bay, which was billed as a tribute to Bob Marley.
CHUCK FISHMAN/GETTY IMAGES

on somewhat overlooked late-1970s singles. Some instrumental and vocal parts were even added after Marley's death. The *Confrontation* album that would have been the third part of the trilogy never got underway, and this wasn't exactly a substitute.

Nevertheless, *Confrontation* was a fairly respectable collection, if not one that ranks with Marley's proper Island LPs conceived and completed as full-length albums. Most of the songs were at about, or not far below, the standard of those that had appeared on *Survival* and *Uprising*, the albums in closest proximity to when most of the material was recorded. Perhaps because the cuts weren't part of a full-length record intended to project a certain mood, there's a nice unforced feel to much of the proceedings, if one that couldn't deliver the same impact that an album like *Exodus* had. Inspired by the term used to describe black soldiers who fought in the US cavalry in the latter part of the nineteenth century, "Buffalo Soldier" even made #4 on the UK charts.

Rita Marley in Kingston, circa 1985. LEE JAFFE/GETTY IMAGES

"The album is diffuse in its impact," cautioned *Rolling Stone*. "Marley's scratchy-soothing vocal style and inimitable phrasing dominate the songs, properly and sometimes powerfully, but the charged atmosphere that came about when he led the Wailers and the magically responsive backup singers, the I-Threes, simply can't be duplicated by overdubs. *Confrontation* is an album of numerous small pleasures—the water-bug delicacy of 'Jump Nyabinghi,' the forceful insight of 'Buffalo Soldier,' the gospel-like adamancy of 'Rastman Live Up'—and it is a valuable, welcome document. But the magical part of Marley's rich legacy is best sought out on previous releases."

"Marley's work was becoming increasingly spotty, but the songs here are consistently strong, if not spectacular," wrote Don Snowden in his *Los Angeles Times* review. "The lyrics reflect a militant, spiritual stance, and a rough passion is apparent in the vocals. The Wailers effectively lock the melodies into tough, spartanly arranged grooves. *Confrontation* isn't the best album in the Wailers' catalogue, but it's an enjoyable, valuable addition. Much of its appeal undoubtedly comes from the opportunity to savor fresh, vital music from one of those rare artists who actually shaped and changed the course of pop music. Those who cherish the music of Bob Marley and the Wailers needn't be embarrassed about adding it to their collections."

CONFRONTATION

Review by Chris Salewicz

On May 11, 1983, the second anniversary of Bob Marley's death, Tuff Gong, through Island Records, released a new Bob Marley album, *Confrontation*. Despite the material's provenance, there was no sense that the album had been scraped together. Some of the tunes were outtakes from the *Survival* and *Uprising* sessions; others had been worked up from demo tapes, with the Wailers and the I-Threes adding overdubs.

"Mix Up, Mix Up" was built from a two-track that had Bob's voice on one track and his scratchy ska-like guitar and a drum machine on the other, and had a rhythm uncannily similar to Marvin Gaye's "Sexual Healing." "Give Thanks," similar in rhythm and melody to "If the Cap Fits" on *Rastaman Vibration*, had been written at the same time as that song; similarly, "I Know" was a *Rastaman Vibration* outtake. "Jump Nyabinghi" came from another two-track demo, and "Blackman Redemption" and "Rastaman Live Up!" were tough, militant tunes that had both been Tuff Gong singles in 1979. "Chant Down Babylon" and "Stiff Necked Fools" balanced out the set. "Trench Town" was another Tuff Gong single, and "Buffalo Soldier," yet another single, was about African Americans who fought for the Union in the American Civil War.

Chris Blackwell, who had produced *Confrontation*, pointed out that "Buffalo Soldier" was a particularly meaningful song. As reggae proclaimed self-determination, American Indians found a soul brother in Bob Marley. Many young Apaches considered him a reborn chief. In Arizona, there was a cult of reverence toward Bob Marley among the Hopi tribe.

As a fierce tropical rainstorm enshrouded in thick clouds his house high in Jamaica's Blue Mountains, Blackwell emphasized to me quite how extraordinary had been Bob's success. "Before Bob," he stressed, "the only thing that anyone with Rasta hair could succeed at was being a carpenter or a fisherman. But

Bob just had it naturally. He was a really exceptional person. When I first met him, I immediately trusted him. People at first would say to me, 'Those guys, the Wailers, are real trouble.' Which usually means that the people in question want to be treated like human beings."

It was Bob's simple, clear perception of life, believed Blackwell, that allowed the musician to realize greatness. In the hamlet of Nine Mile, deep amid the steep valleys of rural Jamaica, his upbringing indelibly stamped basic country truths on Bob Marley, such as the time it takes for things to grow. In his career he would always let time run its course, hardly typical of many hustling, would-be reggae stars. Jah was with him, and he was with Jah, always.

Confrontation did not, however, reflect or even provide many solid clues to what directions Marley might have explored had he lived. "As we'd finished recording *Uprising*, and were heading for *Confrontation*, we were thinking of turning our music into a kind of more Afro-Jamaican style, taking it closer to nyabinghi, [because] we knew it was time to come with that pattern," reasoned Family Man Barrett in *Wailing Blues*. "Bob and I used to discuss it, saying how people were going to come for the reggae, but after they do that now, we were going to move into the nyabinghi, so it was going to take on more of those same chant vibes you hear on songs like 'Running Away,' 'So Much Things to Say,' and 'Guiltiness.'" "Jump Nyabinghi" is the sole track on *Confrontation* that suggests such a fusion, and then only in a mild manner.

LEGEND AND MORE POSTHUMOUS MARLEY RELEASES

Boosted by "Buffalo Soldier," *Confrontation* was a big hit in the United Kingdom, making #5. The continued commercial viability of Marley's music was reinforced when "One Love" hit #5 as a single there in spring 1984. These successes were nothing, however, compared to the sales rung up when Marley's first true greatest hits collection, *Legend*, was also issued that spring. Topping the UK charts for twelve straight weeks, it eventually sold more than twenty million copies. No previous Marley release had come close to a million.

In the United States, *Legend* was slower to take off, only reaching #54 upon initial release, though it became (as it did in most of the world) one of the steadiest catalog sellers in the record business. As of this writing, it's been in *Billboard*'s album charts for more than four hundred consecutive weeks, the fourth longest such run in history. It also served as a gateway to the rest of Marley's catalog, especially the Island albums, half a dozen of which have now been certified "gold" (selling more than five hundred thousand copies in the States).

Why did *Legend* sell so much more than any previous Marley release? Mostly because of the quality of music, of course, but there were other factors at work. The track selection zeroed in on his most popular standards, sticking mostly to his big UK hits, though the omission of "Lively Up Yourself"—one of his best-loved songs, and one of his catchiest choruses—was inexplicable, its lack of success on the singles charts be damned.

More shrewdly, Dave Robinson of Island Records determined through market research, as Chris Blackwell recounted in *Bob Marley:*

Inspired by the term used to describe black soldiers who fought in the US cavalry in the latter part of the nineteenth century, *Confrontation*'s "Buffalo Soldier" reached #4 on the UK charts.

The Untold Story, "that you should keep the word 'reggae' out of it. Reggae had a mixed reaction: some people liked reggae, some people hated it. A lot of what people didn't like about Bob Marley was the threatening aspect of him, the revolutionary side. So the picture chosen was one of the softest pictures of Bob." What Marley himself would have thought of such blunting of his image is open to question, but his revolutionary message was loud and clear enough in some of *Legend*'s songs, such as "Get Up, Stand Up," "Exodus," and "I Shot the Sheriff."

Legend also helped pave the way for the release of more material from Marley's vaults. Exactly how much is there, like so much about Marley, remains open to dispute according to which expert or associate is consulted. Some have claimed there's little in the way of extras, especially completed studio tracks. Others claim there are at least a dozen albums of material, especially if one counts demos and home tapes. Marley's mother later claimed that most of the tapes recorded at her Miami house were stolen shortly after his death.

Most of the unissued Marley recordings to see the light of day, however, have been taken from live concerts. *Talkin' Blues*, *Live at the Roxy*, *Live Forever*, and *Easy Skanking in Boston '78* capture Marley at various points between 1973 and (on *Live Forever*) his very last show in 1980. Other live recordings, as well as other rare odds and ends, have been added to some of the deluxe editions of his Island albums. Some more previously unreleased tracks showed up on the career-spanning four-CD box set *Songs of Freedom*, which went as far back as his 1962 debut single, "Judge Not," ending with a performance of "Redemption Song" at his final concert. Released in 1992, and like many such projects mixing hits and rarities, it became one of the most successful box sets ever, going double platinum (each measure of platinum signifying one million units).

The packaging of the pre-1973 (pre-Island) Wailers catalog unfortunately remains pretty haphazard. Their many non-LP singles are scattered, often on compilations with threadbare, misleading, or entirely nonexistent annotation that seems to treat such essential details as original labels and release/recording dates as closely guarded secrets. Tracks from different eras are sometimes mixed together willy-nilly. Some of the early Studio One cuts have, as Coxsone Dodd admitted, been subjected to overdubs such as, according to a 1994 *Billboard* article, "some high-hat cymbals to increase the 'brilliance of the top end.'" At least most of it *is* available somewhere or other, even if fans have to empty their wallets several times to track down every last item.

As for who exactly makes these decisions, ownership and administration of the Marley

the LPs

LEGEND

Review by Harvey Kubernik

Released on May 8, 1984, the compilation *Legend* encapsulates the remarkable recording career of one of reggae music's most important figures. This iconic collection is not only the perfect introduction to Marley's music but has become an essential part of every Marley collection—not something that can be said of every artist's greatest-hits collections.

Legend also remains the world's best-selling reggae album and one of the best-selling catalog albums, period, exceeding fifteen million certified units in the United States alone and more than twenty-seven million worldwide. In fact, *Legend* has never stopped selling, dominating *Billboard*'s catalog charts for decades.

The collection features classic Marley anthems like "Three Little Birds," "Get Up, Stand Up," and "I Shot the Sheriff." It includes "Redemption Song," "Is This Love," and "Exodus," the title track of the album that had been a turning point for Marley after the assassination attempt in December 1976 and the departures of guitarists Chinna Smith and Donald Kinsey. The *Exodus* recording sessions in London marked the first time the Wailers had used the twenty-four-track format and produced the international hits "Jamming," "Waiting in Vain," and the "One Love/People Get Ready" medley, all of which also appear on *Legend* .

Another notable inclusion is the hymnlike live version of "No Woman, No Cry" culled from Marley's 1975 solo shows at the Lyceum in London, recorded just after he had added American R & B guitarist

Al Anderson to his lineup in an attempt to build a bigger sound for the larger halls he was now playing.

When *Legend* arrived in 1984, it was supported by an international tour that included the I-Three, Ziggy Marley, and the Wailers, who backed most of Bob's 1970s tours. Bob appeared onscreen behind the group. "It was ghostly and unforgettable," recalled Roger Steffens, reggae scholar and author of *So Much Things to Say: The Oral History of Bob Marley* (2017).

"As I lecture throughout the world on Marley's life," Steffens explains, "I find the same response from students everywhere when I ask if they know Bob Marley: 'If you don't know who Marley is when you arrive at college, by the end of the first week, you'll be introduced to *Legend* by all the other kids in the dorm.'"

"'My music will go on forever,' Marley once said. *Legend* is the album that seals the deal.

estate has been contentious, especially in the decade following his passing. As with the messy business and legal affairs of some other great acts in the wake of their deaths and breakups—from Elvis Presley and Buddy Holly to the Beatles, Pink Floyd, and the Sex Pistols—sifting through the fine points of these squabbles is often disheartening. In stark contrast to careers that were fascinating from almost every angle while the performers were active, it's also sometimes quite tedious. Several books could be written about the tugs-of-war over Marley's estate in particular, especially as he didn't leave a will, perhaps believing to the end that he'd miraculously recover from his illness.

Figures concerning how much was passed on to whom, and to whom his assets were passed on, vary about as much as you'd expect, given the ambiguities that followed even some of the basic details of Marley's life to its end. Basically, the estate was initially under the administration of Rita Marley. She resigned that position, however, after being charged with improperly transferring some assets. Legal actions were directed against her by Bob's former managers Don Taylor and Danny Sims, among others. As *Billboard* reported in December 1991, the rights to buy the estate were ultimately awarded to Chris Blackwell's Island Logic company and the Marley family. The figure for which it was purchased, in keeping with the irritating vagueness clouding even some of the most essential details of Marley's career, was reported differently according to the source, but was in the neighborhood of ten million dollars.

EX-WAILERS AND THE ASSASSINATION OF PETER TOSH

More interesting to the majority of Bob Marley's fans than this distasteful bickering over pieces of the pie—which at times also involved his mother and members of the Wailers— was the music being made by the ex-Wailers. Nothing could be the same with Marley gone, of course, but it wasn't long before a Marley-less Wailers were touring the US for a month in late 1984 with the I-Threes and, on some dates, Bob's son David. "It's our work . . . a commitment and a purpose," rationalized Rita in the *Los Angeles Times*. "We see Bob as a shepherd and leader, and we're confirming that the music goes on, never to die. It's a message of love and hope . . . the hope that we will get rid of war and illusions, and that everything will come to a reality in a one-ness. We see that as something that can save the world. Music has that power, and Bob intended to use it as a weapon."

Also missing from the Wailers on this jaunt were Peter Tosh and Bunny Wailer. In the half decade or so after Marley's death, Tosh continued to be one of reggae's leading figures, and one of its most controversial. Although his signing to Rolling Stones Records had

In the half decade or so after Marley's death, Peter Tosh continued to be one of reggae's leading figures, and one of its most controversial.

taken place in a flurry of effusive compliments from both sides (Tosh appears in the Stones' video for "Waiting on a Friend"), by the early 1980s he was publicly complaining about not being promoted or paid as well as he thought he should be. The association between him and the label came to a tawdry end when he lived in Keith Richards's Jamaican home in the guitarist's absence. Expecting the house to be vacated when he came to the island for a visit, Richards was told by Tosh upon arrival that Tosh intended to stay put.

"He pulled this switch on me," said Richards in *Steppin' Razor: The Life of Peter Tosh*. "He said he had a machine gun. I said, 'Well I'm at Mo' Bay and I'm going to be with you in about an hour and a half so you'd better figure out how to put the magazine in it.' And by the time I got there the place was empty."

The incident was in keeping with Tosh's generally growing erratic behavior, which sometimes crossed the line from merely eccentric to truly out there. "He roundly intimidated members of the music press," wrote Lloyd Bradley in *Q*. "Methods included verbal abuse, ignoring them for up to half an hour, not allowing them to use

tape recorders, forbidding photographers to take more than one picture and demonstrating his kung fu prowess by, without warning, lashing out with kicks and punches mere inches from the journalist's face. He gave his age as being anything from 400 to 1,000,000 with a varying number of reincarnations. . . . He maintained that he knew 'Johnny B. Goode' was going to be a hit because he'd been to the pressing plant and talked to it, told it to do well."

Tosh continued making records, however, his next one attaining a greater commercial impact than the ones he'd released through the Stones' label. Issued in 1983, *Mama Africa* was his highest-charting effort in the United States, where it almost made the Top 50. It even had a small hit single, a reggae-fied treatment of Chuck Berry's classic "Johnny B. Goode."

Bunny Wailer, meanwhile, continued issuing albums on his Solomonic label that attracted little notice beyond the reggae world. He had more to gain than Tosh by reuniting with his old bandmate, which he did in the mid-1980s with the album *The Never Ending Wailers*, also featuring ex-Wailers Constantine Walker and Junior Braithwaite, as well as Tosh's son Andrew.

Not issued until 1993, the record included remakes of songs from the earliest part of the Wailers' career, such as "I'm Still Waiting" and "It Hurts to Be Alone." Like many semi-reunion projects, it was more disappointing

INSETS: Issued in 1983, *Mama Africa* was Tosh's highest-charting effort in the US. It even had a small hit single with a reggae-fied treatment of Chuck Berry's "Johnny B. Goode" (French and German pressings seen here).

LEFT: Bunny continued issuing albums and singles on his Solomonic label that attracted little notice beyond the reggae world. Today he is considered a member of the reggae trinity alongside Bob and Peter. JIM RANKIN/*TORONTO STAR* VIA GETTY IMAGE

than it appeared on paper. "The result sounded like haunted-house effects for a cut-rate carnival attraction," was Timothy White's memorable description in *Catch a Fire: The Life of Bob Marley.* Tosh and Wailer again went their separate ways, but Tosh's career was cut short by a tragedy as horrific as any suffered in the extended Wailers family.

On September 11, 1987, three gunmen entered Tosh's Kingston home. They demanded money from Tosh, his girlfriend Marlene Brown, and several of Tosh's friends before Tosh was fatally shot through the forehead by Dennis "Leppo" Lobban. Two others in the house also died from bullets. The Grammy for Best Reggae Album for Tosh's final record, 1987's *No Nuclear War,* had to be awarded posthumously.

A couple weeks later, more than ten thousand mourners paid tribute when Tosh's body, as Marley's had only six years earlier, was laid out for viewing at Kingston's National Arena. In a statement following Tosh's death, former prime minister Michael Manley hailed Tosh as an artist who "gave to Jamaica and the world an unforgettable library of musical works which will be played and sung by many generations of people." Dennis Lobban is serving a life sentence for Tosh's murder.

Like the attempted assassination of Bob Marley, the killing of Peter Tosh is shrouded in controversy as to motives. There's speculation that Lobban—who'd known Tosh for many years and had just completed a twelve-year jail term for robbery and attempted murder—was bitter because Tosh hadn't done more to help him and his family during and after his time in prison.

A selection of 1980s Bunny Wailer LPs and singles released on Solomonic.

Bunny took a swipe at South African Prime Minister Pieter Botha with this 1987 Solomonic single.

Sadly, Tosh wasn't the only Wailer to die by shooting in 1987, as drummer Carly Barrett had been killed in April. In June 1999, original Wailer Junior Braithwaite also met his death at the hand of a gunman, having returned to Kingston years earlier after a couple of decades in the United States.

That left Bunny Wailer as the only surviving member from the trio of Wailers that had been at the core of the group on most of their pre-1974 recordings. Such was Wailer's standing among American reggae fans that he was able to draw almost fifteen thousand to a Madison Square Garden concert in 1986, despite the lack of anything resembling a hit record on his own. He failed to capitalize on his immense cult popularity, however, declining or missing numerous opportunities to promote himself through the media on that tour. At least he, unlike Tosh, has been able to accept Grammy Awards (all three in the 1990s and all in the Best Reggae Album category) as a living performer. A couple of Marley tributes were among his numerous subsequent albums, and he remains an active performer, touring in 2016 to celebrate the fortieth anniversary of his solo debut album, *Blackheart Man*.

Without any involvement from Wailer, the Wailers have remained an active group since Bob Marley's death. Like a lot of bands who've gone on without their leader, however, their lineup has splintered and altered almost beyond recognition. By 2006, Family Man Barrett was the only member who'd played with Marley. A couple years later, Junior Marvin and Al Anderson formed the Original Wailers, though the two guitarists weren't exactly original, having joined in the mid- to late 1970s. The band currently touring under the Wailers name sometimes plays entire sets devoted to specific albums such *Legend*, *Exodus*, *Uprising*, and *Survival*, adding to the feeling of seeing a Marley tribute act.

DESCENDANTS AND MEMORIALS

Several of Bob Marley's children have been far more visible to the average music fan than his ex-backup musicians. Of these, the most prominent by far is Ziggy Marley, who made numerous albums with the Melody Makers in the 1980s and 1990s, and had a couple of his late-1980s efforts hit the Top 30. In the twenty-first century, he's gone solo, maintaining his status as one of reggae's leading attractions, though not quite matching his earlier sales peaks. His younger brother Stephen has also made several well-received albums, and two of Bob's sons by women other than his wife, Rita—Damian and Ky-Mani—have issued records too. None have matched their father's innovativeness, but none of them pretend to stick too closely to their father's style. Rita herself cut quite a few albums, and even Bob's mother, Cedella Booker, got in on the act with some records before her death in 2008.

Some of Marley's kids are also involved in the nonmusical part of what has become a business empire, as Marley now generates the fourth-highest income of any late musician. The estate has administered beverages, coffee, clothing, T-shirts, headphones, and children's books under the Marley brand. There are even four varieties of Marley cannabis for markets in which possession is legal. A portion of the proceeds goes to charity, and the family's nonprofit Bob Marley Foundation has made contributions to numerous humanitarian causes in Jamaica. It's a far cry from the days when Marley and the other Wailers subsisted on weekly three-pound handouts from Coxsone Dodd.

Fans can also pay tribute by visiting several Marley heritage sites in Jamaica. His legendary home at 56 Hope Road was converted into the Bob Marley Museum, its hour-long tour including memorabilia, film footage, and the room where he and others were shot in 1976, bullet holes still visible on the walls. Either separately or on a combo ticket, the still active Tuff Gong Recording Studios is also open for tours that feature some of Marley's instruments and the mixing board used on some of his classic recordings. There's also a Bob Marley Tribute to Freedom section of Universal Studios in Orlando, Florida, where Marley memorabilia can be viewed in a replica of 56 Hope Road.

More off the beaten track, the Trench Town Culture Yard Museum has a small collection of, according to its website, "articles, instruments and furnishing used by Bob Marley." A lot of Wailers history took place in or around the Culture Yard's buildings, where the group sometimes hung out and played and wrote music.

It takes considerably more effort to get to Marley's birthplace, more than fifty miles away in the village of Nine Mile, which now houses the Bob Marley Centre and Mausoleum. This complex includes the modest home in which Marley lived between the ages of six and thirteen, as well as the mausoleum that serves as his final place of rest.

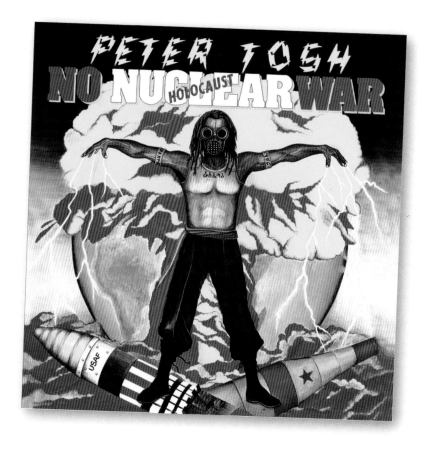

The 1988 Grammy for Best Reggae Album for Tosh's final record, *No Nuclear War*, had to be awarded posthumously.

Bob Marley's true legacy, however, lies not in T-shirts or any of the other souvenirs available. Nor is it in the considerable tourist dollars he generates for a country that, despite progress in many areas, remains home to many residents nearly or just as poor as he was when growing up in Nine Mile and Trench Town. His greatest contributions were in the music he and the Wailers spread around Jamaica, and then the world. More than any other artist, they popularized reggae in all corners of the globe. The form was adopted in areas where the style was unknown before Marley and others brought it out of Jamaica, by artists ranging from African reggae performers such as the Ivory Coast's Alpha Blondy and South Africa's Lucky Dube to twenty-first century American ska-rock bands.

Through his voicing of the struggles and joys of the people of Jamaica, the Jamaican experience—and, by extension, the voice of the Third World, of which Jamaica was a part—was heard to an extent unimaginable when this tiny country declared independence back in the early 1960s. Through his songs, the oppressed minorities he reflected and represented gained one of their greatest voices. His music, like much of the best rock and reggae, helped bring together people of many regions and races who'd had little contact with each other in the first half of the twentieth century.

In one of the Wailers' first and ultimately most widely heard songs, they urged listeners to, with "One Love," and one heart, get together and feel all right. Much work remains to be done, but Bob Marley did much to bring that love between all people of the world many steps closer to reality.

Through Bob Marley's songs, the oppressed minorities he reflected and represented gained one of their greatest voices. GIJSBERT HANEKROOT/REDFERNS/GETTY IMAGES

SELECTED DISCOGRAPHY

This selected discography is not exhaustive, as it would be difficult to compile a complete list of all Bob Marley releases throughout the world. It concentrates on his and the Wailers' most essential recordings, including all of their studio albums and their most notable best-of collections, live recordings, and box sets. It also lists some of the best of the many compilations featuring non-LP material from 1964 to 1972, the years prior to their first Island Records release. The abbreviation *JA* signifies a Jamaican release.

STUDIO ALBUMS

The Wailing Wailers
Released: Studio One, circa late 1965–early 1966 (JA)
Recorded: Studio One, Kingston, circa mid-1964–early 1966
Producer: Clement "Coxsone" Dodd
Musicians: Bob Marley, Peter Tosh, Bunny Livingston, Junior Braithwaite, Beverley Kelso, Cherry Green, Lloyd Knibbs, Lloyd Brevett, Jerome Haines, Jackie Mittoo, Don Drummond, Roland Alphonso, Tommy McCook, Johnny Moore, Dennis Campbell, Carl McCloud, Lloyd Spence, Ernest Ranglin, Richard Ace, Rita Marley, Joe Higgs, Sylvia Richards, Esmond Jarrett, Desi Miles, Hux Brown, Lloyd Delpratt, Bobby Ellis, Trummie Miles, Tony Wilson, Seymour Walker, Lyn Taitt, Vin Gordon, Lester Sterling, Lloyd Robinson, Fred Crossley, Dwight Pinkney, Danny McFarlane, Vision Walker, Headley Bennett
Tracks: "(I'm Gonna) Put It On," "I Need You," "Lonesome Feeling," "What's New Pussycat," "One Love," "When the Well Runs Dry," "Ten Commandments of Love," "Rude Boy," "It Hurts to Be Alone," "Love and Affection," "I'm Still Waiting," "Simmer Down"

The Best of the Wailers
Released: Beverley's, circa mid-1970 (JA)
Recorded: Dynamic Sounds Studio, Kingston, circa May 1970
Producer: Leslie Kong
Musicians: Bob Marley, Peter Tosh, Bunny Livingston, Mikey Richards, Jackie Jackson, Hux Brown, Gladdy Anderson, Winston Wright, Carlton Lee, Reggie Lewis
Tracks: "Soul Shakedown Party," "Stop the Train," "Caution," "Soul Captives," "Go Tell It on the Mountain," "Can't You See," "Soon Come," "Cheer Up," "Back Out," "Do It Twice"

Soul Rebels
Released: Upsetter, circa December 1970 (JA)
Recorded: Dynamic Sounds Studio and Randy's Studio, Kingston, circa August–December 1970

Producer: Lee Perry
Musicians: Bob Marley, Peter Tosh, Bunny Livingston, Dave Barker, Carlton Barrett, Family Man Barrett, Hux Brown, Reggie Lewis, Glen Adams, Lloyd Parks, Ranford Williams, Sticky Thompson
Tracks: "Soul Rebel," "Try Me," "It's Alright," "No Sympathy," "My Cup," "Soul Almighty," "Rebel's Hop," "Corner Stone," "400 Years," "No Water," "Reaction," "My Sympathy"

Soul Revolution
Released: Upsetter, circa mid-1971 (JA)
Recorded: Randy's Studio, Kingston, circa December 1970–March 1971
Producer: Lee Perry
Musicians: Bob Marley, Peter Tosh, Bunny Livingston, Hugh Malcolm, Family Man Barrett, Reggie Lewis, Ranford Williams, Glen Adams, Sticky Thompson, Carlton Barrett, Headley Bennett, Winston Wright, Tyrone Downie
Tracks: "Keep on Moving," "Don't Rock My Boat," "Put It On," "Fussing and Fighting," "Duppy Conqueror V/4," "Memphis," "Soul Rebel," "Riding High," "Kaya," "African Herbsman," "Stand Alone," "Sun Is Shining," "Brain Washing"

Catch a Fire
Released: Island, April 13, 1973
Recorded: Dynamic Sounds Studio, Kingston; Harry J Studio, Kingston; Randy's Studio, Kingston; and Basing Street Studios, London, circa October 1972
Producers: Bob Marley and Chris Blackwell
Musicians: Bob Marley, Peter Tosh, Bunny Livingston, Family Man Barrett, Carlton Barrett, Rita Marley, Marcia Griffiths, Rabbit Bundrick, Wayne Perkins, Tommy McCook, Robbie Shakespeare, Francisco Willie Pep, Winston Wright, Chris Karan
Tracks: "Concrete Jungle," "Slave Driver," "400 Years," "Stop That Train," "Baby We've Got a Date (Rock It Baby)," "Stir It Up," "Kinky Reggae," "No More Trouble," "Midnight Ravers"

Burnin'

Released: Island, October 19, 1973

Recorded: Harry J Studio, Kingston and Basing Street Studios, London, circa April 1973

Producers: The Wailers and Chris Blackwell

Musicians: Bob Marley, Peter Tosh, Bunny Livingston, Family Man Barrett, Carlton Barrett, Earl Lindo

Tracks: "Get Up, Stand Up," "Hallelujah Time," "I Shot the Sheriff," "Burnin' and Lootin'," "Put It On," "Small Axe," "Pass It On," "Duppy Conqueror," "One Foundation," "Rastaman Chant"

Natty Dread

Released: Island, October 25, 1974

Recorded: Harry J Studio, Kingston and Basing Street Studios, London, circa early 1974

Producers: The Wailers and Chris Blackwell

Musicians: Bob Marley, Family Man Barrett, Carlton Barrett, Bernard Harvey, Jean Roussel, Al Anderson, Rita Marley, Marcia Griffiths, Judy Mowatt

Tracks: "Lively Up Yourself," "No Woman, No Cry," "Them Belly Full (But We Hungry)," "Rebel Music (3 O'Clock Roadblock)," "So Jah Seh," "Natty Dread," "Bend Down Low," "Talkin' Blues," "Revolution"

Rastaman Vibration

Released: Island, April 30, 1976

Recorded: Harry J Studio, Kingston and Joe Gibbs Studio, Kingston, circa August–September 1975

Producers: Bob Marley and the Wailers

Musicians: Bob Marley, Chinna Smith, Al Anderson, Family Man Barrett, Carlton Barrett, Tyrone Downie, Rita Marley, Marcia Griffiths, Judy Mowatt, Tommy McCook, Donald Kinsey

Tracks: "Positive Vibration," "Roots, Rock, Reggae," "Johnny Was," "Cry to Me," "Want More," "Crazy Baldhead," "Who the Cap Fit," "Night Shift," "War," "Rat Race"

Exodus

Released: Island, June 3, 1977

Recorded: Island Studios, London, early 1977

Producers: Bob Marley and the Wailers

Musicians: Bob Marley, Family Man Barrett, Carlton Barrett, Tyrone Downie, Seeco Patterson, Junior Marvin, Rita Marley, Marcia Griffiths, Judy Mowatt

Tracks: "Natural Mystic," "So Much Things to Say," "Guiltiness," "The Heathen," "Exodus," "Jamming," "Waiting in Vain," "Turn Your Lights Down Low," "Three Little Birds," "One Love/People Get Ready"

Kaya

Released: Island, March 23, 1978

Recorded: Island Studios, London, early 1977

Producers: Bob Marley and the Wailers

Musicians: Bob Marley, Family Man Barrett, Carlton Barrett, Tyrone Downie, Seeco Patterson, Junior Marvin, Rita Marley, Marcia Griffiths, Judy Mowatt, Vincent Gordon, Glen DaCosta, Winston Grennan

Tracks: "Easy Skanking," "Kaya," "Is This Love," "Sun Is Shining," "Satisfy My Soul," "She's Gone," "Misty Morning," "Crisis," "Running Away," "Time Will Tell"

Survival

Released: Island, October 2, 1979

Recorded: Tuff Gong Studio, Kingston, early 1979

Producers: Bob Marley and the Wailers, Alex Sadkin

Musicians: Bob Marley, Family Man Barrett, Carlton Barrett, Tyrone Downie, Seeco Patterson, Junior Marvin, Earl Lindo, Al Anderson, Rita Marley, Marcia Griffiths, Judy Mowatt, Carlton Davis, Mikey Richards, Val Douglas, Dean Fraser, Headley Bennett, Nambo Robinson, Melba Liston, Luther Francois, Junior Chin, Jackie Willacy, Micky Hanson, Lee Jaffe

Tracks: "Wake Up and Live," "Africa Unite," "One Drop," "Ride Natty Ride," "Ambush in the Night," "So Much Trouble in the World," "Zimbabwe," "Top Rankin'," "Babylon System," "Survival"

Uprising

Released: Island, June 10, 1980

Recorded: Tuff Gong Studio, Kingston, circa late 1979–early 1980

Producers: Bob Marley and the Wailers

Musicians: Bob Marley, Family Man Barrett, Carlton Barrett, Carlton Davis, Tyrone Downie, Seeco Patterson, Junior Marvin, Earl Lindo, Al Anderson, Rita Marley, Marcia Griffiths, Judy Mowatt

Tracks: "Coming in from the Cold," "Real Situation," "Bad Card," "We and Dem," "Work," "Zion Train," "Pimper's Paradise," "Could You Be Loved," "Forever Loving Jah," "Redemption Song"

Confrontation

Released: Island, May 23, 1983

Recorded: Tuff Gong Studio, Kingston; possibly also Dynamic Sounds Studio, Kingston, and Harry J Studio, Kingston; 1977–1980 and April–May 1982

Producers: Bob Marley and the Wailers, Errol Brown

Musicians: Bob Marley, Family Man Barrett, Carlton Barrett, Tyrone Downie, Junior Marvin, Earl Lindo, Seeco Patterson, Rita Marley, Marcia Griffiths, Judy Mowatt, Glen DaCosta, David Madden, Nambo Robinson, Devon Evans, Carlton Davis

Tracks: "Chant Down Babylon," "Buffalo Soldier," "Jump Nyabinghi," "Mix Up, Mix Up," "Give Thanks and Praises," "Blackman Redemption," "Trench Town," "Stiff Necked Fools," "I Know," "Rastaman Live Up"

LIVE ALBUMS

Live!

Released: Island, December 5, 1975
Recorded: Lyceum Theatre, London, July 18, 1975
Producers: Bob Marley and the Wailers, Chris Blackwell, and Steve Smith
Musicians: Bob Marley, Family Man Barrett, Carlton Barrett, Tyrone Downie, Al Anderson, Seeco Patterson, Rita Marley, Marcia Griffiths, Judy Mowatt
Tracks: "Trench Town Rock," "Burnin' and Lootin'," "Them Belly Full (But We Hungry)," "Lively Up Yourself," "No Woman, No Cry," "I Shot the Sheriff," "Get Up, Stand Up"

Babylon by Bus

Released: Island, November 10, 1978
Recorded: 1975–1976, London, and June 25–27, 1978, Pavillon de Paris, Paris
Producers: Bob Marley and the Wailers, Chris Blackwell
Musicians: Bob Marley, Family Man Barrett, Carlton Barrett, Tyrone Downie, Junior Marvin, Seeco Patterson, Al Anderson, Earl Lindo, Rita Marley, Marcia Griffiths, Judy Mowatt
Tracks: "Positive Vibration," "Punky Reggae Party," "Exodus," "Stir It Up," "Rat Race," "Concrete Jungle," "Kinky Reggae," "Lively Up Yourself," "Rebel Music (3 O'Clock Roadblock)," "War/No More Trouble," "Is This Love," "The Heathen," "Jamming"

Talkin' Blues

Released: Tuff Gong, February 4, 1991
Recorded: October 31, 1973, The Record Plant, Sausalito, CA; Lyceum Theatre., London, July 17, 1975 ("I Shot the Sheriff" only); Harry J Studio, Kingston, early 1974 ("Talkin' Blues," "Am-A-Do," and "Bend Down Low" only)
Producer: none credited
Musicians: Bob Marley, Peter Tosh, Joe Higgs, Earl Lindo, Family Man Barrett, Carlton Barrett, Bernard Harvey, Al Anderson, Rita Marley, Marcia Griffiths, Judy Mowatt, Tyrone Downie, Seeco Patterson
Tracks: "Talkin' Blues," "Burnin' and Lootin'," "Kinky Reggae," "Get Up, Stand Up," "Slave Driver," "Walk the Proud Land," "You Can't Blame the Youth," "Rastaman Chant," "Am-A-Do," "Bend Down Low," "I Shot the Sheriff"

Live at the Roxy

Released: Tuff Gong, June 24, 2003
Recorded: May 26, 1976, The Roxy, West Hollywood
Producers: Bob Marley and the Wailers
Musicians: Bob Marley, Family Man Barrett, Carlton Barrett, Chinna Smith, Donald Kinsey, Earl Lindo, Tyrone Downie, Seeco Patterson, Rita Marley, Marcia Griffiths, Judy Mowatt
Tracks: "Trench Town Rock," "Burnin' and Lootin'," "Them Belly Full (But We Hungry)," "Rebel Music (3 O'Clock Road Block)," "I Shot the Sheriff," "Want More," "No Woman, No Cry," "Lively Up Yourself," "Roots, Rock, Reggae," "Rat Race," "Positive Vibration," "Get Up, Stand Up/No More Trouble/War"

Live Forever: The Stanley Theater, Pittsburgh, PA, September 23, 1980

Released: Tuff Gong, February 1, 2011
Recorded: September 23, 1980, The Stanley Theater, Pittsburgh, PA
Producer: none credited
Musicians: Bob Marley, Family Man Barrett, Al Anderson, Junior Marvin, Earl Lindo, Tyrone Downie, Seeco Patterson, Rita Marley, Marcia Griffiths, Judy Mowatt
Tracks: "Natural Mystic," "Positive Vibration," "Burnin' and Lootin'," "Them Belly Full (But We Hungry)," "The Heathen," "Running Away," "Crazy Baldhead," "War/No More Trouble," "Zimbabwe," "Zion Train," "No Woman, No Cry," "Jamming," "Exodus," "Redemption Song," "Coming in from the Cold," "Could You Be Loved," "Is This Love," "Work," "Get Up, Stand Up"

Uprising Live!

Released: Tuff Gong, November 24, 2014
Recorded: June 13, 1980, Westfalenhalle, Dortmund, Germany
Producer: None credited
Musicians: Bob Marley, Family Man Barrett, Carlton Barrett, Junior Marvin, Earl Lindo, Tyrone Downie, Seeco Patterson, Rita Marley, Marcia Griffiths, Judy Mowatt
Tracks: "Precious World," "Slave Queen," "Steppin' out of Darkness," "That's the Way Jah Planned It," "Marley Chant," "Natural Mystic," "Positive Vibration," "Revolution," "I Shot the Sheriff," "War/No More Trouble," "Zimbabwe," "Jamming," "No Woman, No Cry," "Zion Train," "Exodus," "Redemption Song," "Could You Be Loved," "Work," "Natty Dread," "Is This Love," "Get Up, Stand Up," "Coming in from the Cold," "Lively Up Yourself" (first four tracks by the I-Threes, also includes DVD of the concert)

Easy Skanking in Boston '78

Released: Tuff Gong, April 7, 2015
Recorded: June 8, 1978, Boston Music Hall
Producers: Cedella Marley, Jaime Feldman, Matt Solodky, Ziggy Marley
Musicians: Bob Marley, Family Man Barrett, Carlton Barrett, Junior Marvin, Earl Lindo, Tyrone Downie, Seeco Patterson, Rita Marley, Marcia Griffiths, Judy Mowatt
Tracks: "Slave Driver," "Burnin' and Lootin'," "Them Belly Full (But We Hungry)," "The Heathen," "Rebel Music," "I Shot the Sheriff," "Easy Skanking," "No Woman, No Cry," "Lively Up Yourself," "Jamming," "War/No More Trouble," "Get Up, Stand Up," "Exodus"

BEST-OF ALBUMS

Legend: The Best of Bob Marley and the Wailers
Released: Island, May 8, 1984

Tracks: "Is This Love," "No Woman, No Cry," "Could You Be Loved," "Three Little Birds," "Buffalo Soldier," "Get Up, Stand Up," "Stir It Up," "One Love/People Get Ready," "I Shot the Sheriff," "Waiting in Vain," "Redemption Song," "Satisfy My Soul," "Exodus," "Jamming"

One Love: The Very Best of Bob Marley and the Wailers
Released: Island, May 22, 2001

Tracks: "Stir It Up," "Get Up, Stand Up," "I Shot the Sheriff," "Lively Up Yourself," "No Woman, No Cry," "Roots, Rock, Reggae," "Exodus," "Jamming," "Waiting in Vain," "Three Little Birds," "Turn Your Lights Down Love," "One Love/People Get Ready," "Is This Love," "Sun Is Shining," "So Much Trouble in the World," "Could You Be Loved," "Redemption Song (Band Version)," "Buffalo Soldier," "Iron Lion Zion," "I Know a Place"

A two-CD edition of this release includes these tracks on the bonus disc: "Concrete Jungle," "Burnin' and Lootin'," "Rebel Music (3 O'Clock Roadblock)," "Jah Live," "Positive Vibration," "Smile Jamaica," "Natural Mystic," "Punky Reggae Party," "Satisfy My Soul," "Africa Unite," "Coming in from the Cold," "Rastaman Live Up," "Who Colt the Game"

BOX SET

Songs of Freedom
Released: Tuff Gong, October 6, 1992

Tracks: "Judge Not," "One Cup of Coffee," "Simmer Down," "I'm Still Waiting," "One Love/People Get Ready (Original)," "Put It On," "Bus Dem Shut (Pyaka)," "Mellow Mood (Original)," "Bend Down Low," "Hypocrites," "Stir It Up (Original)," "Nice Time," "Thank You Lord (Original)," "Hammer," "Caution," "Back Out," "Soul Shakedown Party," "Do It Twice," "Soul Rebel," "Sun Is Shining," "Don't Rock the Boat," "Small Axe," "Duppy Conqueror," "Mr. Brown," "Screw Face," "Lick Samba," "Trench Town Rock (Previosly Unreleased Alternate Mix)," "Craven Choke Puppy," "Guava Jelly," "Acoustic Medley (Previously Unreleased)—Featuring: a) Guava Jelly, b) This Train, c) Corner Stone, d) Comma Comma, e) Dewdrops, f) Stir It Up, g) I'm Hurting Inside," "I'm Hurting Inside (Previously Unreleased Alternate Mix)," "High Tide or Low Tide (Previously Unreleased)," "Slave Driver," "No More Trouble," "Concrete Jungle," "Get Up, Stand Up," "Rastaman Chant," "Burnin' and Lootin'," "Iron Lion Zion (Previously Unreleased)," "Lively Up Yourself," "Natty Dread," "I Shot the Sheriff (Live)," "No Woman, No Cry (Live at the Roxy)," "Who the Cap Fit," "Jah Live," "Crazy Baldheads," "War," "Johnny Was," "Rat Race," "Jammin' (12" Mix)," "Waiting in Vain (Advert Mix)," "Exodus (12" Mix)," "Natural Mystic," "Three Little Birds (Previously Unreleased Alternate Mix)," "Running Away," "Keep on Moving (London Version)," "Easy Skanking," "Is This Love (Horns Mix)," "Smile Jamaica," "Time Will Tell," "Africa Unite," "Survival," "One Drop," "One Dub," "Zimbabwe," "So Much Trouble in the World," "Ride Natty Ride (12" Mix)," "Babylon System," "Coming in From the Cold (12" Mix)," "Real Situation," "Bad Card," "Could You Be Loved (12" Mix)," "Forever Loving Jah," "Rastaman Live Up," "Give Thanks and Praise," "One Love/People Get Ready (12" Mix)," "Why Should I (Previously Unreleased)," "Redemption Song (Live in Pittsburgh)"

Notes: Four-CD box set with recordings by Bob Marley spanning his entire career, from his 1962 debut single, "Judge Not," to his performance of "Redemption Song" at his final concert on September 23, 1980. Besides including most of his most well-known songs, it also has some previously unreleased material and non-LP singles.

OTHER IMPORTANT COMPILATIONS

The Birth of a Legend
Released: Calla, 1976

Tracks: "Simmer Down," "It Hurts to Be Alone," "Lonesome Feelings," "Love and Affection," "I'm Still Waiting," "One Love," "I Am Going Home," "Wings of a Dove," "Let Me Go," "Who Feels It (Knows It)," "Maga Dog," "I Made a Mistake," "Lonesome Track," "Nobody Knows," "The Ten Commandments of Love," "Donna," "Do You Remember," "Dancing Shoes," "I Don't Need Your Love," "Do You Feel the Same Way"

Notes: Twenty-track compilation, first issued as a double LP and then a single-disc CD, of much of the best material recorded by the Wailers in the mid-1960s at Studio One.

One Love at Studio One
Released: Heartbeat, 1991

Tracks: "This Train," "Simmer Down," "I Am Going Home," "Do You Remember," "Mr. Talkative," "Habits," "Amen," "Go Jimmy Go," "Teenager in Love," "I Need You," "It Hurts to Be Alone," "True Confession," "Lonesome Feeling," "There She Goes," "Diamond Baby," "Playboy," "Where's the Girl for Me," "Hooligan," "One Love," "Love and Affection," "And I Love Her," "Rude Boy," "I'm Still Waiting," "Ska Jerk," "Somewhere to Lay My Head," "Wages of Love (rehearsal)," "Wages of Love," "I'm Gonna Put It On," "Cry to Me," "Jailhouse," "Sinner Man," "Who Feels It Knows It," "Let Him Go," "When the Well Runs Dry," "Can't You See," "What Am I Supposed to Do," "Rolling Stone," "Bend Down Low," "Freedom Time," "Rocking Steady"

Notes: Two-CD compilation of Studio One material from the mid-1960s, with some overlap with *The Birth of a Legend*, and some previously unreleased tracks and alternate takes.

The Toughest (credited to Peter Tosh)
Released: Heartbeat, 1996

Tracks: "Hoot Nanny Hoot," "Maga Dog," "Amen," "Jumbie Jamboree," "Shame and Scandal," "Sinner Man," "Rasta Shook Them Up," "The Toughest," "Don't Look Back," "When the Well Runs Dry," "Making Love," "Can't You See," "Treat Me Good," "Rightful Ruler," "400 Years," "No Sympathy," "Secondhand (version one)," "Secondhand (version two)," "Downpresser"

Notes: Although credited to Peter Tosh, many of the cuts on this CD are in fact Wailers tracks that feature Tosh as singer (and sometimes songwriter). About two-thirds of the material is from the mid-1960s Studio One years; the other half-dozen songs were done for Lee Perry in the late 1960s and early 1970s.

Wail'N Soul'M Singles Selecta
Released: Universal, 2005

Tracks: "Bend Down Low," "Freedom Time," "Stir It Up," "This Train," "Nice Time," "Hypocrite," "Mellow Mood," "Thank You Lord," "Bus Dem Shut," "Lyrical Satirical," "Funeral," "Pound Get a Blow," "Steppin' Razor," "Hurtin' Inside," "Play Play," "Them Have Fi Get a Beatin'," "Fire Fire," "Don't You Rock My Boat," "Chances Are," "The Lord Will Make a Way Somehow," "Hypocrite (vocal channel)," "Thank You Lord (vocal channel)," "Studio Chat"

Notes: Twenty tracks the Wailers recorded for singles on their own Wail'N Soul'M label circa 1967–1968, with a few marginal bonuses. It would be nice if other compilations could gather most or all of their 1969–1972 non-LP singles in as compact a fashion, but while those singles are on various reissues, they're scattered over many different anthologies.

BIBLIOGRAPHY

BOOKS

Booker, Cedella, with Anthony C. Winkler. *Bob Marley, My Son.* Lanham, MD: Taylor Trade Publishing, 2003.

Christgau, Robert. *Christgau's Record Guide: Rock Albums of the '70s.* New York: Ticknor & Fields, 1981.

Clapton, Eric. *Clapton: The Autobiography.* New York: Broadway Books, 2007.

Davis, Stephen. *Bob Marley (Revised Edition).* Rochester, VT: Schenkman Books, 1990.

Farley, Christopher John. *Before the Legend: The Rise of Bob Marley.* New York: Amistad, 2006.

Goldman, Vivien. *The Book of Exodus: The Making and Meaning of Bob Marley's Album of the Century.* New York: Three Rivers Press, 2006.

Grant, Colin. *The Natural Mystics: Marley, Tosh, and Wailer.* New York: W. W. Norton, 2011.

Jaffe, Lee. *One Love: Life with Bob Marley and the Wailers.* New York: W. W. Norton, 2003.

Katz, David. *People Funny Boy: The Genius of Lee "Scratch" Perry.* Edinburgh, Scotland: Payback Press, 2000.

Marley, Rita, with Hettie Jones. *No Woman No Cry: My Life with Bob Marley.* New York: Hyperion, 2004.

Marsh, Dave, with John Swenson, eds. *The Rolling Stone Record Guide.* New York: Rolling Stone Press, 1979.

Masouri, John. *The Life of Peter Tosh: Steppin' Razor.* London: Omnibus Press, 2013.

Masouri, John. *Wailing Blues: The Story of Bob Marley's Wailers.* London: Omnibus Press, 2008.

McCann, Ian, and Harry Hawke. *Bob Marley: The Complete Guide to His Music.* London: Omnibus Press, 2004.

Morris, Dennis. *Bob Marley: A Rebel Life.* London: Plexus, 1999.

Salewicz, Chris. *Bob Marley: The Untold Story.* New York: Faber & Faber, 2009.

Steffens, Roger, and Leroy Jodie Pierson. *Bob Marley and the Wailers: The Definitive Discography.* Cambridge, MA: Rounder Books, 2005.

Taylor, Don. *Marley and Me.* New York: Barricade Books, 1995.

White, Timothy. *Catch a Fire: The Life of Bob Marley: The Definitive Edition—Revised and Updated.* New York: St. Martin's Press, 2006.

MAGAZINES AND NEWSPAPERS

The Beat, 1991 annual Bob Marley Collector's Edition (Coxsone Dodd on "Simmer Down"; Bunny Wailer on Beverley Kelso and Cherry Green leaving Wailers)

Billboard, October 20, 1973 (*Burnin'* review)

Billboard, November 10, 1973 (Marley on "I Shot the Sheriff"; compares reggae to the blues; sees reggae as people's music; American reaction to reggae)

Billboard, November 24, 1973 (Marley on African-American reaction to reggae)

Billboard, July 13, 1991 (Chris Blackwell on *Catch a Fire*)

Billboard, June 18, 1994 (Coxsone Dodd on overdubs on reissues of early Wailers material)

Black Echoes, undated 1981, quoted in *The Life of Peter Tosh: Steppin' Razor* (Peter Tosh on Bob Marley's funeral)

Black Music, January 1975 (Lee Perry on Peter Tosh's writing and Bob Marley)

Creem, May 1973 (*Catch a Fire* review)

Creem, July 1978 (*Kaya* review)

Creem, March 1979 (Keith Richards on Peter Tosh; Peter Tosh on "Don't Look Back")

Essence, January 1976 (Marley on politics)

Fusion, May 1973 (*Catch a Fire* review)

Gleaner, undated in 1978, quoted in *Wailing Blues: The Story of Bob Marley's Wailers* (Marley's political influence in Jamaica)

Guardian, May 12, 1981 (Marley obituary)

High Times, September 1976 (Marley on marijuana and politics)

International Times, May 31, 1973 (*Catch a Fire* review)

Let It Rock, July 1973 (Marley on "Small Axe," "Duppy Conqueror," and "Trench Town Rock"; Marley on recording *Catch a Fire*)

Los Angeles Times, undated 1983, reprinted on Rock's Back Pages website (*Confrontation* review)

Los Angeles Times, September 13, 1984 (Rita Marley on Bob Marley's message)

Melody Maker, February 24, 1973 (Marley on Johnny Nash; preview of *Catch a Fire*; inaccurately reports Bob and Rita Marley aren't married)

Melody Maker, June 23, 1973 (report from *Burnin'* sessions)

Melody Maker, August 11, 1973 (review of Max's Kansas City concert)

Melody Maker, July 26, 1975 (Marley quote about interracial roots; Marley on "I Shot the Sheriff")

Melody Maker, September 6, 1975 (George Harrison on Marley)

Melody Maker, August 11, 1979 (Marley on *Kaya*)

Melody Maker, September 29, 1979 (*Survival* review)

MOJO, August 2002 (Danny Sims on New York DJs' reactions to early Wailers material)

MOJO, July 2011 (Keith Baugh on Marley concert in London in March 1972; Neville Garrick on designing *Survival* cover)

Montreal Star, August 11, 1979 (review of Peter Tosh concert at Theatre St. Denis)

New Musical Express, July 26, 1975 (review of London Lyceum concert)

New Musical Express, June 26, 1976 (review of Hammersmith Odeon concert)

New Musical Express, June 16, 1979 (on Peter Tosh live; Peter Tosh on changes in reggae)

New Musical Express, November 10, 1979 (review of Apollo Theater concert)

New Musical Express, July 5, 1980 (*Uprising* review)

New York Daily News, undated March 1979, quoted in *The Life of Peter Tosh: Steppin' Razor* (review of Peter Tosh concert at Bottom Line)

New York Times, July 23, 1973 (review of Max's Kansas City concert)

New York Times, June 16, 1978 (Marley on *Kaya* and Jamaican politics)

New York Times, June 19, 1978 (review of Madison Square Garden concert)

New York Times, March 9, 1979 (review of Peter Tosh concert at Bottom Line)

New York Times, May 22, 1981 (Marley funeral report)

New York Times Magazine, August 14, 1977 (Marley described as "the Third World's first real superstar")

Option, May/June 1986 (Joe Higgs on teaching the Wailers to sing)

Option, September/October 1988 (Donald Kinsey on joining the Wailers and Bob Marley assassination attempt)

Oui, November 1979 (Peter Tosh on Mick Jagger and Keith Richards)

Playboy, September 1976 (hails Marley and the Wailers as finest band of the 1970s)

Q, November 1987 (on Peter Tosh's eccentric behavior)

Rolling Stone, October 12, 1972 (review of Johnny Nash's *I Can See Clearly Now*)

Rolling Stone, February 15, 1973 (Johnny Nash on not being a reggae singer)

Rolling Stone, April 12, 1973 (*Catch a Fire* review)

Rolling Stone, January 17, 1974 (*Burnin'* review)

Rolling Stone, April 24, 1975 (*Natty Dread* review)

Rolling Stone, July 17, 1975 (review of Chicago 1975 concert)

Rolling Stone, June 1, 1978 (*Kaya* review)

Rolling Stone, October 16, 1980 (*Uprising* review)

Rolling Stone, November 13, 1980 (Marley denies cancer rumors)

Rolling Stone, June 25, 1981 (Marley on Jamaicans recording quickly)

Rolling Stone, July 9, 1981 (Marley funeral report)

Rolling Stone, September 1, 1983 (*Confrontation* review)

San Francisco Chronicle, October 23, 1973 (review of Matrix concert)

San Francisco Chronicle, July 7, 1975, (review of Boarding House show)

Smash Hits, August 7, 1980 (Marley on *Natty Dread*)

Sounds, August 28, 1976 (Peter Tosh on packaging of *Legalize It* album)

Sounds, October 16, 1976 (Chris Blackwell on Bunny Wailer's *Blackheart Man*; Bunny Wailer on original Wailers' common purpose)

Sounds, May 21, 1977 (*Exodus* review)

Sounds, June 28, 1977 (Marley on *Kaya*'s love songs)

Sounds, September 3, 1977 (Marley on punk; Paul Simonon on reggae)

Sounds, undated in 1977, quoted in Vivien Goldman's *The Book of Exodus: The Making and Meaning of Bob Marley's Album of the Century* (Marley on "Smile Jamaica")

Sounds, undated in 1978, quoted in *Bob Marley: The Untold Story* (review of Bingley, England show)

Spear, August 1981 (Marley obituary)

Street Life, May 15, 1976 (*Rastaman Vibration* review)

Time, March 22, 1976 (on Marley's stature in Jamaica; Michael Manley on reggae)

Time, December 31, 1999 (on its selection of *Exodus* as the album of the century)

Times, July 18, 1975 (review of London Lyceum concert)

Village Voice, June 30, 1975 (review of Central Park concert)

DVDS

Catch a Fire (Eagle Rock, 1999)

Marley (Magnolia, 2012)

Rebel Music: The Bob Marley Story (Palm Pictures, 2001)

LINER NOTES

Bundrick, Rabbit, for Bob Marley, *Songs of Freedom* (Tuff Gong), 1992.

Steffens, Roger, for Bob Marley and the Wailers, *Climb the Ladder* (Heartbeat), 2000.

Wailer, Bunny, for *Bunny Wailer Sings the Wailers* (Island), 1981.

WEBSITES

Bob Marley—The Official Site, www.bobmarley.com

Bob Marley Concerts, www.bobmarleyconcerts.com

Bob Marley Magazine, www.bobmarleymagazine.com

Rock's Back Pages, www.rocksbackpages.com

Trench Town Culture Yard Museum, www.trenchtowncultureyard.com

VH1 TELEVISION

Documentary *Peter Tosh: Behind the Music* (August 29, 1999).

AUTHOR AND CONTRIBUTORS

Richie Unterberger has written nearly a dozen rock history books, including *The Unreleased Beatles: Music and Film*; *White Light/White Heat: The Velvet Underground Day-by-Day*; *Won't Get Fooled Again: The Who from Lifehouse to Quadrophenia*; *Fleetwood Mac: The Complete Illustrated History*; and *Jingle Jangle Morning: Folk-Rock in the 1960s*. He was a contributor to Voyageur Press's *The Doors: The Illustrated History* and *Dylan: Disc by Disc*, and has written for numerous publications, including *MOJO*, *Uncut*, and *Record Collector*. He lives in San Francisco.

Garth Cartwright (www.garthcartwright.com) is a New Zealand–born, London-based journalist, critic, and author. He's written for many publications and contributed to Voyageur Press books about Miles Davis, AC/DC, and rockabilly. Garth's own books include *Princes Amongst Men: Journeys with Gypsy Musicians*, *More Miles Than Money: Journeys Through American Music*, and most recently *Going for a Song: The Great British Record Shop as Oracle*.

Gillian G. Gaar has written thirteen books, including *Boss: Bruce Springsteen and the E Street Band: The Illustrated History*, *Hendrix: The Ultimate Illustrated History*, *The Doors: The Illustrated History*, and *She's A Rebel: The History of Women in Rock & Roll*. She was also a contributor to Voyageur Press's *Nirvana: The Complete Illustrated History* and has written for numerous publications, including *MOJO*, *Rolling Stone*, and *Goldmine*. She lives and writes in Seattle.

Pat Gilbert has been writing about music and film for more than twenty-five years. He is a former editor of *MOJO*, the world's biggest-selling music magazine, and currently edits its quarterly offshoot, *MOJO '60s*. Pat is also the author of *Passion Is a Fashion: The Real Story of The Clash*, and has provided sleeve notes for the group's official releases since the late 1990s. In 2010, he visited Jamaica to write a profile of Island Records boss Chris Blackwell. He lives in London.

Dave Hunter is an American musician and writer who has worked extensively in both the United States and Britain. A former editor of *The Guitar Magazine* (UK), his books include *The Guitar Amp Handbook*, *Guitar Effects Pedals: The Practical Handbook*, *Amped: The Illustrated History of the World's Greatest Amplifiers*, *The Gibson Les Paul: The Illustrated History of the Guitar That Changed Rock*, and several others. Hunter is a monthly contributor to *Guitar Player*, *Vintage Guitar*, and *Guitar & Bass* magazines and lives in Portsmouth, New Hampshire, with his wife and their two children.

Harvey Kubernik, a lifelong resident of Southern California, is a veteran music journalist whose work has been published in *Melody Maker*, the *Los Angeles Free Press*, *Variety*, *Goldmine*, *Record Collector News*, the *Los Angeles Times*, and *MOJO*, among others. A former West Coast director of A&R for MCA Records, Kubernik is the author of eight books, including *Canyon of Dreams: The Magic and the Music of Laurel Canyon*, *Neil Young: Heart of Gold*, and *Leonard Cohen: Everybody Knows*. Kubernik saw Bob Marley and the Wailers live six times and interviewed band members once in Hollywood. He lives in Los Angeles.

Chris Salewicz documents popular culture. A senior features writer for *NME* from 1975 to 1981, Salewicz subsequently worked for *The Sunday Times*, *Q*, *MOJO*, and *Conde Nast Traveller*, and newspapers and magazines across the globe. Chris is the author of seventeen books, including the acclaimed *Rude Boy: Once Upon a Time in Jamaica*, *Redemption Song: The Ballad of Joe Strummer*, and *Bob Marley: The Untold Story*. His book *Dead Gods: The 27 Club* analyzes of the deaths of seven twenty-seven-year-old musical maestros, including Amy Winehouse, Kurt Cobain, and Jimi Hendrix.

INDEX

"Things will be OK in the end. If it's not OK, it's not the end."

—Bob Marley